THE PLANTSMEN
OF
ROCHESTER PARKS

A HISTORY OF ROCHESTER'S PARKS

BY
ALVAN R. GRANT

Third edition, September 2014
Published by Arthur Trimble, Rochester NY.

ISBN 9 780692 252932

CONTENTS

Foreword by Arthur Trimble   1

Acknowledgments   3

Prologue   4

Introduction   7

The Dunbar Years   21

The Barney Slavin Years   38

Linkages — Patrick J. Slavin   72

Linkages Continued — Richard E. Horsey   78

Linkages Continued   84

The New Order — Wilbur E. Wright   89

Alvan Roger Grant   100

Bernard E. Harkness   110

Richard A. Fenicchia — Propagator and Hybridizer   125

The Park Merger and the Grant-In-Aid Programs   148

The Horticulture Program Moves to the County   154

Addendum Part 1   207

Addendum Part 2 — A Rambling Update   210

Afterword   216

Appendixes   227

FOREWORD

When the original book *The Plantsmen of Rochester Parks* was published, neither Mr. Grant nor myself had a sense of the book's importance as a part of Rochester's history.

It was only recently brought to my attention by Cassandra Petsos, president of Rochester People for Parks, that only a couple of copies of the original twelve books were still available. She felt that the book should not be lost, but republished in memory of Alvan Roger Grant—a book that Mr. Grant would surely be proud of and pleased with.

At her urging, the work was begun that brought this book into being. With the advances in book-publishing technology, it should become an important addition to the history of the parks and arboreta of Monroe County and the City of Rochester. The original WordPerfect file was still available, and several draft copies of the original manuscript were printed and proofed.

At this point it was decided that the book should be brought up to date and have another addendum written. For that additional addendum we are indebted to Kent Millham. Kent, along with Noelle Nagel, represent the last of the plantsmen and plantswomen of Rochester parks as defined by Mr. Grant in this book.

The paragraph above needs some clarification regarding the word "plantsmen." In the early days of Rochester's parks, the word "parks" was synonymous with "arboreta." In an arboretum, plants are viewed as specimens and classified taxonomically with scientific names. This is the only accepted way to keep a plant properly identified in a way recognizable to a plant scientist anywhere in the world.

As you read the book it is obvious that Rochester's parks were recognized as important arboreta all over the world and famous plant scientists from many countries came to Rochester to

1

see firsthand an outstanding plant collection. With this recognition came the privilege of exchanging seeds, cuttings, and plants with other arboreta.

As the population grew so the use of the parks grew, and the parks became places where nature could be observed and the beauty of trees and shrubs be appreciated. This in turn has required more manpower to be employed in replacing plant material and pruning and mowing to keep the parks beautiful. With the budget constraints currently in effect this has meant less attention to the parks as arboreta.

This shift has affected the scientific aspect of the parks. The availability of a good computer database has made record keeping more efficient and accurate, but the plant-breeding program and the plant and seed exchange with other arboreta has taken a big hit. This in turn will ultimately mean the reputation of Rochester's parks will diminish among the world's great arboreta. Perhaps this is inevitable, but it makes this book even more important as we remember the great accomplishments of "The Plantsmen of Rochester Parks."

Alvan Roger Grant was born in 1917, graduated from Cornell in 1940, resigned as Monroe County Parks Director in March 1977, and died on February 13, 2007. Alvan was one of the greatest of the men he wrote about, the plantsmen of Rochester's parks.

Arthur Trimble, a good friend
September 2014

ACKNOWLEDGMENTS

I wish to express my thanks to a good friend, Arthur Trimble, for his assistance in preparing this manuscript for printing. Without his help, this would consist of approximately 200 pages of crudely typed paper held together with a paper clip.

I also want to thank my wife, Mairian, for her patience during the many hours I spent researching and organizing the material, which I garnered from many different places. Some of these hours could have been spent in more interesting activities.

. . . . . . Alvan Grant

Since this book is being republished after Mr. Grants death it is important to acknowledge the assistance I received in turning the original book into a truly professional book about the history of Rochester's parks.

Georgia Hubbard, a good friend, typed the original document supplied by Mr. Grant into a WordPerfect file which served as the basic file for the book.

The work of editing, proof reading and formatting of the book was done by Andrea Kingston, a volunteer in the library of the Rochester Civic Garden Center. Without her expertise it is doubtful the book would look as professional as befits this important part of parks history. Thank you Andrea.

Kent Millham, a current plantsman of Rochester parks and editor of The International Lilac Journal, proof read the book to insure the accuracy and correctness of the horticultural information. Kent also wrote the last or 3rd Addendum to make the book as current as possible. He also supplied the 'Rochester' lilac picture on the book cover.

The Rochester Democrat and Chronicle Media Group supplied the great picture of Mr. Grant that appears on the back cover

Mary Dougherty, an instructor in book publishing, handled all the details of publishing and distribution of the book; helping to get the widest possible distribution of the finished product.

Marcy Klein, a graphic designer and member of the RCGC board, who produced the beautiful new cover for this 2014 version of the book.

There are many others, all volunteers, staff or fellow members of the Board of the Rochester Civic Garden Center. Without their support and encouragement the book might not have been published.

. . . . Arthur Trimble

PROLOGUE

When I started writing this history of the plantsmen of the Rochester park system, I was thinking primarily of John Dunbar, Bernard (Barney) Slavin, Richard Horsey, Bernard (Bernie) Harkness, and Richard (Dick) Fenicchia. These five individuals made the greatest contributions in achieving for the park system its worldwide reputation as one of the outstanding arboretums in the United States. As I proceeded with the writing, I became aware of other individuals who might be called the supporting cast—they also were plantsmen, although their role in this history was smaller in relation to that of the five men mentioned above and around whom this history has evolved.

I also realized that this writing could not be restricted only to those men who worked with the plants and plant culture. The parks with their geological, historic, and natural features furnish the setting for this history—they provide the stage upon which the action takes place. Consequently, it seemed logical to me, especially in the absence of any other document that outlined the growth and changes that took place in the total makeup of the park system, to incorporate some of these in this narrative.

To be fair to some of the other park men with whom I worked during my tenure, it seems that I should acknowledge their efforts in maintaining the park areas and in performing the many chores that are necessary in the successful operation of a complete park system. Three men in particular are Roger Greiten, Clarence Johnson, and Anthony Mattuci. Each one of this threesome had his own section of the total park acreage for which he was responsible. Through attention to the in-park, day-to-day operation and maintenance of this acreage, they kept the park facilities in good condition for public usage. Also, in cooperation with the plantsmen and working with the park personnel assigned to their areas, they made a contribution to the planting programs within their areas using trees and shrubs obtained from the park nurseries.

In writing this history, I have relied upon material garnered from many sources: newspaper clippings; scrapbooks (my own and Dick Fenicchia's); obituaries (found in the public library); old park reports; histories written by the City Historian, Blake McKelvey; etc. Inasmuch as I have had an association with the park system for almost one-half of the time with which this history is concerned, I have relied upon my memory, and also that of Dick Fenicchia, whose personal relationship with the park system dates back to the mid-1920s, and with whom I worked closely from 1950 until 1977. Dick and I still (in 1994) get together several times each month to visit the parks to observe the plantings at different seasons and to keep ourselves informed about the plant collections. I also learned much about the early development of Durand Eastman and Seneca Parks from visits with Art Blensinger, who began his employment with the park system in 1922 and who, presently 93 years of age, is still making occasional pilgrimages to Durand Eastman Park.

Another factor that influenced me to write this history has been that my career with the park system, which began in 1945, overlapped with that of Patrick Slavin (Park Director, 1930-1950), who worked with the park system from 1890 until his death in 1950, and also with that of Richard Horsey, who was with the park system from 1904 until his retirement in 1950.

Whenever I have used material in this report that should be credited to some other source, I have attempted to identify it immediately by mentioning that source. Hopefully, this has avoided the need for a lengthy bibliography.

Readers of this manuscript may wonder why the title, "The Plantsmen of Rochester Parks," when the county park system appears on so many pages. The story begins in 1888 when Ellwanger and Barry gave to the City of Rochester approximately 20 acres of land to be used for park purposes and required it be developed as an arboretum. This determined the manner in which Highland Park would be developed, and the same pattern was followed as other areas were added to the Rochester park system. This type of development, and the aftercare it called for, required the leadership of true horticulturists such as John Dunbar, Barney Slavin, and others, and has remained a focus for the city-owned areas.

The County of Monroe park areas came into the local scene in 1926 when the Ellison family donated the land now known as Ellison Park. This area and other areas acquired by the county have a different focus than that adopted by the city. The natural environment, although subjected to some minor changes, became the focus for the development of the county parks.

In 1961, the agreement between the County of Monroe and the City of Rochester went into effect. By this agreement, the county took over the operation and maintenance of several city park areas. The actual operation of park (city and county) remained much the same as before. The horticultural development remained within the city-owned areas. Within these areas were the greenhouses, nurseries, herbarium, and special equipment used in development and care of plants—all of which are vital to the work of the plantsmen. Their base of operation would remain within the city-owned areas—consequently, the title, "The Plantsmen of Rochester Parks."

It must be noted that the care of street trees and the maintenance of several city-owned park areas remained under the jurisdiction of the city. These, and the employees who have been responsible for their care, are not included in this manuscript. Over the years, however, the city employees involved in maintenance of these areas have taken good care of these areas, which are scattered throughout the city.

INTRODUCTION

The park system presently enjoyed by the residents of the City of Rochester and the County of Monroe has emerged out of yesterday. It is the product of many wise decisions made by elected and appointed officials coupled with the dedication and hard work of the employees assigned to these areas. The circumstances leading to the creation of a park system for the City of Rochester, and the story of its growth during the first sixty years of its existence, have been well documented by the former City Historian, Blake McKelvey, in the booklet entitled *An Historical View of Rochester's Parks and Playgrounds*. This booklet, published in January 1949 by the Rochester Public Library as part of a series on Rochester history, has been complemented by the publication *A Growing Legacy, An Illustrated History of Rochester's Parks*, also written by Blake McKelvey, now City Historian Emeritus, and published by the Parks Centennial Committee for Education and Interpretation during the Parks' Centennial in 1988. These two publications provide an interesting summary of the growth of the park system and its history from the viewpoint of administrative and recreational programs. The latter publication continues the history from the 1940s to the late 1980s.

During the more than one hundred years of its existence, many reports have been written relative to the growth of the park system, the resources and programs that it offers, and the progress that has been made in the development of the individual park areas. These reports give credit to the various administrators who have directed the activities of this park system but neglect the men in the field who, with their imagination and their hands, converted acquired lands into parks.

We can liken the development of parks to the construction of other public edifices. The difference is in the type of building materials that are used. We think of parks as pieces of natural terrain embellished with trees, shrubs, turf, and floral materials of diverse forms that are arranged in pleasing and manageable patterns to promote use and enjoyment by park visitors. The document in hand will tell the story of the men who actually put these building materials together—those plantsmen within the park system who were most responsible for changing the acquired acres into usable and beautiful parks. These plantsmen reached out beyond their assigned duties and were responsible for innovations in park design as well as for the introduction of many new plant varieties of various genera and species.

An editorial that appeared in the December 5, 1888, issue of *Garden and Forest* announced the beginning of the municipal park system of Rochester, New York, and bespoke of its success as follows:

> Before acquiring any land it has separately taken the professional advice of seven men of experience in the management of public parks: Mr. H. W. S. Cleveland of Minneapolis; Mr. Calvert Vaux and Mr. Samuel Parsons, Jr., of New York; Mr. F. L. Olmsted and Mr. J. C. Olmsted of Brookline; Mr. William McMillan of Buffalo; and Mr. W. S. Edgerton of Albany. It has occasioned some surprise that each of these gentlemen, after making the circuit of the city, should, without conference, have fixed upon the same three localities as most desirable to be secured for park purposes. One of these is a body of high ground commanding a superb distant prospect, a part of the site being a tract of land of twenty acres which Messrs. Ellwanger and Barry, the well known nurserymen, have presented to the city; another, a piece of the celebrated Genesee meadows above the city; the third, a portion of the great wooded gorge of the Genesee below the City.

In the September 15, 1897, issue of this same periodical, there appeared an article written by a Mr. O. E. Orfet, a visitor to Rochester from Massachusetts, which stated:

> There is much of horticultural interest in Rochester in its many large and famous nurseries, and the fine system of parks that has recently been formed is already a credit to the city. This system includes Genesee River Gorge, a feature unique in its way and of inestimable value for its

magnificent scenery, and the gorge has been made secure to the public, for all time; the South (Genesee Valley) Park, with its broad pastoral views; and the more highly developed Highland Park, where it has been the object to have every species of deciduous shrub that will grow planted according to its botanical affinity. This has been accomplished in a most happy manner on sloping hillsides that prevent monotony and give easy access by grassy walks.

What a remarkable testimony, when one realizes that the Rochester park system had its beginning only nine years previous, in 1888. The credit for this reputation at such an early date can be attributed to several sources. First, there was the Ellwanger and Barry Nursery firm, which came into existence in 1840. It was in May of that year that Patrick Barry, who had emigrated from Ireland in 1836, joined with George Ellwanger, an immigrant from Germany in 1835, to form the nursery firm. They named their business "The Mount Hope Botanical and Pomological Gardens" and offered for sale "A fine collection of Fruit and Ornamental Trees, Flowering Shrubs, Greenhouse and Hardy Herbaceous Plants, Bulbous Flower Roots, Double Dahlia, etc., etc." They guaranteed delivery of plants, "packed so they can be transported to any part of the country. Gardens laid out and skillful gardeners furnished at short notice." They also announced, in an advertisement that appeared in the September 1840 issue of *Genesee Farmer* (from which the quoted material was taken), that "a regular Botanical and Pomological Garden will be found of which due notice will be given to the public so that they may visit and inspect it."

The nursery prospered and for over fifty years made shipments of nursery stock, via the Erie Canal and the Albany and Buffalo Railroad and thence by lake steamer, to many customers throughout the country. The nursery grew rapidly in size from the original seven acres in 1840 to 650 acres in 1871. As well as shipping thousands of plants from the nursery, Ellwanger and Barry collected plant specimens from all over the United States and Europe for testing within Mt. Hope Gardens. Some of these are still growing today at the Mt. Hope properties, now part of the University of Rochester.

George Ellwanger and Patrick Barry became leaders in civic affairs and made many contributions to charitable institutions within Rochester. They were concerned about the lack of public lands for use by the residents of the city and offered to donate nineteen acres of land around the Highland Reservoir to the city for park purposes. Twice, in 1882 and again in 1883, city officials refused their offer. However, in January 1888, after an election where some new officials were elected to office, the gift was somewhat reluctantly accepted. There were certain restrictions in the deed that determined how the land should be developed. Three of these restrictions that are pertinent to this manuscript are as follows: "the City must employ a competent landscape engineer to make plans and drawings for the park; the park must be maintained in the style of a park of the first class; and the collections of hardy trees and shrubs must be planted to form an arboretum." These restrictions were accepted by the Common Council of the City at its meeting on January 17, 1888.

Ellwanger and Barry also promised to furnish two plants of everything growing within their nursery for planting in this park. This gift of plant materials, coupled with the expressed desire of Ellwanger and Barry (as stated in the deed) that an arboretum be established in Highland Park, was to have a great influence upon the development of the entire park system.

Another major contribution of the Ellwanger and Barry firm, at least indirectly, was the supply of experienced plantsmen who would be recruited for work within the developing park areas as the nursery business began to wind down within the Rochester area. Unfortunately, there is no record of many of these individuals that can be referred to; however, through conversations with some former park employees whose employment dates back many years, this author garnered information about some of the earlier plantsmen in the park system. There have also been some career overlaps that give continuity to this story.

Another great contribution was made by "a group of patriotic citizens whose sole aim in their efforts was to provide pleasure and innocent diversion for present and future generations, to add to the attractiveness of the city, and to provide perpetual breathing places which might contribute to the moral uplifting, physical development and health of our inhabitants." Most active among this group were Dr. Edward Mott Moore, Councilman George W. Elliott, and Bishop Bernard McQuaid. As a result of the persistent efforts and unselfish zeal of this group of citizens, the state legislature, on April 17, adopted Legislative Act of 1888, entitled "An Act to Authorize the Selection, Location and Acquisition of Certain Grants for Public Parks and Parkways In and Near the City of Rochester and to Provide for the Maintenance and Establishment Thereof."

This act authorized the creation of a Park Commission consisting of twenty-one members to which it gave certain powers and responsibilities as quoted in the act:

> The said Park Commissioners shall have power to select and locate such grounds in or near the City of Rochester, as may in their opinion, be proper and desirable to be reserved, set apart, or acquired for one or more public parks and parkways located between such public parks, and approaches thereto, and streets connecting the said parks, and for this purpose may take any part or parts of existing streets and change the lines thereof.

The act further defined the terms of the commissioners and authorized the issuing of bonds in the amount of $300,000 by the Treasurer of the City of Rochester "in such amounts as, from time to time, may be needed for the purchase of land." Section 25 of the act provided "that the Common Council, every year, grant said Park Commission such amounts of money as it shall require and, as to said Common Council shall approve reasonable and just for maintenance of said park or parks, parkways, approaches thereto, and streets connecting the same, and for keeping in repair the improvements and structures therein and for providing a suitable office for the Commission and necessary police protection for maintenance of small parks in said City and care of shade trees in said small parks and the streets, avenues and alleys of the City, from the general fund of the City." There were other provisions in this act; however, the ones quoted seem to be most pertinent to this story.

The Park Commission held its first meeting on May 7, 1888. Among the 21 commissioners appointed by the mayor were many of those individuals who had been leaders in the struggle to have parks established in Rochester. At the meeting, Dr. Edward Mott Moore, Sr., was elected President of the Board; Henry F. Huntington, Treasurer; and W. F. Peck, a nonmember, Secretary.

The Park Commission laid the foundation for what was to be achieved over a period of many years and in doing so they won the applause of the people and the confidence of the municipal authorities. Their achievements belong to the formative or preliminary stage of the Rochester park system, but the credit for the marvelous expansion, development, and exquisite culture that characterize our parks and are admired by all today must be shared with those who came into the contest in later years. The original board was happy in the selection of lands for park purposes but, for years, these lands remained unattractive for want of proper adornment, a process that was slow and unappreciated by the public. This was natural—trees, shrubs, and ornamental plants take time to grow into beauty. The steps that must be taken in preparing the land for park development and use are tedious and slow operations and, extended over wide areas of land, performed under the stress of inadequate funds and shorthanded labor required forbearance of the critical public whose unsympathetic attitude was anything but encouraging to those pioneer commissioners.

In June 1888, the park commissioners took a very important action when they hired Calvin C. Laney as a surveyor of the park properties. Mr. Laney, who was born in Waterloo, New York, on February 18, 1850, attended public school there until he was thirteen years old. He then continued his education at the Friends Academy in Union Springs and later at a private school in

Poughkeepsie. After this he attended Waterloo Academy for two years. During the next two years he helped his parents in their grocery store while teaching school. In 1871 and 1872, he worked with an engineer corps surveying a railroad through Seneca County. This was the beginning of an eighteen-year career in working on the construction of railroads in various parts of New York, Pennsylvania, Vermont, Illinois, and Nebraska. Because of his ever-increasing knowledge and expertise, he earned several promotions. In 1882, he was division engineer, supervising the building of the Pine Creek Railroad from Stokesdale Junction to Williamsport, Pennsylvania, and in 1885, he was superintendent in charge of construction of the Beach Creek Railroad from Jersey Shore to Clearfield in Pennsylvania. In 1887, he supervised the building of 80 miles of railway for the Kansas City and Omaha Railroad. During these years, he also spent some time working on the construction of bridges in Buffalo, New York (1876), and in making topographical maps in Rochester (1876, and again in 1886). In 1887, he was called to San Diego, California, to make surveys of Coronado Beach. On June 25, 1888, he began his career with the Rochester park system—a career that extended until 1928. With the hiring of Calvin Laney, the Park Commission gained a man not just well versed in surveying and some types of construction but also one experienced in the supervision of men. The type of experience he would bring to his position with the Rochester parks would prove to be of great value in the building of this park system.

On June 27, 1888, the commissioners made a visit to Buffalo, where parks had been in existence for twenty years. The Buffalo Park Board members advised the newly formed Rochester Park Commission as follows: "First select your landscape architect and abide by his judgment on the selection of sites for your parks; also, purchase all the land needed at once and do not appreciate values that you may be obliged to pay for in the future."

The Park Commission heeded the advice regarding the selection of a landscape architect. After reviewing proposals received from several experts, at a meeting on October 8, 1888, the commissioners formally agreed to employ Frederick Law Olmsted and Son, "at a compensation of $5000 for three years service from the date of his first visit."

Frederick Law Olmsted, Sr., recognized today as the founder of park planning and landscaping in America, earned his reputation as a result of his work in planning and creating Central Park in New York City. This park, begun in 1857 and completed in 1863, became the "starting gun" for the park movement, which spread rapidly to every major American city. After 1863, Olmsted, with his partner Calvert Vaux, and later in independent practice, trained the majority of designers and planners who were to shape the country's physical growth throughout the late nineteenth century. As a consultant hired by the Rochester Park Commission, Olmsted was specifically charged with providing advice in the locating and development of a park system for the City of Rochester. He considered the Genesee River to be Rochester's fairest asset with a natural setting that should be preserved. He recommended that priority be given to the purchase and development of two large parks straddling the river at points north and south of the center city. These two parks were North Park (later named Seneca Park) and South Park (later named Genesee Valley Park).

In a report of the Board of Park Commissioners, dated 1888-1889, under the subheading "Highland Park," it is stated, "Mr. Olmsted looked upon the landscape before him and marked out its adaptation and special effect." Relative to Seneca Park, he said, "In this park we have the incomparable efforts of nature in one of her finest opportunities," and about Genesee Valley Park, his remark was, "I wish to make a restful place for the people of Rochester." Along with the work on these three parks, during the next three decades, the firm of Olmsted (F. L. Olmsted, Sr., retired from professional practice in 1895) would have input into the designs and plans for Franklin Square, Jones Park, Lakeview Park, Madison Park, Brown Square, Riley Triangle, Maple Grove (at that time, considered part of Seneca Park west of the river, now Maplewood Park), Cobbs Hill Reservoir and Park, Warner Tract (now part of Highland Park), and the Parade Grounds. The Olmsted firm also made a contribution to the layout of Durand

15

Eastman Park, particularly the lakes and the road pattern within this park.

In assigning the priority for acquisition and development, Highland Park was bypassed because of the expense and difficulty envisioned in obtaining more land for addition to the 20 acres given by Ellwanger and Barry. However, in a letter from Edward M. Moore, dated March 18, 1890, Mr. Moore informed Olmsted, "We have decided to purchase the land around the reservoir, precisely as you have laid it out."

Frederick Law Olmsted and members of his firm advised in the selection of areas for parks and in the design of several of the park areas, particularly Highland Park, Genesee Valley Park, Seneca Park, and several smaller areas. There is no evidence that he or any member of his firm were ever actively involved in any of the plantings in these areas; however, in the designs, Olmsted did recommend areas where plantings should be made, and where existing plants should be retained or removed as part of the design. Frederick Law Olmsted had a "definite feeling for the land, for living plants and for the union of the two in an organic whole," and this feeling is reflected in the plans that he developed during his career.

It is in Highland Park where the results of Olmsted's foresightedness in design (proposed in 1890-1892) are most evident today. To a large degree, the theme for Highland Park had been set by Ellwanger and Barry and confirmed by the Park Commission, as mentioned earlier. While conforming to the concept of an arboretum, Olmsted managed to incorporate his design with the development that was already underway. Although this park is surrounded, in fact hemmed in, by residential development, one gets the feeling that one is well away from the city. Olmsted recommended that the pinetum (the plantings of pines, spruce, firs, and other tall-growing evergreen trees) be planted on the small slopes that rise above both sides of the curving roadway from Goodman Street South to Mt. Vernon Avenue so that the towering trees now create the impression that you are driving through a wooded canyon such as is found in mountain country. The gentle curving of the road adds a feeling of suspense as one drives through the park and provides a constantly expanding vista to the beholder.

Elsewhere in the park, various collections of plants of different genera and species are separated by open spaces. This intermingling of open space and planting areas is ideal in an arboretum setting and provides a visible opportunity to observe a particular planting without interference from competing plantings. Perhaps one reason Highland Park earned its reputation as an outstanding park of Olmsted design is that the recommendations made by Frederick Law Olmsted for this park meshed so closely with ideas held by John Dunbar, who was hired in 1890 to take charge of the horticultural development of the Rochester parks. Both of these men, Olmsted and Dunbar, favored the manmade pastoral landscapes so common in England. John Dunbar had worked on several large English estates before coming to America, and Frederick Law Olmsted was greatly influenced by what he observed during several visits to England, especially by People's Park in Birkenhead.

A letter written to Frederick L. Olmsted, Jr., on December 1, 1910, by Calvin C. Laney, Superintendent of Parks, reads as follows: "We are going to build a new show greenhouse at Highland Park. A lady has left $20,000 to build it. We would like your advice in regard to the location." This greenhouse, now known as the Lamberton Conservatory, was completed in 1911 at the site recommended by the Olmsted firm.

Unfortunately, very little mention of Frederick Law Olmsted appears in the annual reports of the Rochester Park Commission. Consequently, much of the information about him that appears in this narrative was derived from correspondence between members of the Park Commission and staff members of the Olmsted firm. This information became available through research undertaken at the Library of Congress by a local woman interested in the preservation of Olmsted-designed areas.

The professional input by the Olmsted firm provided an outline for the development of the Rochester park system; however, the actual development was accomplished by park employees working in the field under the supervision of a few inspired and dedicated men. It is the accomplishments of these men, the true plantsmen in the department, that have resulted in the parks that this community enjoys today.

With the park commissioners actively engaged in the acquisition of the land for the two large parks north and south of the city, Calvin C. Laney was immediately at work surveying these properties and preparing contour maps that would be used by the Olmsted firm as it began its program of providing plans and designs for the new park areas. The two large parks referred to originally as North Park and South Park were soon given the names of Seneca Park and Genesee Valley Park.

While making the original surveys of these park areas, as well as of Highland Park, Laney was making lists of all the various trees and shrubs that could be found growing within western New York. These lists would be referred to frequently when the planting program within the parks became a reality. Mr. Laney assumed responsibility for the first planting to be undertaken in the park system. Using his lists, he hunted for healthy specimens to plant within the new park areas.

Genesee Valley Park, in particular, was an assemblage of former farms. During the summer of 1889 and continuing from then on, Laney engaged laborers in the task of clearing out existing hedgerows, fences, and undesirable trees and shrubs. Guided by advice from Olmsted, meadows in Genesee Valley Park were prepared for seeding, the trees in the picnic grove were thinned out, and about one-quarter mile of road was graded. Although the acceptance of the original twenty acres of land at Highland Park predated the acquisition of land in any other location, it was Genesee Valley Park where the first significant development took place.

Thousands of young plants were planted under the general supervision of Calvin Laney in accordance with plans received from Olmsted, who indicated that masses of foliage were needed as accents in the pastoral landscape, to furnish shade for the picnic areas and the trails, and to screen out the railroad tracks running along the eastern boundary and cutting through the park west of the river.

It is important to mention, at this time in this story of the plantsmen in the park system, that signing the park payroll on April 1, 1890, as a member of a crew of laborers working in Genesee Valley Park, was a 17-year-old Irish lad by the name of Bernard (Barney) Slavin. Despite his age, he was soon made an assistant foreman of the crew, and very shortly after, he was appointed foreman. It is important to remember the name Barney Slavin, because he will play a major role in this brief history.

In 1889, the park commissioners created the position of Superintendent of Parks and immediately appointed Calvin Laney to the position with recommendations offered by Frederick Law Olmsted, who was impressed by the knowledge, leadership, and skills exhibited by Mr. Laney. Calvin Laney was always appreciative of the contributions made by the park commissioners in the development of the park system. In a speech he made in 1937, Calvin Laney mentioned the first land purchase for parks as follows: "In accordance with the recommendations of the landscape architect, Frederick Law Olmsted, the Park Board made land purchases of property along the Genesee River and property near Mt. Hope Reservoir. It is important to note the conscientious study given to the locations." In another section of this same speech, he said, "This overseeing of the parks was a labor of love to the commissioners. Not a day went by that they did not ride out to inspect the work that was accomplished. That work and the efforts of those who afterward became members of the Park Board constitute one of the brightest chapters in the history of our city for they gave unselfishly of their time and efforts to make the Rochester Park system one of the best in the world." Also, "In the complexities of a large city there came a time when it seemed best to make the parks a department with a supervisory head and the Park Board became a thing of the past."

It is interesting that two of the three men who served as the supervising heads of the park system for the next 13 years would have the title of Park Commissioner. Two of these men would have formerly served on the Park Commission; these were Alexander Lamberton, who would serve from 1915 until 1918, and William S. Riley, who served from 1918 to 1925. When Riley retired in 1925, Calvin Laney was appointed Park Commissioner, serving until his retirement in 1928. At that time the park system was established as the Bureau of Parks, which the new city charter placed under the Commissioner of Public Safety.

Calvin Laney had been charged with supervising the building of an urban park system. In addition to the surveying of newly acquired areas, he laid out roads and walks and was responsible for the general development of the areas. Aware that the Park Commission had determined that Highland Park would be developed as an arboretum, and without any training or experience in horticulture and landscaping, Mr. Laney realized that he lacked the knowledge needed for the proper horticultural development of the park areas. Consequently, in April 1891, he took the very significant step of hiring John Dunbar to be Assistant Superintendent in charge of the horticultural development of the Rochester parks.

Before proceeding with more details concerning the career of John Dunbar relative to the Rochester parks, it seems pertinent to mention that the careers of John Dunbar and Barney Slavin, the two men who made the greatest contributions to the early development of horticulture in these parks, paralleled and intermeshed with one another. In this story their careers will be reported on separately to avoid the conflict that this author would have in trying to report fully about each of these individuals at the same time. Inasmuch as John Dunbar arrived in Rochester in 1891, fully prepared by training and experience to undertake the responsibility for which he was hired, while Barney Slavin, although hired before Dunbar, was still learning (much from

Dunbar, as well as from self study) and gaining the experience that would lead him on to great achievements in horticulture, John Dunbar's career will be reported on first.

To a great extent, in this document, where the writer makes reference to the local parks, he may mention the park system. There may be instances, however, where the terms "Park Department" or "Park Bureau" will be used. Please realize that the three terms are interchangeable; the difference in terminology is the result of changes in the structure of the local government.

THE DUNBAR YEARS

The hiring of John Dunbar was to be an important factor in gaining for Rochester its reputation as a center for horticulture as early as 1897. Dunbar's early background had prepared him for the challenge that was before him. He was born in Rafford, in northern Scotland, on June 4, 1859. After completing his formal schooling in his late teens, he apprenticed on the estate of Sir William Gordon Cummings near Altyre, Elginshire. This estate contained an extensive collection of deciduous trees, shrubs, and conifers. All branches of horticulture were intelligently conducted there. He became a journeyman gardener at the age of twenty and during the next eight years worked on three major estates, including Blenheim Castle, the birthplace of Winston Churchill at Woodstock, Oxfordshire. Here he was foreman of a large tropical plant department. Thus, in England and Scotland, he had gained broad experience and attained a degree of proficiency that well fitted him for the career that was ahead of him in America.

At the age of twenty-eight, he came to the United States to work at Dosoris, the Long Island estate of Charles Anderson Dana, editor of the *New York Sun*. Here he served as assistant to William Falconer, a fellow Scotsman, who had attended the same village school in Scotland. Mr. Falconer was eight years older than Dunbar and had come to the United States thirteen years prior to Dunbar's arrival. He had already made a reputation as a leading horticulturist in this country while serving as head gardener at Dosoris. Calvin Laney learned about Dunbar through correspondence with William McMillan, a Park Commissioner in Buffalo, New York, who was acquainted with Mr. Falconer. Evidently in response to a letter from Calvin Laney, McMillan wrote, in a letter dated April 6, 1891, as follows:

I am sorry to say I do not know of any man competent for the place you offer. I have a young man, a thorough gardener, with good training both in Scotland and here, but not so thoroughly posted on nursery stock as one should be to fill your bill properly. He came to me this spring on purpose to get fuller knowledge on this very branch. I pay him $1.75 per day. He is not married. He is very intelligent and ambitious and would probably suit you if you were not likely to do any special propagation or planting for another year. But he is not worth $65 per month as yet.

So I have taken the liberty to notify Mr. William Falconer of Glen Cove, Long Island, who is more likely to know of some capable man for such a position than anyone else in America. If he knows of such a man I have asked him to ask the candidate to make a direct application to you himself.

Mr. Falconer, in a letter to Mr. McMillan dated April 8, 1891, wrote as follows:

My dear Mr. McMillan,

In answer to yours of the 6th inst., W'd say: I have a likely young man and I believe he c'd fill the Rochester place very well. He is Scotch, from near Forres, about 32, tall, strong, intelligent, and of exceptional good moral character. He has been here with me for about four years, came directly to me here from England and has never been anywhere else in this country. He served his apprenticeship as a gardener at Altyre (Sir William Gordon Cummings place) near Forres, and afterwards worked as a journeyman gardener in several private gardens in England. During the first year he was here I had him take care of the fruit trees, and since then he has had the greenhouses to look after, and, in my absence, take full charge.

He wishes to leave here to better himself financially; also he wants to get married, but would like to get a permanent place before taking this step. His name is John Dunbar.

While here he has had an excellent opportunity of acquainting himself with all manner of outdoor work peculiar to a large ornamented estate, and the best chance in the country for posting himself in trees, shrubs and other hardy ornamental plants.

If you think he might be a suitable person, I'd advise that Mr. Laney see him personally before making an engagement.

Very sincerely yours
/s/ Wm. Falconer

And in a note enclosed with the foregoing letter, Mr. Falconer writes:

My dear Mr. McMillan,

The enclosed letter explains itself and you can use it as you wish—send it to Mr. Laney if you see fit. I We'd advise that Dunbar sh'd not make application for the place till after I hear from you.

You know that all Scotch gardeners bro't up in country places get an outside training, in this respect differing a good deal from English gardeners who usually are strictly greenhouse men; at the same time all gardeners of all countries have a leaning toward a greenhouse. To be an absolutely outdoor man who knows much about plants of any kind, be they trees, shrubs, or anything else is a very difficult matter indeed.

Now Dunbar is a real good man, faithful, vigorous and can handle men. He is a teetotaler and an active churchman. Indeed I think you will go a long way before you can get a better one. At the same time, where it is possible at all, I believe in both parties seeing each other and understanding each other perfectly.

In making application for a situation the applicant is apt to blow pretty strong about his qualifications, and, if need be, with the aid of others, get up the blow to a pretty stiff breeze; and it often happens that the poorest quality has the most wind. A personal interview checks this sort of thing.

With kindest regards

Very sincerely yours
/s/ Wm. Falconer

A letter from Buffalo, New York, dated April 10, 1891,
follows:

Dear Mr. Laney,

Have just rec'd the enclosed letter from Mr. Falconer. From
what he says I believe Mr. Dunbar is just the man for you.
From further talk with the man on the park here I find he
would not suit, so you need not think of him. I advise you
show Mr. Falconer's notes to some of your leading
Commissioners, and advise that the man be sent for, for a
personal interview as Falconer suggests. For my part if in
your place I would not hesitate to engage him off hand. He
is no doubt willing to come for the wages offered—$65 (per
month) with house, or Mr. Falconer would not suggest him.

At Falconer's place there are about 1200 different species of
hardy trees and shrubs.

Yours truly,
/s/ Wm. McMillan

A letter from Buffalo, New York, dated April 15, 1891, from
William McMillan to Calvin Laney includes the following: "I have
yours of yesterday and have at once enclosed it in a note to Mr.
Falconer, telling him to send on Mr. Dunbar as suggested in your
note." Also: "I am personally glad of your decision to send for
Dunbar, as he has had exceptionally fine training for the work you
propose for him. I am confident he is just the right man."

It was with the arrival of John Dunbar in Rochester in
April 1891 that the horticultural work in this park system really
began. The first serious planting was undertaken in the spring of

1892. Ellwanger and Barry made a sizable donation of plants from their nursery, and Dunbar had ordered shipments from nurseries in different parts of the United States, Great Britain, France, Belgium, and Germany. About 1,500 species and varieties of shrubs were procured and planted. Included were 100 varieties of lilacs, which became the nucleus for Rochester's now famous lilac collection. With Superintendent Laney's support, Dunbar established a small nursery in Highland Park where plants could be held until permanent sites were selected and prepared.

In 1896, consistent with plans previously made by F. L. Olmsted, John Dunbar planned and supervised the planting of an extensive collection of conifers along both sides of the road (Pinetum Road) through Highland Park from Goodman Street to Mt. Vernon Avenue. He was especially proud of the 109 varieties of coniferous evergreens that were thriving in this location by 1898. This collection included needled evergreens of pine, spruce, fir, arborvitae, and juniper, also deciduous species of larch and cypress. The 1898 report of the Park Commission mentions the extension of Highland Park from Highland Avenue to Elmwood Avenue being cleared of native growth and planted with grass, with some part of it reserved for nursery purposes. This was done under Mr. Dunbar's supervision. During 1899, he prepared planting beds at the foot of the embankment east of the Children's Pavilion (this was located in the circle on top of the hill at the end of Reservoir Avenue) by removing the native soil to a depth of two and one-half feet and replacing it with pure humus (peat) drawn in from a nearby deposit discovered in the Pinnacle Hills. The planting of rhododendrons, azaleas, and other ericaceous plants in these beds commenced in 1900.

John Dunbar was officially appointed to the position of Assistant Superintendent of Parks in 1891 and served in that position until his retirement in 1926.

The combination of Laney and Dunbar was of great value to the City of Rochester in the development of a new park system. Laney, with his background in construction work and in the preparation of land areas for special usages, which he had acquired while involved in surveying and in railroad work, and Dunbar, with his special knowledge of plant materials and other aspects of horticultural work, made a perfect team for the development of a park system, especially one that was dedicated to the establishment of an arboretum.

John Dunbar could not singlehandedly convert the terrain at Highland Park into an outstanding botanical park and arboretum. He furnished the knowledge and leadership needed in getting the job done and, consequently, is credited with the results. This does not mean that he avoided tackling any of the backbreaking work involved in the planting of large trees or in the maintenance of the parks. Mr. Richard Horsey, who, beginning in 1908, worked closely with Dunbar in Highland Park, said that Dunbar "had no use for shirkers. At one time when he thought that men assigned to cutting overgrown materials with scythes were goofing off, he took a scythe and led them for a halfway. They were tired out trying to keep up with him."

To supplement the manpower assigned to Highland Park and to assist in the preparation of planting beds and in the actual planting program, manpower was drawn from Genesee Valley Park. In charge of the Genesee Valley crew was the young Irishman, Barney Slavin, who had earned promotion to foreman by the hard work and dedication with which he addressed assigned chores. Working with an experienced gardener such as Dunbar provided Barney with the grooming and the inspiration that would steer him into a lifetime involvement with park and horticultural work. The careers of these two men, Dunbar and Slavin, would run parallel to each other for over thirty years—each man made outstanding contributions that brought much renown and prestige to the Rochester parks.

Beginning in 1895, Dunbar was sending reports on the performance of plants growing within Highland Park to various horticultural journals. Among these were a series on trees and shrubs in bloom at Rochester that were sent to his old friend, William Falconer, who edited the journal *Gardening*. Another popular outlet for his writings was *Garden and Forest*, a favorite journal of Charles Sprague Sargent of the Arnold Arboretum and Harvard University. Professor Sargent was a world-famous horticulturist. His curiosity aroused by these reports from Rochester, Sargent visited Rochester in the autumn of 1899 to see for himself the wealth of plant materials that he was reading about. He was so impressed with what he observed in Rochester that he made a series of annual visits that would continue for twenty years. During the first few years, Dr. Sargent, accompanied by some of the park commissioners and, of course, Calvin Laney and John Dunbar, toured the parks in horse-drawn buggies. These tours centered on Highland Park, but also grew to include Genesee Valley Park, Seneca Park, Maplewood Park, Durand Eastman Park, and Cobbs Hill Park. During the evenings, after a long day spent in the parks, when Sargent was in town, some of the commissioners and park staff would gather at the Powers Hotel to listen to and to be inspired by the distinguished visitor from Boston. The friendship for Rochester parks, which was engendered first through Dunbar's articles and then through the personal contacts that Laney and Dunbar enjoyed with Professor Sargent during his visits, proved to be of great value to these parks.

Beginning in 1902, the Rochester park system became the fortunate recipient of Dr. Sargent's generosity as he sent large consignments of trees and shrubs raised from seeds and cuttings at Arnold Arboretum for planting in Rochester. Much of this material had originally been collected in western China by an employee of the arboretum—the famous botanical explorer and plant collector, Ernest Henry Wilson, who also visited Rochester upon several occasions. Ernest Wilson was commonly known as "Chinese" Wilson because of his many plant-collecting expeditions in China.

A heavy burden was being placed upon the park staff as the parks continued to expand. As new acres were added to Highland Park and Genesee Valley Park, and, even to a greater degree, to Seneca Park, these areas had to be landscaped in harmony to agree with the older sections. Until 1904, Seneca Park was considered to occupy both sides of the river. With the acquisition of Maple Grove during this year the area west of the river was split off and Maplewood Park came into existence. John Dunbar, with some cooperation from members of the Rochester Rose Society, established a special rose garden in this area.

The first greenhouses within Highland Park were constructed in 1904 when one greenhouse, 100 feet long by 20 feet wide, and another, 100 feet long by 11 feet wide, were built. These greenhouses, located at the southwest corner of Highland Avenue and Goodman Street South, were placed under John Dunbar's supervision and were used as propagating houses where plants for planting throughout the parks were started. A third house, 100 feet long by 11 feet wide, was added in 1905. This "lower greenhouse range," as it was to remain until the 1960s, was completed in 1916 with the construction of the "Palm House," 100 feet long by 28 feet wide. The lower greenhouses were opened for public visitation, and for several years prior to the construction of the Lamberton Conservatory (dedicated in 1911), Dunbar supervised the growing and exhibiting of seasonal plant displays in the larger of the two original houses. With the construction of the conservatory, John Dunbar had a new outlet in which to display the results of his skill in floriculture. The conservatory became the "show houses," while the lower greenhouse range was where all of the plants for display at the conservatory were raised, as well as serving as the propagating center for all types of plants used throughout the whole department.

The three older parks had now become four, and their acreage, which was 631 acres in 1902, had grown to 1,006 by 1915. In addition, several new parks now made their appearance. The nucleus for Cobbs Hill Park was given in 1905 by George Eastman and a few other public-spirited citizens. Along with other plantings in this area, the lilac collection was expanded to a substantial degree at Cobbs Hill Park.

Having noticed some differences in growth of some individual specimens of hawthorns that appeared in abundance in the Rochester-Monroe County area, Dunbar had been studying them. He mentioned these studies to Calvin Laney, who, in turn, called them to Dr. Sargent's attention. Because of his intense interest in the taxonomy of plants, Sargent became vitally interested in Dunbar's studies, and a lasting friendship developed between the two men. Sargent encouraged park officials to engage in "more extensive botanical research, such as exploring the nearby areas for specimens of Hawthorn." The list of specimens was soon expanded to include other genera such as elm, hickory, blackberry, alder, shadbush, linden, plum, and other native plants. These explorations were extended to other areas in Western New York, Western Pennsylvania, Southern Missouri, Western Arkansas, Eastern Oklahoma, Southern Ontario, Central and Southern Ohio, Western Kentucky, and Northwest Texas.

John Dunbar's training during his apprenticeship and, also, through the experience he had acquired while working on estates in England and under Falconer at Dosoris, included the keeping of accurate records relative to the various plant materials. These records stated the sources from which the plants were acquired, dates of planting, and the locations within the parks where the various plants could be found. The maintenance of records such as these is an important function of any arboretum and is assigned as a separate responsibility of a trained botanist or taxonomist. In effect, these records would become a valuable asset of the park system and would justify its classification as an arboretum.

Realizing that it could be impossible for John Dunbar to continue to supervise the development of the parks and at the same time maintain an accurate system of records, Dr. Sargent encouraged the development of a herbarium within the Rochester park system with a trained and experienced botanist or taxonomist in charge. As well as being the depository for the planting records, the herbarium would house the horticultural library and would also contain specially prepared sheets or folders of dried plant specimens collected by the park staff. These herbarium sheets would be available for study purposes to assist in the determination and substantiation of the botanically correct names of plants.

Mr. Richard E. Horsey, who became an employee of the park system in 1904, was assigned the responsibility of keeping the records and maintaining the herbarium. Mr. Horsey was more a student of plants than a grower. However, his contribution to the park system was a valuable one that will be described in more detail as this history progresses.

In late July 1908, after complaining about the oppressive heat that was prevalent in Rochester during that summer, and under the pressure of an ever-increasing burden in the development of an ever-growing park system, Dunbar suffered an ailment that placed him in a sanitarium in Canandaigua for much of the year. During his absence, the supervision of Highland Park was taken over by Richard Horsey, who was made foreman of the park. Although Barney Slavin was, at that time, engaged in the supervision of Seneca Park and the newly acquired Durand Eastman Park, he and his crew made several trips to Highland Park to assist in some of the planting and maintenance of that area.

After recovering from this one period of hospitalization, Dunbar returned to work in the parks until his retirement on January 1, 1926. During his entire tenure with the parks, he was faced with a constant challenge; park areas were being added and landscaping and plantings were needed in the development of these areas. Also some of the trees and shrubs, planted in earlier years, were requiring more care, such as pruning, spraying, and general cultivation.

Other events were happening at about this time that greatly increased the responsibilities assigned to John Dunbar. Several of the city squares that had been acquired as early as 1826 (Franklin Square) and 1837 (Washington Park, Jones Park, Madison Park, and Plymouth Park) had been reviewed by the Olmsted firm, and plans for renewal of the earlier landscapes were prepared. Cobbs Hill Park (152.407 acres) had been acquired by gift and purchase during the years 1905-1911. Edgerton Park (32.387 acres) became city property in 1910 as a result of property exchange. During 1903, the movement for playgrounds for the youth of the city and for general recreation areas was initiated with the development of Brown Square Playground (designed by

31

the Olmsted firm). During the 22 years that followed (until Dunbar's retirement on January 1, 1926), 16 more playgrounds were developed. The park staff, under the leadership of Calvin Laney and John Dunbar and, beginning in about 1912-1913, Bernard Slavin, were called upon to assist in some of the planting and landscaping of these areas.

Another factor that had a real influence upon Dunbar was the assignment, in 1903, of Barney Slavin to the developing of Seneca Park. With this change in staff at Highland Park, Dunbar lost his "right-hand man." Dunbar was also called upon to assist in the preparation of many plants for moving to Seneca Park from the Highland Park nursery.

In 1910, a nursery with 23,000 trees and shrubs raised at Highland Park was established on the Frost tract in Genesee Valley Park (on the west side of the river). This was the result of a cooperative effort by John Dunbar and Barney Slavin, who brought his "gang" from Seneca Park to assist in this program.

In 1910, George Bahringer, a former nurseryman, joined the staff as a foreman assigned to Highland Park. Although he could in no way replace Barney Slavin, with his insatiable thirst and drive for horticultural knowledge, Bahringer was a very dedicated and competent park employee. He had a reputation of being a real expert in the pruning of trees and shrubs. Although he spent most of his time in Highland Park, Bahringer was often called upon for special jobs in other park areas. He was of great assistance to John Dunbar in the maintenance program within Highland Park and also in the planting at Cobbs Hill Park, which, in effect, became a horticultural annex to Highland Park.

A gift (in lieu of back taxes) of the old Warner estate added forty acres to Highland Park in 1909. This made possible the development of some active recreational features, including a toboggan slide. (Citizens of today, familiar with Highland Park, may find this hard to believe, although for years the Lily Pond has been a popular ice-skating rink.) Dunbar planted a collection of American oaks, hickories, and maples along Robinson Drive between South Avenue and Mt. Hope Avenue, together with hawthorn and a few other species.

The Rochester parks continued to grow at a rapid rate. Very early in its history, it was discovered that the limited acreage of Highland Park would not be able to hold all of the plant materials that could be grown in this geographical region. Consequently, many plantings of botanical interest were expanded into Genesee Valley, Seneca, Durand Eastman, and Cobbs Hill Parks.

In an article that appeared in the July 1915 *Bulletin of the New York Forestry Association,* John Dunbar stated, "At present we have 297 species and varieties of Lilacs—a collection of Rhododendrons, Azaleas, and other ericaceous plants— Crabapples, Cherries, Plums, Redbuds, Bush Honeysuckles, Shad trees, Snowdrop trees, Dogwoods, Viburnums, Mockoranges, Deutzias, Spireaes, Roses, and other conspicuous flowering shrubs and trees in sufficient quantities so bloom seems of super- abundant profusion. . . . numerous trees, shrubs, and vines—about 3800 in number—some of the principal genera are Pines–67, Spruce–50, Fir–30. We also maintain an Herbarium—so far as we know, the park system of Rochester is the only municipal park system in the world where complete systematic collections of hardy trees and shrubs of the North Temperate Zone have been successfully acquired and placed under cultivation and answering all the purposes of a scientific institution."

When the Trustees of the Ellwanger and Barry Nursery decided in 1918 to terminate their business, several of their employees found employment in the park system. Because most of them had homes located in the general neighborhood of Highland Park, they were assigned to work in that area. With skills that had been honed by their nursery experience, they were well prepared to make a real contribution to the continuing development and maintenance of this park. Unfortunately, records of these men are not readily available. However, foremost among them was a German immigrant, Frederick Ahrens, who had been chief propagator for the nursery firm. He was one of the men mentioned in the old advertisement of the nursery which stated, "Gardens laid out and skillful gardeners furnished at short notice."

Mr. Ahrens's daughter-in-law, now in her nineties, remembers that when she married Fred Ahrens, Jr., in 1925, she was told that her father-in-law had planted Kodak Park. Unfortunately, she could not furnish any biographical information about him, and this author has not been able to find any such material.

Mr. Ahrens was assigned to the greenhouses, where he was immediately involved in a program of propagating plants for both Dunbar and Slavin. He was particularly skilled in the raising of plants for conservatory display, and consequently worked closely with John Dunbar. Barney Slavin found Ahrens to be "quite set in his ways" and not willing to share any of his "secrets of the trade" with Barney. This, of course, did not please Barney, who was always trying to increase his own knowledge in all aspects of horticulture. As a result, he was willing to let Dunbar have "full sway" in making use of Ahrens. Mr. Ahrens also worked in close cooperation with Richard Horsey, whose responsibility at that time was maintaining all plant collections in good condition. Horsey would constantly review all plants growing within the various collections and would give Ahrens a list of those which he felt were in need of propagation.

Fred Ahrens's proficiency in the propagation of plants was well known throughout the horticultural world. Upon request from Liberty Hyde Bailey, Dean of Agriculture at Cornell University and author of many books dealing with horticultural subjects, including the six-volume *Standard Cyclopedia of Horticulture*, Ahrens wrote a section entitled "Propagation of Coniferous Evergreens" for inclusion in Bailey's book *Cultivated Evergreens*.

As well as devoting his work hours to the creation of a park system, John Dunbar was also active within the community, organizing flower shows and assisting garden clubs. Shortly after he planted the rose garden in the newly acquired Maplewood Park at the corner of Driving Park and Lake Avenue, he was a cofounder of the Rochester Rose Society and served as its president for a number of years. He was actively involved with the Western New York Horticulture Society and served as its botanist.

For over thirty years, he wrote reports on the plants that were growing within the parks. These were published in various horticultural journals. He contributed to the chapters on *Berberis, Crataegus,* and *Rhododendrons* in the *Standard Cyclopedia of Horticulture* published by L. H. Bailey. In 1923 he collaborated with other plantsmen in writing the chapter on the "Cultivation and Propagation of Conifers," the chapter on "Adaptation of Conifers," and the chapter entitled "Broad-leafed Evergreens," which appeared in the book *The Cultivated Evergreens,* edited by Bailey. In the September 22, 1923, issue of the *Florists Exchange and the Horticultural Trade World* he wrote "The Latest News About Lilacs." In this article he described thirty of his lilac seedlings. He mentions 'General Sherman,' which "has immense, many shouldered, upright clusters of single flowers of which the color might be described as creamy lavender as being his best lilac and one of the most beautiful lilacs in cultivation."

Although the lilac collection represents only one of the many plant collections in Highland Park, it is this collection that has brought to John Dunbar his most lasting fame. In 1892 he established a small collection of lilacs in Highland Park near the corner of Highland Avenue and Goodman Street South. Little did he dream at that time that someday this collection would be expanded to cover many acres and become one of the outstanding floral displays in Western New York. Soon after planting these lilacs in the park, Dunbar started a program of raising lilacs from seeds that he collected from some of the French hybrids within the collection. By selecting from the seedlings, he was able to introduce thirty lilac cultivars. These can be classified into four groups according to the names he gave them. These are as follows:
1. The Rochester group—seven named after individuals connected with the parks in some way and two named after members of his family.
2. American personalities—statesmen, authors, and inventors—eight in this group.

3. The Army and Navy group—six generals and one admiral.
4. Presidents—six U.S. presidents—included in this group is 'President Lincoln,' for many years considered to be an outstanding blue lilac.

These introductions were not all made at the same time, but were spread out over a period of approximately twenty years.

John Dunbar's interest in the introduction of new plant materials was not limited to lilacs alone. He was also responsible for the introduction of several plants of other genera. He designated these selections by initial and number (for example, JD 100). However, four of his selections were named for him by other plantsmen (two by Rehder and two by Sargent). These are *Carya Dunbarii*, the Dunbar Hickory; *Cornus Dunbarii*, the Dunbar Dogwood; *Crataegus Dunbarii*, the Dunbar Hawthorn; and *Prunus Dunbarii*.

John Dunbar retired on January 1, 1926. Upon his death on June 1, 1927, at the age of 68, the professional journal *The Florists Exchange and Horticultural Trade World* noted that "he had suffered from an illness which was the primary cause of his retirement from the post of Assistant Superintendent and Arboriculturist of the Rochester Park Department with which he had been continuously connected for more than thirty-five years."

His friend, William Falconer wrote, "John Dunbar's work at Rochester has a national reputation and admiration, and is a living lesson to everyone interested in landscape effects and a knowledge of trees and shrubs and their adaptation for ornament and use. His intimate and friendly association with Dr. C. S. Sargent and the Arnold Arboretum gave him opportunities for observation and investigation almost unique, and the Rochester park system appreciating this advantage, afforded ample space for appropriate plantings; the living truth to all who wished to see and learn."

It is interesting to note that in the latest book about lilacs (*Lilacs, the Genus Syringa*), published in 1988, the author, the late

Fr. John L. Fiala, writes as follows: "Dunbar's 'President Lincoln' lilac was considered for many decades as the 'bluest lilac known.' Dunbar's 'General Sherman' is an outstanding lilac even today and should be included in every worthwhile collection. In bud a deep lavender, it opens to a pearled, creamy pale lavender, a treasure of beauty. It was Dunbar's choicest which somehow the garden writers and the commercial nurseries missed." Fr. Fiala also includes 'General Sherman' in his listing of "Lilacs of Special and Unique Color Classification." About this classification, Fr. Fiala writes, "There are a few lilacs in a classification all their own. These have some new characteristics not ordinarily found in lilacs." Other Dunbar lilacs named by Fr. Fiala as being of considerable merit include 'A. B. Lamberton,' a violet-lavender; 'President Roosevelt,' a purplish red; 'General John Pershing,' an azure blue; 'President John Adams,' a double white; 'Henry Clay,' a rather showy white; and 'Alexander Hamilton,' a violet-lavender.

Fr. Fiala also had this to say about Dunbar and his lilacs: "Not all of his lilacs can presently be found among the plantings in Highland Park. However, there is a bronze plaque honoring his memory. This is located at the Pansy Bed which is surrounded by choice lilacs." The plaque reads:

JOHN DUNBAR
CREATIVE BUILDER OF THE ROCHESTER PARKS
APRIL 1891 TO JANUARY 1, 1926
HE STARTED THE HIGHLAND PARK LILAC COLLECTION
THIRTY-ONE NAMED VARIETIES
WERE ORIGINATED BY HIM
RAFFORD ELGENSHIRE SCOTLAND 1857 - ROCHESTER 1927

Some of John Dunbar's success in building Highland Park into a world-renowned arboretum must be attributed to the friendship that he engendered with Professor Charles S. Sargent of Harvard University's Arnold Arboretum, as previously mentioned. Sargent became a constant advisor and a contributor. Highland Park was one of the testing grounds selected by Sargent for the woody plants from north and west China when "Chinese" Wilson and other botanical explorers and collectors were channeling their seed introductions through the Arnold Arboretum.

Also, prior to 1919, when plant quarantines were established, European and Asiatic nursery lists were combed for plants to add to the collections in Highland Park and Durand Eastman Park. By perusing the interesting records that are on file in the park herbarium, one can learn that many plants were obtained from nurseries in France, England, Holland, Russia, Japan, and Germany, some as early as 1892.

John Dunbar had brought to the Rochester park system a trained and perceptive mind, which was needed during the early stages of its development. Because of his training and knowledge, he not only set an example for the younger men who had become associated with the park system, but he also furnished them with on-the-job training that enabled them to continue the work he had started in Highland Park and equipped them to move out into other areas while he concentrated on Highland Park. Foremost among these young men was the young Irish lad, Bernard (Barney) H. Slavin, who, only seventeen years old at the time, started his park career on April 1, 1890, one year before Dunbar came to the park system from his position at the Dana estate on Long Island.

THE BARNEY SLAVIN YEARS

Bernard H. Slavin was born in Ireland to Mary and Arthur Slavin in 1874. When he was seven years old, the family immigrated to Canada, locating near Peterborough, Ontario, where his father worked in a lumber camp for two years. He earned enough money there to bring his family to Rochester, where they lived for a few years on Oak Street. During this time, Barney attended public and parochial schools for four years. This was the extent of his formal schooling. However, in later years he was tutored at home and he spent hours studying all of the material he could find relative to horticulture and plant materials. Also, during the years 1910 to 1915, realizing that it would benefit him to have a broader knowledge, he spent many more hours on academic subjects.

From Oak Street, the family moved to a red brick farmhouse (since razed) which was located on the Benjamin M. Baker farm on East River Road. This property, within a few years, became part of Genesee Valley Park. Barney's father managed this farm for Baker, and Barney worked there as a farmhand for a short time. He then worked as a farmhand for David Bell, part of whose farm on West Henrietta Road was condemned by the State of New York when the Barge Canal was built.

Barney left farming to try railroading. It had a romantic appeal to the young Irishman, even though his work was mostly confined to cleaning and coaling locomotives in the roundhouse of what was the Rochester-to-Olean spur of the Pennsylvania Railroad. Barney told the story that he might have stayed in railroading except for his mother. "One day I was ordered to serve as an emergency fireman on a wrecking crew that went to Portageville to clean up a wreck. There I saw a trainman with both legs cut off. I told my mother what I saw and she pleaded with me to quit railroading." He gave in and, at 7:30 A.M. on April 1, 1890, signed in at Genesee Valley Park, where he went to work with "pick and shovel" as a 15-cents-per-hour, 10-hour-per-day laborer. This was the start of a career in park work that would continue for 52 years. "Pick and shovel" included all of those chores that Calvin

Laney expected the laborers to perform during the early 1890s: removing hedgerows that separated the old farm lots from each other, grubbing out stumps, stone picking, preparing land for seeding, building roads and trails, and planting trees and shrubs.

Of interest to note is that Barney's brother, Patrick, twelve years old at the time, also began employment with the park system, starting as a water boy working with a crew in Genesee Valley Park and ending his park career sixty years later while serving as Director of Parks. More about Pat later in this history.

Barney Slavin entered into park work with great enthusiasm. Although somewhat slight in build, he had the strength of a young bull and no assigned task was too tough for him. Despite his age (seventeen when he first signed the payroll), he was soon made assistant foreman of the crew, and shortly thereafter, foreman. As Barney in later years said about himself, "I was just a green lad who had to be tough to boss a gang of husky lumbermen who came in from the woods to work in this new river park." Barney learned a great deal about plants by working with them and by studying about them in whatever reference books he could find. Some idea of the outdoor laboratory in which he worked and learned can be garnered by looking at the record of the plant materials that were planted in Genesee Valley Park during his first year on the job. Ten thousand five hundred native shrubs, fifty-eight thousand trees, plus an additional ten thousand willows were planted.

This listing contains many more plants than the average person learns to identify during an entire lifetime. Barney challenged himself to become familiar with these before his eighteenth birthday. The hardwood trees were planted for permanence (many of those planted at this early date are still standing); softwoods were planted as nurse trees to protect the hardwoods until they became well established. In addition to these trees in the young forest plantation that screened out the railroads and East River Road along the eastern boundary of the park, 493 specimen trees, in small groups or as single specimens, were planted along the drives and walks, in the meadows, and along the river banks. These consisted of scarlet maples; silver maples; Norway maples; lindens; white, red, bur and pin oaks; butternuts; liquidamber; buckeyes; tulip trees; nettle trees (hackberry); American elms; cucumber trees; Babylonian willows; Wisconsin willows; black willows; European white birch; white ash; American beech; mulberries; and white hickories. The river banks were planted with basket, long-leaved, shiny-leaved, golden-barked, and black willows, and indigo shrub to prevent erosion of the banks. In addition to the deciduous trees, 1,280 evergreen trees consisting of hemlock, red pine, and white pine were planted along the banks of the small creek (Red Creek) that flows through the park. These evergreens were planted for the purpose of making the shallow valley of the creek appear somewhat deeper and somewhat like a ravine. The plans for all of this planting embodied the theories of Olmsted; however, the planting was accomplished by Barney Slavin and his "gang of lumbermen."

As he planted, Barney was learning not just the names and the characteristics of the plants but also how to use them effectively. What he could not learn from field observations during the ten-hour workday he picked out of reference books after work. Barney and his "gang" established a nursery in Genesee Valley Park west of the river and, under the direction of Calvin Laney, gained experience in the laying of agricultural tile and the grading of swales in the solving of drainage problems. This was more than work for Barney; it was an education that would serve him well in future years.

During 1891, Barney and others from Genesee Valley Park were called to Highland Park upon several occasions to assist in preparing areas for planting. Again, in 1892, Barney was at Highland Park, where he assisted in the planting of the many trees and shrubs that Dunbar had received as a gift from Ellwanger and Barry Nursery, and by purchase from several European nurseries. Among these plants were the first 100 lilac varieties that Dunbar had ordered from France. In later years, Barney could say that he planted some of the first lilacs in Highland Park.

In 1895, Superintendent Laney and his assistant, John Dunbar, in recognition of the industry and potential of this young Irish American, transferred Barney to Highland Park on a permanent basis. He was made foreman of this park in 1901. At this time Highland Park contained just slightly more than fifty acres. A nursery was maintained on land south and west of the reservoir, and it was here that Dunbar propagated and raised many of the plants for planting on all of the new park lands that were constantly being added to this new park system. Working with Dunbar, Barney became familiar with the techniques and procedures of propagating plants and with various nursery practices.

The work of developing the ever-growing Rochester park system was becoming more demanding as additional acres were being added to the existing parks and new areas were being acquired. Many new small parks (miscellaneous neighborhood squares and circles, including grassy and tree-planted street malls) were being placed within the system. These needed special attention because of their locations scattered throughout the city. It was impossible for Laney and Dunbar to be personally involved in all of this development and, at the same time, direct the maintenance of those areas that were already developed. Laney was busy directing the surveying of new park properties as they were added. He also had become more involved in dealings with the park commissioners and with other administrative work. The continuing task of developing the arboretum at Highland Park was consuming most of Dunbar's time. The commissioners were anxious to develop Seneca Park. Consequently, in 1903, Barney Slavin was sent there to "get the job done."

At Seneca Park, Barney had as a guide the park plan prepared by the Olmsted firm and also some limited supervision from Calvin Laney and John Dunbar. It was Barney Slavin, however, who accepted the challenge and converted this acreage along the Genesee River into an outstanding linear park. Originally Seneca Park embraced both sides of the river. During 1904 it was decided to operate each side as a separate entity and, consequently, Barney was busy in the two parks at the same time.

He found 125 different species of trees and shrubs growing naturally within Seneca Park (east of the river).

An early task was the grading of the slope east of Trout Lake, the small spring-fed pond located in the lower park area north of the present zoo. With his crew, Barney moved many surplus pine trees from the Highland Park nursery to plant on the barren slope that resulted from this grading project. Several hundred oak trees in various species were also taken from the park nurseries at Highland Park and planted in a border along the railroad that limits the eastern boundary of this park. A small number of chestnut trees, as well as post, shingle, and pin oaks, were planted in various locations throughout this park, and much scrub growth that obstructed views of the river was cut out. Along with this horticultural work, Barney also developed the city's first ice-skating rink and sledding facilities at Seneca Park.

For many years, Barney Slavin and his family lived in a city-owned house located on a knoll within Seneca Park near the present Ridge Road (Veterans Memorial) bridge. During these years Barney maintained correspondence with Jackson Dawson of the Arnold Arboretum. Mr. Dawson was a famed propagator and was considered to be a "plant genius." He shared many of his secrets with Barney. It has been reported by Betty Keiper (at one time Garden Editor for the *Rochester Times-Union*) in the December 1947 *Journal of New York Botanic Garden*, that during the years when his residence was within Seneca Park, "seed flats filled the Slavin cellar, spilling out into his kitchen, and into his dooryard, high above the spectacular Genesee River Gorge." After a day's work in the parks, Barney spent many hours at night working in his "home nursery." This was his hobby, a true labor of love. The only compensation he received for it was his own satisfaction, especially in germinating seeds of some of the woody plants that were most difficult to germinate.

When he was not in the Rochester parks working with his plants Barney might be found somewhere in the countryside near Rochester or throughout Western New York State wandering through woodlands and combing the hillsides for something unusual in the plant world. He joined with John Dunbar in increasing the collection of *Crataegus* (hawthorn) in Genesee Valley Park to the largest collection of this particular plant in the world. Beginning in 1906, partly in compliance with recommendations made by Professor Sargent, Barney expanded his exploration trips into Pennsylvania, and then into the southwestern and midwestern United States, where he was especially engaged in looking for new and interesting species of hickory, plum, hawthorn, shadblow, crabapple, and oaks. At that time Professor Sargent was writing his *Manual of Trees*, and the assistance given by his "Rochester connections" proved valuable.

Beginning in 1908 and continuing throughout his career, Barney recorded in field books the observations that he was making on his trips. All woody plants and their culture were of interest and "worth a look" by Barney. The following excerpt from one of his notebooks written during 1948 (when he was reviewing and rewriting some of his notes written years earlier) gives an insight into the persistence and sagacity with which he undertook those trips to observe and collect plants:

> In the summer of 1902, at the request of Dr. Charles Sprague Sargent, Director of Arnold Arboretum, I went to the Niagara Falls to look for and find, if possible, *Hypericum kalmianum*, a little yellow flowering shrub (was lost in cultivation); that is now 46 years ago. [Note: Barney was writing in 1948 about his trip in 1902.] This little shrub was reported at the falls and also at Wind-mill point on the Canadian side of Lake Erie by one Judge Day of Buffalo. Twenty-three years earlier, that is 69 years ago now. [Note: Barney is referring to 1879.] I failed to find it at the falls, but while in company with the superintendent of Victory Park I came upon a few bushes of a very fine fruiting *Daphne mezereum* and with the blessings of the superintendent I gathered a few seeds which were planted and from these several generations were raised and planted in the different Parks in Rochester. But now to get back to *Hypericum kalmianum*, from the falls I went to Fort Erie and from there to Wind-mill point by way of a narrow gauge

railroad. Then alighted and walked back to Fort Erie. On the way back I found *Hypericum kalmianum* in abundance on the sandy beach of Lake Erie on the Canadian side. I pulled up several hundred seedlings and brought them back and they were sent to the Arnold Arboretum gardeners and to various other places and some were planted in Highland Park, Rochester, New York and to sum up this was all done in one day by the old time. B. H. Slavin.

In 1907, Henry S. Durand and George Eastman presented a gift of 484 acres of land along Lake Ontario in the Town of Irondequoit to the City of Rochester, "to be used as a public park forever." This acreage was named Durand Eastman Park in honor of the donors. Subsequent acquisition brought the acreage to 499 acres.

The natural terrain in this park originated as a delta deposited by the Genesee River. Subsequent erosion had converted it into a series of steep-sided, narrow valleys. At the time of its acquisition by the city, most of the once-cultivated land within its bounds had been abandoned due to low productivity of the soil. As it has been described elsewhere, "it included swamps, gullies, plateaus of blow-sand, hill-sides, treeless ravines, and about 100 acres of peripheral forest."

Barney's younger brother, Patrick, was sent to Durand Eastman Park to take charge of developing this new area. As Barney later commented, "Pat fell flat on his face." Within two months, the task of developing this nearly barren land into a park was assigned to Barney, adding it to the responsibilities he already had at Seneca Park. This new park area was a desolate sight. A member of the then-functioning Park Commission who viewed the area with Barney remarked, "I don't know why you bother with it. You'll never make anything out of it."

Barney retained his headquarters at Seneca Park but split his time between the two areas, taking some of his laborers with him to Durand Eastman Park to assist in converting this new area into the unique park it was to become. He placed Seneca Park under the foremanship of Claude Leake, who, although not a plantsman, followed Barney's directions in getting the work done during Barney's absences. In 1910, with his dual responsibilities, Barney was promoted to Assistant Superintendent of Parks, a title he shared with John Dunbar, who held the title from 1891 until his retirement in 1926.

In later years, Slavin had this to say about his relationship with John Dunbar: "Mr. Dunbar and I made a good team. He had a lot of experience and was a national figure in our field. Both of us disliked political interference and kept as far away from politicians as possible. There was a lot more politics in the park board after Dr. Moore's death than there was when he was president." (Dr. Moore died in 1902. William S. Riley was appointed to fill the vacancy on the board, and Alexander B. Lamberton became the new president.)

Slavin said that one day he met a very worried Dunbar in the corridor of the building in which the park office was located. He inquired what the trouble was, and Dunbar said, "They want to get rid of me." Slavin was astonished. He knew that Dunbar was as completely dedicated to the parks as he was himself and he had a great respect for the Scotsman's knowledge of botany and horticulture. "If I have to go," Dunbar told Slavin, "I hope you'll succeed me as assistant superintendent." "I won't," Slavin answered, "If they're foolish enough to fire you, I'll quit."

The wisdom of some of the park board members prevailed over the political machinations of others, and Dunbar remained in his post until his retirement in 1926, working in collaboration with Slavin to bring ever-increasing prestige to the Rochester parks. The two men worked together for years without disagreement. They were unalike in all ways except in their devotion to the parks. "Mr. Dunbar knew how to use garden tools as well as I did, though he had never been a park laborer," Slavin said. "We could both take a tool and show the men how a job should be done."

During the years when Durand Eastman Park was first being developed, transportation to this area was often difficult.

Automobiles were somewhat scarce at that time, and the park was about six miles "as the crow flies" from the center of the city. Some park personnel referred to it as "Siberia." At times transportation between the two parks was by means of horse and wagon, a time-consuming journey.

One member of Barney's "gang of laborers" was a gardener by the name of Louis Fenicchia, who had acquired his nursery experience and skills in Italy before immigrating to the United States. After working with Barney for a short time, assisting with the planting at both Seneca and Durand Eastman Parks, Louis resigned from the city payroll and started out on his own, working for several local estates where he could earn more money. Louis was the father of Richard A. Fenicchia, who, in the mid-1920s, became a park employee doing propagation and nursery work under Slavin's direction. Later in his career, Dick Fenicchia would serve as Superintendent of Horticulture for the Bureau of Parks, and beginning in 1961 for the Department of Parks of Monroe County.

The development of Durand Eastman Park was a challenge of herculean proportions for Barney Slavin, a challenge that he had been preparing for during his eighteen years in the park system. The transforming of 500 acres of inhospitable, steep-sloped land into an outstanding park became an obsession for this man who loved working with plants. The experience and knowledge he had acquired, coupled with his inquisitive mind and a rare power of observation, had developed within him a certain philosophy relative to the use of plant materials that would guide him in the development of this area. He believed that a park should be designed in a manner whereby it would serve as a living textbook, offering visitors the opportunity to see and touch not just a few species of shrubs, trees, and other plants, but thousands. He had the foresight to see that, being close to the lake, the park could support many varieties of plants that would not survive the climate only a short distance inland. The tempering effect of the lake created microclimates that made this possible. Barney had spent many hours observing plants in their native habitats and, in his planting of park areas, he arranged them as naturally as possible. He believed in the proper use of open space, perhaps something that he had gleaned from exposure to the plans developed by Frederick Law Olmsted, who was a great believer in interspersing open space throughout his designs. In his plantings, Barney also provided for vistas that would result in a greater perception of beauty in the landscape.

Slavin's landscapes are distinctive in the imaginative choice of taxa. He had an eye for the unusual landscape. Rather than depending on standard, well-known, and tried species, he planted colorful exotics, such as mountain silverbells, yellow buckeyes, oriental fringe trees, Japanese horsechestnuts, and paperbark maples in the foreground of the plantings where they would stand out against a background of native and more commonly planted trees. This is particularly noticeable in his treatment of hillside plantings, where the native plants act as backdrops in the general landscape picture. He was ingenious in the manner in which he combined plants to provide the greatest interest for the casual park visitor.

That Barney Slavin was successful in meeting this challenge is attested to by the worldwide reputation that Durand Eastman Park earned among horticulturists who would come from all parts of the world to see and admire this park and its store of plant materials. Although there was some limited input from the Olmsted firm relative to the location of roads and the construction of two small lakes, the development of the park was left up to Barney. He would meet regularly with Calvin Laney to review problems of engineering, but at Durand Eastman Park, Barney was the on-the-job engineer as well as the chief planter.

Perhaps the following material quoted from the 1911 *Annual Report of the Rochester Park Department* will give some idea of the scope of Barney's accomplishments during his first few years at Durand Eastman Park:

> Nearly one hundred of its acres are a noble forest of white pine, hemlock, chestnut, ash, red maple, white, red and black oak, black and yellow birch, black cherry, beech, tulip

tree, sassafras, and dogwood. Three and one-quarter miles of walks and drives have been constructed and two small lakes have been created by placing dams at the end of natural ravines. [Note: No small feat when one considers that this work was accomplished with horse-drawn equipment.] Bison, deer, elk, tahr, camels, and llamas wander over the rolling land, scarcely knowing that they are confined. Thousands of trees and shrubs have been planted in various parts of the park. Rhododendrons, Azaleas, and other plants that will not thrive in limestone soil (the native soil throughout this region) have been planted in selected sites within the park and are doing well. A grove of 1200 nut trees has been planted in the northwest corner of the park. This planting includes hickories, butternuts, black walnuts, Japanese and Persian walnuts, and several varieties of chestnut. In this park is a nursery in which many choice trees and shrubs not obtainable from commercial nurseries are grown for planting throughout the parks as needed for landscaping of these areas.

It is interesting to note that in May 1913, George Eastman signed an indenture giving permission to the City of Rochester to appropriate a portion of the land formerly donated to the city for Durand Eastman Park for "the purpose of maintaining a collection of wild animals and wild fowl therein" and to permit a duly incorporated Zoological Society to provide wild animals and wild fowl for the said park for exhibiting but under the immediate control and disposition of said Zoological Society, its officers, and agents. Dr. Durand also agreed to sign a similar indenture.

As can be correctly determined by reading the quoted material taken from the 1911 *Annual Report* as cited above, Barney Slavin had not only been engaged in a massive planting program and in the construction of several miles of paths and roadways over a very difficult terrain, but he had also been preparing an area for hoofed animals—an area that would become well known as the Durand Eastman Park Zoo.

While working with John Dunbar at Highland Park, Barney had observed that, in growing trees and shrubs from seeds, some of the resulting seedlings might be cultivars (plants with some different characteristics from the parent plants). This was further substantiated while Barney was on plant exploration trips, where he would occasionally find a plant specimen that varied somewhat from the type, perhaps in the color of its flowers or fruit, in the overall shape of the tree, or even in the orientation of its branches. As a result of these observations, he planted thousands of seeds that he collected from selected species and, by maintaining a constant surveillance over the resulting seedlings, he discovered that variations might even be found within a flat of seedlings of a single species.

Very early during his assignment to Durand Eastman Park, Barney established a nursery on a plateau in the park off Log Cabin Road north of the Huntington Hills properties. Within a very few years, he started a second, considerably larger nursery on property owned by the city sewage treatment plant. This property is contiguous to the park on the west. It was at these two nurseries that he specialized in growing trees from seeds. By selection he was able to discover many new and interesting forms of different plants. Using his own special propagation procedures, he produced a number of tall, slender trees especially adapted to planting along city streets, where there may be limited space for growing trees with fuller crowns.

A bill to abolish the Board of Park Commissioners and to create a Department of Parks under the mayor of the city passed the legislature in February and was signed by Governor Whitman on March 3, 1915. On March 8, Mayor Hiram H. Edgerton appointed A. B. Lamberton, who had been President of the Board of Park Commissioners continuously since the death of Dr. Edward M. Moore in March 1902, as Commissioner of Parks, and a few days later Commissioner Lamberton appointed William S. Riley, the third vice-president of the late board, to the position of Deputy Commissioner of Parks.

At this time, Barney Slavin was given the additional title of Superintendent of Street Trees, and the duties of that position were added to his already heavy workload. He now had a "ready market" for the thousands of trees of special form that he was producing in his park nurseries. When these reached adequate size for moving out of the nurseries, they were planted along the streets and in city parks. Included among these were Slavin's Ascending American Elm; his upright Norway maple; a specially selected red maple; a fastigiate form of linden; a hybrid maple resulting from a cross of *Acer leucoderme* and *A. saccharum*; and his hybrid oak, a cross of *Quercus cerris* and *Q. acutissima*. The latter three were planted within Durand Eastman Park. Examples of the others may still be found at various locations throughout the city. Perhaps one of the best examples is the planting of upright maples that can still be seen in the approaches to Veterans Memorial Bridge on Ridge Road. Also, the planting of these maples along both sides of Westfield Street, between Brooks Avenue and Chili Avenue, was a classic example of fitting the right trees to a narrow street. Barney also experimented with exotic trees for planting along the city streets, using species such as purple European beech, mountain silverbells, Eastern sycamore, and Amur corktree. The fact that many of these are still thriving in the locations where he planted them speaks well of his success.

That Barney Slavin was a real pioneer in the use of "tailored trees" was attested to in a article written by Jacob Gerling, an employee of the Rochester park system from 1933 until 1961. In this article, which appeared in the January-February 1960 issue of the *Garden Journal*, Jake discussed the problems that can arise from the planting of "king-sized trees" along city streets:

> Much of our present and immediate future distress could have been avoided if "a voice crying in the wilderness" almost a half-century ago had been heeded. This voice was that of Bernard H. Slavin, retired Superintendent of Parks in Rochester, a man whose keen foresight, inherent ability and earnest devotion to his work characterized more than fifty years of outstanding service in the development of

Rochester's nationally known parks. As early as 1915, Bernard Slavin realized that overgrown trees, far too closely placed, were becoming an expensive nuisance on city streets, and thousands of gaunt skeletons marking the ruthless spread of chestnut blight, then well on its way toward total destruction of this valuable species, alerted him to the fallacy of using one species too freely in City-street planting. [Note: Another factor to be considered was the constant conflict of large trees with power lines.] Bernard Slavin was the first city arborist to actually do something about the worsening situation. His noteworthy accomplishment in the selection and use of well-suited street trees is evident today on many of Rochester's streets. In these plantings, small trees, fastigiate and columnar forms, have proved their worth in coping with the limiting factors present on so many city streets, and maintenance costs are but a fraction of that required by outsized trees. Outstanding among the improved forms used so successfully in Slavin's early test plantings are *Acer platanoides erectum*, *Tilia americana fastigiata*, and *Ulmus americana ascendens* (his own introductions), and the columnar Sugar Maple. For smaller species types he selected *Sorbus alnifolia*, *Tilia cordata*, *Ostrya virginiana*, and flowering trees of the genera *Magnolia*, *Malus*, and *Halesia*.

Although Barney's main concern was Durand Eastman Park, he could no longer devote as much time to it as he wanted to. Consequently, he was somewhat relieved in 1920 to find a man whom he could trust to carry out his directions. This man was Martin Trott, who came to the park as a laborer. Recognizing that Trott had the necessary attributes to handle a crew of park employees, Barney very quickly appointed him to the position of foreman. The Trott family moved into the old Durand house (formerly a country house owned by Dr. Durand). Barney would appear there almost every morning before 7:30 A.M. to go over plans with Trott.

It is revealing of Barney's interest in Durand Eastman Park, and of Trott's respect for Barney, that Trott never claimed to have planted any part of this park without mentioning that he worked under Barney's directions. During his tenure in Durand Eastman Park, Trott also assisted in the development and operation of the golf course and the hoofed-animal zoo. In 1938, he accepted the position of Superintendent of Hamlin Beach, which had just become a state park. Here he supervised Civilian Conservation Corps crews in the building of many of the facilities and improvements in that area. Martin Trott remained at Hamlin Beach State Park until 1942. At that time he returned to employment with the City of Rochester and became foreman in charge of the small city parks.

As Assistant Superintendents, John Dunbar and Barney Slavin, working under the Superintendent of Parks, Calvin Laney, shared in earning for the Rochester park system a worldwide reputation as a center for horticultural excellence. Dunbar concentrated his efforts on Highland Park, where, with cooperation from Arnold Arboretum and other horticultural centers, he was able to assemble the many collections into an outstanding arboretum. He also continued to give attention to the development of Genesee Valley Park, Cobbs Hill Park, and several of the small park areas, especially those scattered throughout the southern side of the city.

Barney Slavin, on the other hand, especially after his appointment to the position of Superintendent of Street Trees, spread his talents over a wider area of the park system. He was now (from 1915 and into the 1920s) not only engaged in the development of three major parks (Durand Eastman, Seneca, and Maplewood), and in the planting and care of trees on the city's streets, but also active in the development of some of the smaller park areas and playgrounds.

In 1919, the City of Rochester purchased the 35 acres of Ontario Beach Park. Beginning in 1873, and constantly changing as "improvements" were made, this originally rugged, undeveloped area had become crowded with a mélange of dancing pavilions, shooting galleries, beer gardens, amusement rides, food stands, and approximately 40 "hotels." After this clutter of building and facilities was razed, the area was assigned to Barney Slavin for conversion into a city park. His development of the area was simple but well conceived. A walkway, parallel to the lake front, was built, separating the sandy beach area from the greensward that was established between it and Beach Avenue. Over 100 American elm trees were planted in this lawn area to form an open grove of trees that provided shade for swimmers who wanted to escape from the hot rays of the sun and for the many other visitors who flocked to this area on hot summer days to enjoy lake breezes and vistas that, because of the natural shape of the trees, were unimpeded even for people passing by on Beach Avenue.

In January 1922, twenty-year-old Arthur Blensinger began employment as a laborer assigned to Seneca Park, where he worked under the park foreman, Claude Leake, who was a favorite of Barney's despite the fact that he knew very little about plant materials. Leake could manage a crew to Barney's satisfaction and consequently would get the job done as per Barney's orders.

When Leake was killed in an automobile accident in 1927, Art Blensinger was promoted to foreman at Seneca Park. Art was the living embodiment of the word "woodsman." Consequently, he was of great assistance to Barney in the laying out of footpaths and trails in Seneca Park, and also in Durand Eastman Park, where he remembers that the Seneca crew went upon many occasions to assist in the continuing process of developing this area. Art remained in Seneca Park for sixteen years until 1938 when, because of a political maneuver that benefitted a ward leader, he was sent to Highland Park to assist the foreman there, and the ward leader was given the job of foreman at Seneca Park. Art remained at Highland Park for about one year before being reassigned as foreman at Durand Eastman Park, where he remained until his retirement in 1972.

During the spring and fall of 1924, a massive planting program was undertaken on the 120 acres of land that had been a gift to the city for addition to Genesee Valley Park in January 1908 by Miss Frances Baker. This planting, which coincided with the expansion of the golf courses in this park, was under Barney Slavin's supervision. Many of the plants used came from his Durand Eastman nurseries. To a degree, this was a homecoming for Barney because it was on this former farm land that he had labored under his father's direction prior to 1890. Over 5,200 trees and shrubs were planted. A large percentage of these are still thriving. Many of the 550 oak trees in nine different species furnish welcome shade to golfers during a hot summer day when the sun is high in the sky. The 100 *Nyssa sylvatica* (also known as tupelo or sourgum) provide rich, red color in the fall, as do the dogwoods and some of the maples. Thirty different species of trees and shrubs were used, some as freestanding specimens, others as components in the borders along the roadsides and the property lines.

During the mid-1920s, many changes were taking place. As mentioned earlier, Calvin Laney was appointed Park Commissioner in 1925, a position he retained until his retirement in 1928. John Dunbar retired in the spring of 1926, and shortly thereafter Barney Slavin was appointed Superintendent of Parks.

Barney Slavin's theater of operations now became the entire park system. Because of the success he had experienced with the nurseries he had developed in Durand Eastman Park, he remained intensely interested in the propagation of plants and was always on the outlook for new cultivars. Realizing that the greenhouse range at Highland Park was a useful facility in the propagation of plants, Barney had been relying more and more upon cooperation from John Dunbar and Fred Ahrens. Although he greatly admired Ahrens for his skill in propagation, he found him to be very difficult to work with. Barney was looking for someone who would more willingly work under his direct supervision.

In 1925, Barney found that person, a young man whom he had known as a boy, Richard A. Fenicchia, a son of Louis Fenicchia who had worked in Barney's crew in the early development of both Seneca and Durand Eastman Parks. Dick remembered Barney visiting with his father upon several occasions over the years and said that "Barney would pick me up and toss me in the air when I was a small boy." By 1925, when he was 17 years of age, Dick had gained considerable experience in gardening and horticulture while working with his father in the small nursery that Louis had developed, and also while assisting his father on the several estates that he maintained for the owners. During those learning years, Dick also developed a feeling and a love for plants, which is inherent in a true plantsman.

In any conversation with Dick about plants or parks, one quickly learns that Barney Slavin had a real influence in promoting Dick's interest in plants and in stimulating him to thoroughly research the culture of plant materials. Dick credits Barney with being the vital force in the development of the plant collections within the Rochester parks. Perhaps one of Barney's greatest accomplishments, however, was in realizing that Dick Fenicchia, then a lad still in his teens, had an inborn feeling or sensitiveness for plants coupled with a searching mind that directed him in learning as much as possible about each plant with which he had contact.

Barney assigned Dick to the greenhouses, where, under Barney's direction, he was immediately involved in a program of propagating plants of many different genera and species. Here Dick came in close contact with Fred Ahrens, whom Dick remembers as being an excellent propagator, perhaps "one of the best in the world, because of his former position with the Ellwanger and Barry Nursery. . . . He could get a pencil to form roots." Dick found Ahrens to be very secretive about the methods he used in propagation: "He never wanted anyone to observe him at work and disliked being watched when he was working with plants." Consequently, Dick developed his own methods of propagation.

After Barney observed Dick making a cross of *Viburnum rhytidophyllum* with *V. lantana*, he decided to get Dick involved in a program of plant hybridization with special emphasis on rhododendrons and azaleas. During the next few years in the late 1920s and early 1930s, Dick hybridized over 200 species of these.

Barney Slavin instilled in Dick the importance of keeping accurate records of his work—a log showing the plants he used with all dates being recorded—when he made the crosses, the date the resultant seeds were harvested and planted, when germination was first observed, type of media used, any special treatment given to cuttings when placed in media, etc. From these records we can now learn that one of the first sowings of azalea seeds by Dick was made on December 3, 1927. Two seedlings from this sowing were selected for further propagation and were perpetuated throughout the years by cuttings that were rooted and grown on, and at the time of this writing in 1993 there are some of these selections still being used in the Easter displays at Lamberton Conservatory.

With Barney's encouragement and support, Dick continued his propagation work and hybridization experiments until April 1934, when he was dismissed from employment with the city. There had been a political change in city government, and Dick refused to change his enrollment in order to hold on to his job. In fact, when Barney asked him to make the change, Dick answered, "I'll go down with the ship," and Barney was forced to terminate him. This might be interpreted as an irrational action of a young man. However, this was not true with Dick. It simply demonstrated the sense of loyalty and the adherence to his principles that had always been characteristic of him. He continued to visit the greenhouses as a volunteer, devoting spare time to the care of some of the plants in which he had a special interest, until he realized that his efforts and his presence were not appreciated by those employees still assigned to the greenhouses.

Dick Fenicchia has the following to say about Barney Slavin:

> Under Slavin's administration, phenomenal advances were made in the Rochester parks. The Lilac collection was expanded to its present size. This expansion took place along Highland Avenue from a location about opposite Laney Road to the property line of St. John's Home. Thousands of trees and shrubs were planted, as well as new

hybrids and forms of lilacs. Magnolias, conifers, maples and other genera were selected. Slavin landscaped Durand Eastman Park single-handedly; drawing plans for roads, conifer plantings and an arboretum. The site of the Pinetum was underlaid with a network of drainage tiles to drain the former marsh land. Thousands of American beech, oak, conifer, Sarvistree, paper birch, nut trees and katsura trees were planted. His landscapes are distinct in their choice of taxa and their excellence. He had an eye for the unusual. Rather than planting standard well known and tried species, he used colorful exotics, such as mountain silverbells, yellow buckeyes, oriental fringetrees, Japanese horsechestnuts and paperbark maples. He also developed Seneca and Maplewood Parks, and Cobbs Hill Park, and planted a large number of unusual oaks in Genesee Valley Park. At that time, newly discovered species and varieties of many plants were arriving at Arnold Arboretum. Each taxon that they received, they would, in turn, send at least one plant to the Rochester parks. New taxa also arrived from American and foreign nurseries and from the U.S. Department of Agriculture.

Slavin collected trees in Oklahoma which he introduced in the local parks. In addition he was in charge of planting street trees. Slavin pioneered the practice of planting grafted clones on streets. he also experimented with exotic species for streets. Some of these were the purple European Beech, Mountain Silverbell, Eastern Sycamore and the Amur Corktree. He had outstanding success with all of these; many are still thriving today. Barney Slavin started all of the major plant collections found within Durand Eastman Park. These included magnolias, conifers of all types, cherries, plums, lindens, oaks, yews, white and pink forms of flowering dogwood, viburnums, and many other trees and shrubs.

During the late 1920s, Barney schooled Dick Fenicchia with a set of recommendations that he felt should be followed in park areas. These are as follows:

1. Never raise a tree by cutting the lower branches. Barney believed that the natural characteristics of trees should not be tampered with. Man can destroy the inherent beauty that nature creates.
2. Cut no tree that can be saved. Many trees will naturally "make a comeback" from injuries if given a chance to outgrow them.
3. Plant some trees with bare roots; others with root balls. Observe and study the natural composition of trees. Those with major tap roots are harder to transplant than those with a network of fibrous roots. Prepare trees ahead of time by root pruning. When filling in a planting hole with loose soil, after you have properly set the plant, whether bare-rooted or balled-and-burlapped, tamp the soil well, using your heels as a tamper. Tamping with the front (or toe) of your booted foot does not do a good job. Use your heels!
4. Plant hillsides with background plants of native species. Observe "how nature does it" without man's involvement and follow the example. Try, as far as possible, to copy nature's pattern. Exotic trees can be planted with the native ones serving as background.
5. Leave open spaces in the right places. This is especially important where the use of areas by people is encouraged.
6. Open up vistas in the right places. Vistas open up the plantings so that the sun can enter the areas that otherwise might be closed in and dark, thereby allowing nature to develop more colorful and beautiful scenes for the visitor to enjoy. Vistas should focus the eye of the beholder on some special feature, perhaps a body of water or a special planting. Vistas also bring the sky into the living picture that one is observing.
7. Collect and plant many seeds. Observe the resulting seedlings carefully, keeping your eyes open for variations. By selection, you may discover a plant entirely different in some characteristics from others in the same seed lot—perhaps more upright or denser in form than the plant from which you collected the seed. Give the selection room to grow, then propagate from it by cuttings or graft to perpetuate the new characteristics.

In late 1929, Charles B. Riatt, who had been named Director of the Bureau of Parks under the Commissioner of Public Safety, was removed from that position and Patrick Slavin was appointed to succeed him. The two "farm boys" who had "grown up" in the park system, beginning in April 1890 when they first became park employees, were now in a position to supervise the entire operation of the Bureau of Parks, Pat as administrator of the several divisions of the bureau and Barney in charge of the parks with the many plant collections. Pat was more of a politician than was his brother Barney. Consequently, he did not mind the association and machinations with city officials and other political figures with which he had contact.

Barney, on the other hand, was still "Mr. Parks." His duties kept him in the out-of-doors, moving from park area to park area, supervising the continuing development and the maintenance of all of the areas.

The original landscape at Durand Eastman Park was changing each year as new plant materials were added under Barney's supervision. For example, in 1918 a complete collection of native and foreign crabapples had been planted in this park. Also, 1,000 Japanese cherries in seventy varieties were planted in the Durand Eastman Park nursery. These would later be planted in several locations throughout the park to provide accent in front of the background of coniferous trees. In total, 400,000 trees and shrubs had been planted. Most of these were hardy native plants, including many conifers and broad-leaved evergreens. In 1919, two long beds of rhododendrons totaling 600 plants were planted near Zoo Road. Eight beds of *Daphne mezereum* (1,500 plants) were set out, and 97 choice and rare evergreens were planted in the vicinity of Zoo Road. On the slope at the south corner of Zoo Road and Lakeshore Road, 2,850 viburnums were planted. The bank was mulched and pegged to prevent the sliding of the soil. The planting continued during the following year, when another 522 viburnums were planted to hold the high slope along Zoo Road, and the bank of Eastman Lake where it borders the main road was planted with 435 viburnums. An unsightly and dangerous slope at the Wisner

Road entrance of the park was graded and seeded. Also, during 1919, some cutting out was begun in an effort to establish new trails. In 1932, nine additional holes of golf were added to bring the course to eighteen holes.

For a period of a few years in the late 1920s and early 1930s, Barney's son Arthur D. Slavin, a graduate of the University of Notre Dame, worked as a horticulturist in the Bureau of Parks in Rochester. During these years he spent many hours under the direct supervision of Dick Fenicchia, assisting in the propagation program. He also worked many hours assisting Richard Horsey with taxonomic duties in the herbarium. In November 1931, he attended the conifer conference sponsored by the Royal Horticulture Society in England, where he presented a paper entitled, "Some Conifers Growing in the United States." This report, 150 pages long, was printed in book form for the Royal Horticulture Society in 1932, with its author listed as Arthur D. Slavin, M.S., Horticulturist in the Bureau of Parks, Rochester, New York. The report begins as follows:

> The best cultivated conifers in the United States are found principally in the private or public collections. Such collections, when compared to the natural life span of much of the material contained in them, are quite young. Perhaps the oldest pinetum in this country is located at the Hunnewell Estate in Wellesley, Massachusetts. It was established during the middle part of the nineteenth century. The next oldest is at the Arnold Arboretum, Jamaica Plains, Massachusetts. This was begun about 1886. Most of the material described in this paper is growing in the two pineta of the Bureau of Parks, Rochester, New York. The older collection is in Highland Park and was first planted in 1896. The second and larger of the two is in Durand Eastman Park. This pinetum had its beginning in 1912. As may be easily seen, scientific collections of conifers in America are, at least from a dendrological point of view, recent developments.

This report of Arthur Slavin's discussed 20 genera and 345 species of conifers and did much in bringing worldwide fame to the Rochester parks and also to John Dunbar and Barney Slavin, the two men most responsible for the planting of the two Rochester pineta.

Soon after returning from this conference, Art Slavin accepted a position with the U.S. government, working in land conservation. During the Dust Bowl days in the 1930s, he was assigned to projects in the State of Kansas. Dick Fenicchia remembers that thousands of seedling trees raised in Barney's park nurseries were sent to the Dust Bowl areas to be planted where they might aid in soil erosion control.

Beginning early in its history, the Rochester park system distributed thousands of seeds, plants, trees, shrubs, scions, and cuttings to hundreds of botanical and horticultural institutions throughout the United States and many other nations. Large quantities were also given to commercial nurseries (usually in trade for plant materials) and private plant collectors, mostly in the United States and Canada.

One of the most significant events occurred during the 1930s. Throughout spring and summer, thousands of woody plants were propagated under Barney's supervision within the park greenhouses and nurseries. A boxcar filled with these materials was sent to the New York Botanic Gardens to augment its collections. Rochester was as instrumental in establishing some other arboretums as the Arnold Arboretum was in helping Rochester. Large numbers of cuttings and rooted woody materials were sent to the National Arboretum in Washington, D.C.; Somerset Parks Commission, Somerset, New Jersey; and the Royal Botanic Garden in Hamilton, Ontario, Canada. Live inspected plants and cuttings were sent to botanical gardens and arboretums in England, France, Holland, Germany, Poland, and Czechoslovakia. Most of these species were difficult to propagate from seed. The dissemination of plants also played a part in spreading the fame of the Rochester park system throughout the world.

A newcomer to the Park Department in 1933 was Jacob (Jake) Gerling, who began employment as a 55-cent-per-hour laborer assigned to Durand Eastman Park. He was soon promoted to the position of park foreman. Jake's career with the parks cannot be classified with that of anyone else. According to several former park employees who were in a position to observe Gerling's performance, he was never actively involved in park work, at least in a manner comparable to Art Blensinger or Martin Trott. He developed a close relationship with Barney Slavin, was able to learn the details of Barney's horticultural experiments, and managed to get custody of Barney's field books in which much information about his various plant discoveries was recorded. Perhaps Jake's main contribution to the horticultural work of the park system was his publicizing of Barney's work. During his first 20 years with the park system, Jake collected about 5,000 slides of plant materials and park landscapes, which he used in lectures before local garden clubs and professional nursery organizations across the country. He also wrote many articles about selected trees for various nursery and gardening periodicals. These articles dwelt mostly on plants discovered and propagated by Barney Slavin. Excerpts from some of his writings appeared earlier in this history.

In 1940, at an occasion marking Barney's fiftieth year with the Rochester Park Department, the Lakeshore Garden Club passed a resolution recognizing his contributions to horticulture and parks, which read, "He has achieved a civic and aesthetic natural monument of which Rochesterians are justly proud."

Barney was horticultural advisor for many area garden clubs and conducted many tours throughout the various parks, showing off his "babies" to park visitors. He also "entertained" many professional horticulturists and educators during visits they made to Rochester with the express purpose of walking through the park areas with Barney. They were always properly impressed by the great wealth of plant materials they found thriving in this park system. In 1942, the Federated Garden Club of New York State presented Barney with its Silver Achievement Award for "his contributions to horticulture through his service to the parks."

Barney Slavin's retirement in April 1942 marked the completion of 54 years of acquisition and development of the Rochester park system. Much that has been written about these formative years recounts the activities of those individuals who were responsible for the administration of the parks, and the contributions they made in acquiring land were necessary and of great value to the community. However, from a horticultural viewpoint, and one that considers the assembling of those "building blocks" that actually make up the living park areas, due consideration should be given to the two plantsmen, John Dunbar and Barney Slavin, who contributed the most in converting the acquired acres into serviceable and beautiful parks. In respect to them and their accomplishments, this period in park history can rightly be called the Dunbar-Slavin years.

In many ways, it was Dunbar, the trained and experienced plantsman, who set the pattern for the horticultural development of the parks. But, as Betty Keiper once expressed, "Although as a botanist and a horticulturist, Barney was self taught, he had certain natural endowments: a keen plantsman's curiosity, imagination, intuition, enthusiasm, and a deep artistic appreciation of the plant world. Benefitting from his apprenticeship under John Dunbar, he expanded the park development far beyond Dunbar's expectations and dreams." Miss Keiper, writing in the *Rochester Times-Union* in April 1942, further stated, "Barney Slavin made intensive studies of plant materials in this area and aided botanists in recording new varieties. His work in the parks resulted in the development of distinctive new forms of plant materials."

At the time of Barney's retirement after 16 years as Superintendent of Parks, Public Safety Commissioner Thomas C. Woods said in saluting him, "During your 52 years of service in the Rochester park system, you have contributed in a large measure to the happiness of our citizens and the growth of our city. The fame of the Rochester park system has spread from coast to coast and is recognized by all as a very distinct factor in the phenomenal growth and development of our city through the years."

Barney continued to receive awards after his retirement. In 1945, the Rochester Museum of Arts and Sciences elected him as a Fellow and presented the following citation: "By sheer force of an inspired understanding, you groomed a wasteland into a garden of surprising beauty, enabling your city to give its people a new and enthralling area for recreation, inspiration, and health at every season of the year."

In an article published in the December 1947 *Journal of the New York Botanic Garden*, Betty Keiper stated, "There are at least 38 species and varieties in Rochester parks under BHS numbers which might well be given formal designation and introduced into use. . . . The greater number of these are among the Magnolias, Rhododendrons, Azaleas, and Chinese Lilacs." Foremost among the plant forms that he named were the two upright trees formerly mentioned in this article. "The crowns of these trees are confined to somewhat narrow growth and consequently are excellent for planting on narrow city streets." In this article, Miss Keiper described Barney Slavin as a "great American Plantsman—a discoverer and producer of new plants." She also stated, "One of the most notable of the new forms of plant materials was the Katherine crabapple, a double-flowered, light pink variety which he named for his daughter-in-law."

In October 1959, the American Horticulture Council, in national session in Rochester, awarded Barney its F. H. Bartlett medal in recognition of half a century of service to horticulture.

In November 1959, he was cited by the Western New York Arborists Association for pioneering in the selection, propagation, and use of better adapted species of trees and shrubs for city streets. This citation read as follows: "At the time, the Rochester Parks Department was unable to supply funds for the vast amounts of materials needed. Bernard H. Slavin grew literally millions of trees and shrubs at practically no cost."

The job that had faced Barney could not be done overnight nor in several years by importation of nursery materials. City fathers, always monitoring the city budget, were not prepared for any great outlay of funds. Slavin thought in terms of seeds, cuttings, and long nursery rows within the parks. The seeds and cuttings came from other Rochester parks (primarily Highland) and from other horticultural collections throughout the nation, as well as from plant hunters such as "Chinese" (Ernest) Wilson, who foraged for new plants throughout China, Tibet, and other areas.

Commercial nurserymen who seldom looked with favor on government had no criticism of Slavin's activities because it was through him and his nurseries that many obtained propagating stock of plants that were available only from collections such as those in Rochester. Slavin cooperated with the commercial nurserymen as well as with the other arboretums by distributing quantities of seeds, cuttings, and scions. Some even were sent to other countries. The largest of his institutional distributions was a 10,000-pound shipment of seeds and small plants to the Royal Botanical Garden at Kew, New London, England, in 1931.

Several times after this author had joined the Rochester park system in 1945, Barney Slavin would call and say, "I want to show you something in the parks. Pick me up." From observations made during these visits, I got the impression that Barney was a crusty old Irishman. Dick Fenicchia, who knew him much better than I, would agree to a point and then he would add that Barney was always fair with everybody.

His crustiness shows up in some notes he made in the margins of a copy of City Historian Blake McKelvey's *An Historical View of Rochester's Parks and Playgrounds*, published in January 1949. On the first page of this publication, Barney had written, "I pioneered in all of the Rochester parks, beginning as a laborer in Genesee Valley Park, and was made Assistant Foreman in six weeks."

No mention is made of Barney in this publication until page 11, where McKelvey wrote, "Bernard H. Slavin, Dunbar's successor as foreman at Highland Park, took over the larger task of developing Seneca park in 1903. He specialized in growing trees from seed and following Dunbar's techniques." Barney wrote in the margin at this point, "I never followed Dunbar's techniques because I considered my own the best."

McKelvey wrote on page 12, "Patrick Slavin soon became the first foreman of Durand Eastman Park while Horsey received the same appointment at Highland Park." Barney's remark here was, "Yes, and Pat was the first to give it up the same season in 1908. Yes, but Horsey never done the foreman's work but remained in the Herbarium where he was consulted about plants."

On page 17, McKelvey wrote, under the heading of "The Park Commissioner (1915-1918), "Bernard H. Slavin was made superintendent of street trees—an important new position which promised more effective supervision." Barney wrote, "I was made Assistant Superintendent of Parks in 1910 and given the additional work of supervising the street trees in 1915."

Mr. McKelvey wrote about Charles B. Raitt, who was appointed Director of the Bureau of Parks in 1918. Mr. Raitt was removed in 1929 following an accidental drowning at the opening of the Ontario Beach season, and Patrick Slavin was appointed the new director. Writing about this appointment, Mr. McKelvey had this to say: "Patrick Slavin managed to safeguard the city's valuable horticultural estate throughout the lean years." Barney's response was, "Pat done nothing to safeguard horticulture."

After reading McKelvey's *Historical View*, Barney sent the following letter to Blake McKelvey:

February 11, 1949

Dr. Blake McKelvey
City Historian
Rochester Public Library
115 South Avenue
Rochester 4, New York

Dear Dr. McKelvey:

I have read with great interest your recent article in the January issue of "Rochester History", giving a historical view of Rochester parks and playgrounds. Inasmuch as there were several erroneous statements in your article, I am writing at this time to give you a detailed statement of the development work done in the Rochester Park system, from the time that I first entered the employ of the City of Rochester as a laborer at Genesee Valley Park in 1890 until my retirement as Superintendent of Parks in 1942.

When I first became employed as a laborer at Genesee Valley Park, Calvin C. Laney was Superintendent of Parks. Genesee Valley Park was nothing more than a grazing pasture and it was our lot to clean out all of the buildings, fences, orchards, etc., that are a "part and parcel" of a farm and to convert the farm into the park as it is today.

I remained at Genesee Valley Park until 1895, at which time I was transferred to Highland Park, as a foreman. Here again we followed the same process in transforming the acreage into what is today Highland Park. Planning of the work at Highland Park was done by the noted landscape architect, Frederick Law Olmsted of Boston, and under the supervision of one of his assistants I executed and supervised the original planting of the shrub collection at Highland Park. I also supervised the road building from Reservoir Avenue to Goodman Street and from Highland Avenue to Elmwood Avenue, after the city had acquired a new tract of land to the south. I remained at Highland Park for a period of eight years until most of this development work had been completed, at which time I was transferred to Seneca Park as a foreman, where we again followed the same procedure of development work as had been done at Genesee Valley Park and Highland Park.

In 1908, Patrick Slavin was made foreman of Durand Eastman Park, but he retained this title for only a period of a few months. He was succeeded for a short while by various employees in the department, until 1910 when I was appointed Assistant Superintendent of Parks to Mr. Dunbar.

As Assistant Superintendent of Parks, I was responsible for the general supervision of all of the parks in the City and in addition, thereto, was requested to develop Durand Eastman Park, which I did, but with more expertness, and, therefore, made it the wonder of all of the Rochester Parks.

In 1915, in addition to my other duties as Assistant Superintendent, I was asked to help clean up the street trees and for a period of about fourteen months supervised the street tree work.

I would like to take exception to several of the statements in your article, notable, that I followed Mr. Dunbar's technique in this development work. With due respect to Mr. Dunbar's knowledge, I think it only fair to state that I followed my own technique in developing Durand Eastman Park, as well as the various varieties of shade trees, plants, shrubs and innumerable other items connected with the horticulture of our park system.

You also write in your article that it was Commissioner Riley who was responsible for converting Ontario Beach into a recreation center. This project was initiated by Mayor Edgerton, who directed me in carrying it through to a successful conclusion.

I also feel that Miss Gertrude Hartnett is deserving of more recognition, since throughout my many years of service, and especially after I was made Superintendent of Parks in 1926, I found her to be the most dependable employee in the park office.

I have written you these suggestions not as criticisms, but in a spirit of helpfulness, so that if a permanent record is ever made of the history of the park system in the City, proper recognition shall be given to the personnel mostly responsible for making Rochester's beautiful parks famous throughout the country.

Very truly yours,

Bernard H. Slavin
103 S. Washington Street
Rochester 8, New York

During July 1949 there appeared in the *Rochester Municipal Journal* an article that stated in part, "Durand Eastman Park may almost be called a monument to Bernard H. Slavin who retired in 1942 after devoting 52 years of his life working in, promoting, and developing the parks of Rochester. . . . When the land at Durand Eastman was acquired, it consisted of about 75 acres of natural woods with the rest of the acreage a conglomeration of weedy fields, abandoned barns, no longer used roads, steep banks and as Bernard H. Slavin put it 'God knows what'. Barney accepted the challenge presented by the elements described and naturalistically developed the area into an outstanding park."

Bernard H. Slavin died on March 29, 1960, in a nursing home in Elbridge, New York, where his son, Arthur, maintained his residence. Barney considered Durand Eastman Park to have been his greatest achievement. He left behind in Rochester a contribution to its heritage that can never again be equaled. He also left to the park men who followed him a challenge to be ever mindful of the park areas and, particularly, of the plant materials of which these parks are created. In his own words, he was "always ready to fight for his babies, the parks, at the drop of a hat."

Before moving on to the next section in this narrative, there are two more former park employees who should be mentioned. William Lloyd Edson began employment in 1912 as an assistant to Richard Horsey in the herbarium and in the labeling of plants throughout Highland Park. Perhaps he became best known through the weekly columns about birds that appeared in the *Democrat and Chronicle* for more than 50 years. He began carefully compiling notes of his bird observations in 1912, and these notes are still the basis for local ornithologists' knowledge of the bird population in Monroe County. He served for several years as president of the Burroughs Audubon Nature Club and of the Genesee Ornithological Society, which was formed in his home in 1938. He left park employment in 1934 and worked briefly for the Department of Public Works before moving on to industry. Mr. Edson died in 1967 at the age of 71.

The second employee to be mentioned at this point is Kenneth Power, who had been a classmate of Art Slavin at Notre Dame, from which he graduated in 1927. He became a park laborer assigned to Highland Park, where he performed various tasks under the direction of the park foreman and Barney Slavin. He remembers working in the greenhouse with Dick Fenicchia and also with Fred Ahrens in the nursery at Durand Eastman Park. Ken's real and lasting contribution to the history of the park system is the photography he performed under the direction of Barney Slavin. Many of the photographs for which he was responsible are presently stored in the archives of the City of Rochester. Ken remembers taking about 1,000 slides, 200 of which were in color.

He remembers that Art Slavin left the employ of the city in 1932 to "go out west," where he went to work for the federal government. After about two years, Art returned to New York state, bought a farm near Elbridge, and started a nursery.

Ken Power left the park system in 1934 and went to work for the old Board of Supervisors and later became Deputy County Clerk. He was appointed to the position of Election Commissioner in 1960 and continued in that position until his retirement in December 1972. Ken's photographic work will remain as a record of many of the rare plants that could be found (and many still can be) throughout the Rochester park system, particularly in Highland and Durand Eastman Parks.

Up to this point in this history, special credit has been given to Calvin Laney, John Dunbar, and Barney Slavin for the creative leadership they furnished in the horticultural development of the park system. Some employees who were of great assistance to these pioneers have also been mentioned. There are two more early pioneers in the horticultural aspects of the park development who are deserving of special attention. These are Patrick Slavin, brother of Barney, and Richard E. Horsey. Their careers will be reviewed in the order in which they became employees of the park system. It must be mentioned that the careers of these as well as several others, previously mentioned as assisting John Dunbar and Barney Slavin, continued long enough to overlap by a few years the careers of younger men who were to become involved after World War II. They are the linkages between the park plantsmen of the 1890s and those who followed beginning in the 1940s.

LINKAGES — PATRICK J. SLAVIN

One of these "linkages" was Patrick J. Slavin, who, in 1890 at the age of twelve, began employment at Genesee Valley Park as a water boy and messenger under Calvin Laney. Mr. Laney soon became so impressed by the industrious attitude and apparent love for park work exhibited by young Patrick that he promoted him to laborer and transferred him to Highland Park, where he worked under the supervision of John Dunbar during those years when the lilac collection was still in its formative stages. In 1906, upon recommendations from Dunbar, Pat was promoted to assistant foreman and one year later to foreman. When the development of Durand Eastman Park was begun in 1908, Pat was transferred to that new park as its first foreman. Although Patrick was a productive worker and could handle a crew of laborers, he lacked the creativity, the imagination, and the knowledge of plants that was needed in the development of this park. Within two months, Pat was transferred to Genesee Valley Park, where the work was more routine in nature and where he was on familiar ground. The challenge of developing Durand Eastman Park was then assigned to Pat's brother, Barney. However, upon several occasions Pat and a crew of laborers from Genesee Valley Park were sent to Durand Eastman Park to assist in the building of roads and trails. To a large degree, this work was accomplished by the men using horses and horse-drawn equipment, such as dump wagons, slip scrapers, and stone boats. In some instances heavy logs, rigged so that they covered the width of the road, were dragged by horses to serve as leveling bars. Pat's farm experience, gained when he was a young boy working with his father on the Baker farm, had prepared him for this type of work.

At Genesee Valley Park, he supervised the culling out of overgrown plants that had been growing in this area before city ownership and also from earlier plantings. He also made new plantings under the supervision of John Dunbar, who, for several years, in company with Calvin Laney would regularly visit this park to check on the progress being made. Perhaps the greatest contribution that Pat made in the development of Genesee Valley Park was in the construction of roads and pathways.

In 1915, when the twenty-man Park Commission was abolished and Alexander Lamberton was appointed Commissioner of Parks, he named Pat Slavin General Foreman of the parks. In this position, Pat was involved in the development, planting, and maintenance of the small neighborhood parks and squares, such as Jones Park, Plymouth Park, Washington Square, and others. In 1922, Pat Slavin was appointed Assistant Superintendent of Parks by Calvin Laney, and in 1930, two years after Laney's retirement, Pat was named Director of Parks to replace Charles B. Raitt, whose tenure as director had been brought to a close as a result of a drowning at Ontario Beach.

The Bureau of Parks under Pat Slavin's jurisdiction consisted of forty-eight playgrounds; thousands of trees on city streets; Mt. Hope and Riverside Cemeteries; eighteen parks, including Genesee Valley, Highland, Seneca, Maplewood, Durand Eastman, Cobbs Hill, and Ontario Beach; and a number of smaller areas. The parks named above, except for Ontario Beach, were all components of the Rochester arboretum, which had become well known by 1930 in horticulture circles throughout the world. Also within these park areas were two zoos (a hoofed-animal zoo at Durand Eastman and a more complete one at Seneca that housed some exotic animals), two beaches (Ontario and Durand Eastman), three outdoor swimming pools and a natatorium, three eighteen-hole golf courses (two in Genesee Valley and one in Durand Eastman), tennis courts (in Genesee Valley, Highland, Maplewood, Cobbs Hill, and Seneca Parks), and, of course, scores of picnic shelters, miles of roads and trails, and several waterways and pond areas.

To a large degree, the decade of the 1930s was an inopportune time to be Director of Parks. The Great Depression was in full swing, and with drastic cuts in the city budget, many park workers were discharged. Pat was able to obtain some assistance from special federal programs (WPA, CWA, etc.); however, this was somewhat restricted to the care and maintenance of park structures. It was the maintenance of park plantings that really suffered. Many plantings made in early years were reaching maturity and were in need of thinning out and pruning. Others, especially under-plantings in wooded areas, had grown to the extent that they were crowded and so dense with growth that they were beginning to obscure the views that had previously accounted for much of the beauty within the park areas. The ongoing plant propagation and nursery program, which provided the plants needed to safeguard the integrity of the plantings throughout the arboretum, was barely operating. Fred Ahrens retired during the early 1930s because of poor health, and Richard Fenicchia, who had been doing propagation work for Barney Slavin, resigned during this same period due to political changeovers. The fact that Pat Slavin was able to keep the parks functioning during this period was due greatly to his brother, Barney, who continued as Superintendent of Parks until his retirement in 1942. Also sharing the credit was a cadre of park foremen who were loyal to the Slavins and dedicated to their assigned areas. Foremost among these were the "old timers": Martin Trott, who returned to the Rochester park system in 1938, Art Blensinger, Jake Gerling, George Bahringer, and Richard Horsey. Also of great assistance were Elmer Ingerick, who acted as "troubleshooter" for Pat, moving into any situation where some special attention was needed (among other assignments for Elmer was Acting City Forester); the greenskeepers at the two golf courses, Bill Lyons at Genesee Valley and Carl Lawrence at Durand Eastman; and Fred Murray, at Genesee Valley Park, who was always prepared to provide assistance wherever it was needed within the department.

Barney's retirement in 1942 created a real vacuum in the leadership of the park system, which was in need of a general park landscape renewal or renovation. In 1943, Pat Slavin recommended that William Pitkin, a local landscape designer and nurseryman, be appointed to the position of Superintendent of Parks to replace Barney.

William Pitkin had received a degree in landscape architecture from Cornell University in 1911. Before joining the Rochester Park Bureau, he had been president of Chase Brothers Nursery and later of Chase Pitkin Nursery. The experience he brought to his position with the Park Bureau did not really prepare him well for facing up to the budgetary restrictions he would experience while working for the City of Rochester. Here he was expected to provide leadership in a renovation program that would restore the parks to the grandeur they had exhibited before the Depression years. In the beginning of his career with the department, Mr. Pitkin concentrated his efforts in "opening up vistas" in Durand Eastman Park, where he relied greatly upon Art Blensinger and his skill as a woodsman. Mr. Pitkin also benefitted from information provided by Richard Horsey relative to the many plant collections throughout the park system. With this knowledge, he could begin to devise a plan for the renovations and replacements needed within the arboretum. Unfortunately, with the advent of the war, most of that program was placed on hold.

During the late summer of 1945, Wilbur E. Wright, who had served with the U.S. Air Force in the European theatre of operations, was hired as a special assistant to the director of parks. Little did Pat realize that this young veteran would be the man to succeed him as Director of Parks. In November 1945, another World War II veteran, Alvan R. Grant, was hired as plant propagator. The careers of these two, Wright and Grant, although they followed different courses, paralleled each other. Each man would eventually serve as director of parks for the Monroe County Department of Parks.

The personalities and ideologies of Pat Slavin and William Pitkin never really meshed. Pat often bypassed Pitkin by discussing park plans and policies with other employees instead of with Pitkin. Also, "on the sidelines" with ready criticism of some of the work being undertaken in the parks was Barney Slavin, who, although retired, was still visiting the parks regularly, "keeping his eyes on his babies." In the margin of one of the pages in his copy of Blake McKelvey's booklet entitled *An Historical View of Rochester's Parks and Playgrounds*, where Mr. McKelvey had written about the pruning program for improvement of the park landscape, Barney wrote, "This situation after seven years is worse than ever." Criticism such as this was reaching Mr. Pitkin. Another factor that distressed Pitkin was that the city, because of budgetary problems, had adopted a "hold-the-line" fiscal policy that blocked any real improvement program in the parks. Also, Pitkin, the "schooled outsider," was never fully accepted by the park employees, who were accustomed to "movement from within the ranks." Frustrated and disgusted, Pitkin resigned early in 1950.

Although Alvan Grant had been hired to carry on the plant propagation program, as a result of a Civil Service test given during late 1949, he was promoted to Assistant Superintendent of Parks in March 1950, and once again there was no one to continue the propagation program that was so vital to the continuation of the arboretum and to the planting program in all of the city parks. In 1950, Pat Slavin sought out and rehired Richard A. Fenicchia, who had been away from the department since 1935. Dick immediately took over the propagation program and continued with it until his retirement in 1978.

In late April and early May every year, Pat Slavin would visit Highland Park daily, including Saturdays and Sundays, to see the lilacs. He would attempt, with assistance from Richard Horsey and other park employees, to determine a date for Lilac Sunday as early as possible so that the word could be spread throughout New York and Ontario, Canada, thereby giving potential visitors an opportunity to plan their trips to "the lilacs."

It was common practice with Pat Slavin to begin each day shortly after 7:00 A.M. with a tour through some of the parks and along some of the city streets. During spring or fall planting seasons he would have his chauffeur (driver for his city-owned vehicle during his late years as director of parks) park the car along a street where trees had been newly planted. He would get out of the car and attempt to pull one of these trees out of the ground. If he succeeded, he would then trace down the planting crew responsible for that planting and lecture the men about how a tree should be planted by careful and firm tamping of the soil around and over the tree roots.

Pat enjoyed saying that he was older than some of the rhododendrons and azaleas that he had helped John Dunbar plant in Highland Park before the turn of the century.

On May 26, 1950, Patrick Slavin died unexpectedly, the result of a stroke. This was just two days before Lilac Sunday, which he had declared on May 24. An editorial printed in the May 27, 1950, edition of the *Times-Union* stated, in part, "Known affectionately as 'Pat Slavin' to Rochesterians, young and old, he was responsible for bringing to its present development the park's lilac collection which has earned the city fame from coast to coast—Rochester's parks were his life and his identification with them was so complete that he remained as Director through every change in city administration. The beauty of their neat, flowered pathways will remain a fitting memorial to him in death. On May 31, 1950, Wilbur E. Wright was appointed to succeed Mr. Slavin as the Director of Parks."

Patrick Slavin is to be remembered more as an administrator than as a plantsman. However, his early experience and training in the field remained with him throughout his entire career. He retained a sentimental attachment to Genesee Valley Park, not only because he lived out that way as a boy (on the Baker farm, later to become part of the park) and got his first job there, but because he felt that its broad spread of level meadows and green grass were more attractive than the more rugged grandeur of Durand Eastman.

LINKAGES CONTINUED — RICHARD E. HORSEY

Richard E. Horsey has been mentioned previously in this brief history when his career intermeshed with those of others who were active in the development of Rochester's parks. Inasmuch as he made significant contributions to the horticultural history of this park system, he is remembered as one of its real plantsmen. Richard Horsey was born in Oxford, New York, on July 1, 1883. His family moved to Florida and he started public school in Aviate, Orange County, Florida, when he was five years old. Because his family moved often, he attended schools in various parts of the United States. The longest period was in Cedartown, Polk County, Georgia, where he attended school from age nine to fourteen. He graduated from School #52 in Buffalo, New York, at the age of sixteen, completing nine grades.

Shortly thereafter, the family moved to Rochester, and it was here that he learned botany and "plant lore" while working in a commercial greenhouse under Mr. James Bishop, an English-trained florist and botanist. After working approximately two years with Mr. Bishop, Horsey obtained employment with Green's Nursery Company at its offices located on Wall Street, just a short walk from Highland Park. Because of his intense interest in botany, he spent much of his time during lunch hours and before and after work studying the plants in the park. In 1904, after two and a half years with the nursery, he quit to accept a job as a laborer assigned to Highland Park, where he was in daily contact with John Dunbar and both of the Slavins. Here he had the advantage of meeting and exchanging notes and information about plants with the many visitors from colleges, universities, arboretums, and other institutions who were constantly making pilgrimages to the Rochester parks to observe the plant materials.

On April 14, 1908, he was appointed foreman of Highland Park and, although not actually serving in that capacity for much of the time, held that title until his retirement in 1949. (Note: There were few titles for various jobs within the park system until the 1940s, when Civil Service classification first was introduced into municipal government in the city.) From 1908 until he retired,

Mr. Horsey lived in a city-owned house within Highland Park, "next to the Pansy Bed," surrounded by lilacs. It was here that he and Mrs. Horsey raised their family of three sons and a daughter. Residence in the park was a convenience when it came to the study of plants, and of birds, which Horsey adopted as a hobby. It also placed a demand upon him. He was subject to call at any time, day or night, for the slightest reason, and his weekends were never his own. Park visitors, unable to find some specific plant, would knock on his door, asking for assistance, or might even stop to lodge a complaint because a label was missing or some litter had been dropped along a path and the complainant wanted it removed. His advice to new, young employees was, "If you want any life of your own, never live in a park house."

During his tenure of 41 years with the parks, Richard Horsey was a dedicated student of plant materials. Like Barney Slavin, he had an inquisitive mind and a retentive memory. Because of these natural gifts and the wealth of knowledge about plant materials that he was able to assimilate, he, very early in his time with the parks, earned the respect of other scientists for the contributions that he made in the fields of botany, horticulture, and ornithology. He was especially well known for his ability to key out and identify plants. When, as a result of a recommendation made by Dr. Sargent, the park herbarium was established, it was Richard Horsey whom John Dunbar and Calvin Laney selected to take charge of it. Mr. Horsey became a "walking-talking encyclopedia or catalog" of the many plants within the Rochester arboretum, as the parks had become known in horticultural circles. He led innumerable tours for the many groups of students who traveled each year from Cornell, Syracuse School of Forestry, Alfred, Rutgers, Niagara School of Gardeners, and other schools of horticulture to "walk through the park with Horsey." Many of them returned upon many occasions after graduation to seek Mr. Horsey's advice relative to specific plants and to seek his assistance in identification. He maintained active correspondence with curators, propagators, and botanists from all of the other arboretums, many colleges, and other schools of horticulture. Many commercial nurseries also sought his aid.

Mr. Horsey helped in the development of the Highland Park lilac collection. He was an active collaborator in the first "Lilacs for America Survey," conducted in 1941 by the Committee on Horticultural Varieties of the American Association of Botanical Gardens and Arboretums. Mr. Horsey was an assiduous and persistent record keeper. With his field record books in hand, he made daily surveys of the various plant collections, making notes on the condition of specimens. He would then prepare lists of plants that were in need of replacement or that might be in need of special disease- and insect-control measures. These lists were then turned over to the staff members responsible for performing the necessary tasks. Through cooperation by the botanist and the propagator or nurseryman, the plant collections were kept at a high standard. Mr. Horsey's real accomplishments were the organization of the plant records and the building up of the herbarium collection of preserved specimens of plants, which he collected in the field and processed for filing.

During the years 1906 to 1927, at the urging of Professor Charles S. Sargent, Mr. Horsey made botanical and plant-collecting trips throughout Western New York, Western Pennsylvania, Ohio, and Eastern Kentucky. These trips averaged from seven to ten days and were made yearly in both spring and fall. Although he was always on the lookout for rare or threatened plants from which he could secure propagating wood, his main purpose was to gather material for herbarium purposes. Cuttings taken from the plants showing twig, leaf, and flower characteristics would be taken back to Rochester, where he would meticulously dry, press, and mount them on herbarium sheets. Some of these sheets prepared over seventy years ago are still in good condition.

Richard Horsey was a somewhat retiring and a very modest man. In speaking about his career in the parks, he was quoted as saying, "I was responsible for seeing that things were properly labeled." Mr. Horsey prepared for publication many memoranda on the care and culture of various plants as well as lists, giving expected dates of flowering and fall coloration, which were in great demand by local residents who wanted to plan visitations by out-of-town family members or friends at a time when the various floral displays would be at their best. A partial list of articles and notes written by Richard Horsey from 1917 to 1943 contains the following:

- "Hardiness of Coniferous Evergreens As Shown by the Severe Cold Winter of 1917-18," published in *Horticulture*, January 1919.
- "The Singleleaf Pine—Notes and Photograph," published in *Horticulture*, January 1925.
- "Lilacs in the Rochester Parks (1938)," mimeographed at Cornell University for the use of the students in Ornamental Horticulture.
- "Shrubs and Trees Attractive to Birds (1940)," for Charlotte High School, Department of Science, Horticultural Unit.
- As a collaborator for the United States Department of Agriculture, Bureau of Entomology, Washington, D.C., effective March 1, 1934, notes on insects for the *Insect Post Survey Bulletin*.
- "Bird Distribution in Eastern Kentucky," published in *The Auk*, a publication of the American Ornithologists' Union, January 1922. Notes on birds were contributed to *The Auk* from 1919 to 1943.
- "Tree Sparrow Migration: A Comparison"—A remarkable parallel was seen between the experience of Mr. Wendell P. Smith at Wells River, Vermont, and Mr. Horsey's, relative to the tree sparrow. Printed in the *Bulletin of the Northeastern Bird-Banding Association*, July 1926. This material was later printed as part of an article published as "Tree Sparrow Returns and Migration" by Mr. Smith in the *Bulletin of the Northeastern Bird-Banding Association* in January 1927.

In 1942, in recognition of his work in the field of botany, Mr. Horsey was made a Fellow of the Rochester Museum of Arts and Sciences.

To a large degree, after Barney Slavin's retirement in 1942, Mr. Horsey took over the responsibility for maintaining correspondence with other arboretums and horticulturists on behalf of the Department of Parks. All questions relative to horticulture and plant materials were referred to him for reply. In many instances he prepared responses for signing by the director of parks or by the superintendent, who admittedly lacked the knowledge of plant materials possessed by Mr. Horsey.

During his last four years with the park system, Richard Horsey spent many hours with Wilbur Wright and Alvan Grant, both of whom had joined the park system in 1945, schooling them on the importance of the arboretum and the horticultural wealth of the parks. Although his health was failing, he still could climb the slopes at Highland and Durand Eastman Parks, keeping pace with the younger men as he lectured them about the history and merits as well as the botanical value of each plant. In January 1948, Bernard E. Harkness, a young botanist who had already earned recognition as one of the country's leading horticulturists, started employment with the Rochester Park Bureau.

Mr. Horsey, who was planning to retire in 1949, would now prepare Bernie Harkness for the role he was to play as Horsey's successor. This was a wonderful experience for both men—Horsey was delighted and amazed at the knowledge Bernie was bringing with him, and, during the 20 months that remained before Horsey's retirement, Bernie had the opportunity to see and study the plantings with someone who had been with the park system prior to the planting of many of the specimens.

At a retirement party for Mr. Horsey in September 1949, he was presented with a portfolio of letters that the team of Wright, Grant, and Harkness had solicited from friends and associates of Horsey's throughout the horticultural world. Excerpts from two of the letters that were in that portfolio express the high regard in which Mr. Horsey was held by his peers in the fields of botany and horticulture. John C. Wister, Director of the Arthur Hoyt Scott Horticultural Foundation, Swarthmore College, wrote, in part:

> You should be very proud of all your part in this [refers to the development of the arboretum] and I know that you are very happy to look back over the long term of years and see

what you have accomplished. The many visitors you have had from all parts of the country are ample proof of the importance of your work and the appreciation in which it is held by all who are interested in gardening.

Also from Mr. Wister's letter: "It has been your knowledge and devotion to the plants that has enabled the new people to take hold and go on."

The dean of all the horticulturists in this country, and perhaps in the world, Liberty Hyde Bailey, wrote in part:

Dear Mr. Horsey:

The Rochester parks have been notable for many years because of the excellence of their plant materials and the care with which the nomenclature and records have been kept up to date. You have been largely responsible for this excellence. Your work and devotion are well known to plant lovers, who realize that you have made outstanding contributions in the horticultural field. Of course you will continue to live with these interests and they will be themselves a contribution to your happiness.

Cordially yours, with best wishes.

After 45 years of service with the Rochester park system, Mr. Horsey retired in September 1949. He then moved to East Rochester, where he organized a private herbarium of dried plant specimens native to Western New York. This was donated to the New York State University at Geneseo in 1965.

In 1954, he was made an honorary member of the Rochester Academy of Science. During the annual Lilac Festival in 1962, he was presented with the Rochester Parks' Public Service Award for his "work and notes on the hundreds of varieties of Lilacs in the park system."

LINKAGES CONTINUED

"The old changeth, yielding place to new"—this often-quoted line from Alfred Lord Tennyson's "The Passing of King Arthur" might well describe what was taking place in the Rochester park system during the 1940s. During the first fifty-two years (1888-1940) in its history, the acreage in the parks had grown from the original nineteen acres in Highland Park to approximately 2,000 acres in 1938, and that acreage was distributed throughout twenty-four parks and thirty-seven playgrounds. During this same period, park employees with leadership provided by Calvin Laney, John Dunbar, and the Slavins (Barney and Pat) had shaped the acquired acreage into a well-developed park system.

It was good fortune that there was some overlap of these park pioneers with some of the younger men who were remaining to carry on with the horticultural program. Wilbur E. Wright, who succeeded Pat Slavin as Director, had been a "right-hand-man" for Pat for approximately five years and, consequently, was well acquainted with the responsibilities he was inheriting. Alvan Grant had been working closely with Richard Horsey in the program of renovating the plant collections throughout the park areas. Bernard Harkness had been schooled by Richard Horsey for over a year in the duties of the taxonomist and herbarium curator. In 1950, about one month before he died, Pat Slavin was successful in bringing Richard Fenicchia back to employment with the park system, a move that would prove to be almost providential in the effect it would have on the future of the park system and its arboretum. Also, the change in stewardship for the park system as it emerged out of the 1940s and into the 1950s was made easier by several other employees who had worked with the Slavins prior to World War II and who would continue their careers for ten or more years into the last half of the century.

One of these was Martin Trott, who left the Rochester park system in 1938 to work on the development of Hamlin Beach State Park. Shortly after his return to employment with the Rochester park system in 1942, Martin Trott was quoted in the *Democrat and Chronicle*: "Most of the large scale planting of Durand Eastman is over. Most of the hillsides have been filled. Virtually every variety of tree and shrub which will grow in this climate is to be found somewhere in this park."

Martin was assigned to the position of foreman in charge of the small city parks and squares. Although these, in total, represented very little acreage within the park system, they were scattered throughout the city, where they attracted the attention of neighbors who were quick to criticize if there was any sign of neglect or poor maintenance. Some of them, because of their highly visible locations, were constantly under public scrutiny— Washington Park, Anderson Park, and Plymouth Park were good examples of these. Because of their prominent locations, these all needed special year-round attention, such as lawn care and gardening in spring, summer, and fall; care of public sidewalks during winter months; and, of course, pickup of litter year round. At times, Trott and his crew were called upon to participate in the maintenance in other park areas, such as assisting in preparing Highland Park for the annual Lilac Time festivities and the removal of spent lilac blossoms when Lilac Time was over. Martin Trott continued in this position until his retirement in the spring of 1950.

Art Blensinger continued to work at Durand Eastman Park, where, after his regular forty- to forty-eight-hour week, he could often be found on Sundays wandering throughout the park with a pruning saw and shears removing overhanging branches along trails or looking for seedlings of flowering cherry, sassafras, dogwood trees, etc. He would dig these up and transplant them to other areas in the park where he felt they would add color and provide a "better show" for the park visitors. Art was an excellent custodian of the natural environment in which he worked. He remained Park Supervisor at Durand Eastman Park until his retirement in 1972 after fifty years of service in the Rochester park system.

Also at Durand Eastman Park, until his appointment as one of the two Assistant Superintendents of Parks in March 1950, was Jacob Gerling. Jake depended upon Art Blensinger to get the park work done while he studied the plants that Barney Slavin had developed and placed in the nurseries at Durand Eastman Park. Jake accomplished a great deal in public relations and promotion of the Rochester park system through publicizing Barney Slavin's many horticultural accomplishments. He wrote about Barney's pioneering work with smaller, upright, and compact trees for planting on city streets, where space and visibility were a factor. In an article that appeared in the December 1952 issue of the *Garden Journal*, published by the New York Botanic Garden, he cited the need for a new view on street trees in light of modern city conditions and new developments relative to insects and diseases. He pointed out that a tree's resistance to disease should be one of the chief qualities to be considered in choosing a tree for planting along city streets.

On June 1, 1954, when a major reorganization of the Rochester Park Bureau went into effect, Jake was appointed Superintendent of Building Maintenance for the bureau, a position he held until his retirement in 1961. In November 1959, Gerling was cited by the Western New York Arborists Association at a meeting at the State College of Forestry in Syracuse for "achievements in the promotion and use of better adapted species of trees for functional and ornamental service" and for "recognition of successful efforts in furthering the work of Barney Slavin."

For many years Jake was an active member in the Society of Municipal Arborists, where he became friendly with a forester from Cleveland, Ohio, who was promoting "tailored trees." Jake supplied him with many scions taken from some of Barney's introductions. In publications of the Society of Municipal Arborists, Jake gave full credit to Barney Slavin as a pioneer in the selection, propagation, and use of better-adapted species and forms of trees for more practical service on city streets. "Barney, as early as 1915, realized the need for smaller maturing type trees. . . . Alerted by Chestnut blight, Barney also preached against using only one genus too consistently." For twenty years, based upon Barney Slavin's work, Gerling advocated the theme of using trees that "fit the space."

87

Other key people who were of great assistance in making the change from the "old order to the new" were the two golf course supervisors, William Lyons (Genesee Valley Park) and Carl Lawrence (Durand Eastman Park), and the supervisor of Genesee Valley Park, Fred Murray. Bill Lyons and Carl Lawrence should also be considered as plantsmen, perhaps of a very special kind inasmuch as their chief responsibilities were centered on the care of the entire landscapes that comprised their respective golf courses: trees, shrubs, and grasses of different species, the maintenance of which required special skills and knowledge. Fred Murray, Foreman and later Park Supervisor of Genesee Valley Park, was always ready with his crew to assist in planting programs throughout the entire park system. This often resulted in Fred working overtime or on Sundays to keep up with the maintenance of his own park. As he said, "It's one of the hazards of living within a city-owned house in a park."

Not to be forgotten is Elmer Ingerick. When he started employment with the city in 1914, he was listed as a teamster. His duties at that time could be compared to those performed by a tractor operator today, except in many ways, the teamster was more versatile. With his team of horses, he was a unit that performed many tasks within the parks. Dependent upon the appropriate horse-drawn equipment, this work-unit moved soil for use in grading or in the greenhouses, hauled gravel used in constructing roads and paths, mowed lawns, plowed and fitted nursery land, cleared snow from ice-skating rinks, moved trees and shrubs, removed tree stumps, and the list could continue. Elmer was the dean of the park teamsters, and when roads and trails were being graded and constructed throughout the various parks from Genesee Valley to Durand Eastman, Elmer was on the job, supervising the other teamsters.

Both of the Slavins, having been farm boys during the 1880s and into the 1890s, had worked with horses and were well aware of their value and the value of the teamsters in the development of park areas. During the years that Pat Slavin was a foreman in the parks, he became increasingly dependent upon Elmer Ingerick, who was not only an excellent teamster but also very capable of supervising other men. Elmer was a "jack of all trades," and as Pat's responsibilities grew, he promoted Elmer to foreman and called upon him many times to tackle those emergencies that would occasionally spring up. When, during the mid-1940s, the grounds at Mt. Hope Cemetery appeared to be somewhat ragged, Pat assigned Elmer to "take over and clean it up." Elmer soon organized the "cemetery gang" into a more efficient workforce and managed to greatly improve the appearance of this historic area.

In 1950, Elmer was transferred from Mt. Hope Cemetery to the position of City Forester. He fulfilled the duties of this position until a reorganization of the Park Bureau in 1954 brought Calvin Reynolds in as City Forester. Although Elmer wanted to retire at that time, he agreed to act as an assistant to Reynolds for a short period of time while Calvin Reynolds adjusted to his new responsibilities. Elmer retired later in 1954 and went to work in a supervisory capacity for Monroe Tree Surgeons until his untimely death, the result of an automobile accident, in January 1959.

THE NEW ORDER — WILBUR E. WRIGHT

Wilbur E. Wright began his career with the Bureau of Parks during the summer of 1945 as a special aide to the director of parks. He had served as a navigator on a U.S. Air Force plane that was shot down over Europe and had been provided with sanctuary by an underground group opposed to the German forces. After his safe return to friendly forces, this experience led to his early discharge from active duty. Before entering the armed services, Wilbur had majored in horticultural studies at Farmingdale Agricultural and Technical College of the New York State University and at Cornell University. During his first few years with the park system, he spent considerable time "on loan" to the Rochester Housing Authority, supervising the landscaping and planting of the grounds at the housing complexes it was developing.

Whenever possible, he toured the various parks with Richard Horsey in an attempt to become familiar with the plant materials for which these parks were noted throughout the horticultural world. Horsey was a good teacher; in addition to discussing the botanical characteristics of plants, he would recant some history about the parks. Upon many occasions, Wilbur was meeting and conferring with Pat Slavin, often meeting with him at his home on Saturday afternoons, when they would spend several hours discussing problems and plans associated with the Bureau of Parks.

Meanwhile, William Pitkin, the Superintendent of Parks, had become frustrated with the many problems he was encountering within the parks, partly due to the city's budgetary policies, but also to the lack of cooperation he felt he was experiencing within the Park Bureau. Pitkin resigned early in 1950 and moved to Asheville, North Carolina, where he resumed private practice in landscaping design and counseling.

Shortly before Pitkin's resignation, a Civil Service examination was called for the position of Assistant Superintendent of Parks. Inasmuch as Wilbur Wright was a provisional appointee to his position as aide to Pat Slavin, he was not permitted to take the promotional exam. As a result of this examination, Jacob Gerling and Alvan Grant were each appointed Assistant Superintendent. The parks were divided into two districts: Jake Gerling was assigned supervision over Durand Eastman Park, Ontario Beach Park, and Seneca Park, and Alvan Grant was assigned Highland Park with the greenhouses and conservatory, Cobbs Hill Park, all of the small city parks and squares, Genesee Valley Park and its golf courses, Maplewood Park, and all city ice-skating rinks except the ones at two city playgrounds.

Pat Slavin's death on May 26, 1950, ended the 112 years of combined service that the Slavin brothers had devoted to the Rochester park system. On May 31, 1950, City Manager Louis B. Cartwright appointed Wilbur Wright to the position of Director of Parks and Playgrounds to succeed Pat Slavin. In this position, which also carried the title of Deputy Commissioner of Public Safety, Wilbur would administer a bureau (of the Public Safety Department) with such different divisions as playgrounds and cemeteries. On many days he would have very little contact with horticulture. Perhaps his most frequent contact with plants was with the trees growing along the city streets. Unfortunately, his efforts were directed there because of Dutch elm disease, which had reached Rochester.

Wright was immediately immersed in a campaign to save the elms that so gracefully adorned many city streets. He convinced the city administration and the council that new equipment was needed, more manpower had to be employed, and purchase of replacement trees should be included in the program. He initiated a vigorous program of spraying to gain control of the elm leaf beetle, which was the agent carrying the disease from tree to tree. Out on the streets supervising the actual work was City Forester Elmer Ingerick. During the early 1950s, Elmer removed hundreds of elm trees from city streets and, at the same time, pruned thousands of trees to remove broken, dead, or diseased branches to protect the citizenry of Rochester from damage caused by falling branches. During 1952 alone, 1,567 trees were removed because of storm damage, 22,000 trees were sprayed in the constant war with diseases and insects, and thousands were given some corrective pruning. During the 1950s, many new trees were planted, an average of 1,200 per year, to replace those that were removed.

Wilbur Wright consulted with other park men and city foresters from those areas of the country that had experienced the spread of Dutch elm disease before it reached Rochester. He also met with nurserymen, as well as botanists and tree experts from various colleges and universities, as he searched for those species of trees that would best replace the elms. In developing his overall plan to restore and renew the city tree plantings, he sought input from the New York State Department of Agriculture, Syracuse University, and Cornell. Ginkgo (male tree), hornbeam, Bradford pear, Chinese scholar-tree and others, as well as new forms of maple, ash, linden, and locust were recommended and purchased.

At the Disposal Plant nursery in Durand Eastman Park, which Barney Slavin had started in 1908-1910, Wilbur and Elmer supervised the preparation of several acres for the planting of trial blocks of two-year-old seedling trees, which were constantly under their surveillance to determine their value for future use as street trees.

Despite all efforts, although the program of spraying, pruning, and removal of diseased elms probably helped to slow the spread of the disease, within a few years all of the elms along the city streets had been removed. Meanwhile, the seedling trees in the trial blocks at Durand Eastman nursery had grown to a proper size for planting along the city streets.

Beginning with his appointment to the position of Director of Parks, Wilbur Wright was much involved in bringing improvements to the recreation program administered by the Division of Recreation and Playgrounds, which was part of the Bureau of Parks. He instituted a program of improving the methods and operations in this division by establishing an annual Training Institute for Playground Personnel, receiving assistance in this from various agencies of the Rochester Chamber of Commerce.

Just as Pat Slavin had done, Wright attempted on a daily schedule to visit some of the areas for which he was responsible. During late April and early May, he frequently visited Highland Park before 8:00 A.M. to meet with Bernard Harkness and Alvan Grant for a quick tour through the lilacs. His goal was to announce the dates for Lilac Time at least two weeks in advance of peak bloom so that the word could be spread throughout the eastern part of the country and Canada.

During Lilac Time 1951, a large silver cup was presented to Wilbur Wright, representing the City of Rochester, by Paul F. Freese, editor of *Popular Gardening* magazine. This cup, the first in a series of awards by that magazine, was inscribed:

Awarded to the City of Rochester
for the Beauty of its parks
by Popular Gardening—1951

In making the presentation, Mr. Freese stated that he was "particularly impressed by the educational value of Rochester's famed lilac display" and that "it was that aspect of the city's system that his magazine was emphasizing in the award." He also said, "The parks here, and particularly the lilacs, are powerful stimulants to the beautification of home gardens and grounds. . . . The way the shrubs are planted and the complete labeling of every variety are a great help to the home gardener, for they enable him to study the different varieties and to select just what he wants for his own plantings."

The horticultural programs within the parks were being maintained under the supervision of Gerling and Grant, the two Assistant Superintendents, with assistance from Art Blensinger (Park Supervisor of Durand Eastman Park) and Richard Fenicchia (Superintendent of Horticulture) operating out of Highland Park, where he was deeply engaged in an active program of propagation and plant breeding.

Of real significance during the early half of the 1950s was the final step in the emergence of the Park Bureau from dependence upon horses and horse-drawn equipment. This had really started with the Forestry Division many years earlier out of necessity to have motorized vehicles with which to move about on city streets. The same steps were taken on the golf courses when tractors took over from horses in pulling the mowing equipment and power-driven lawn mowers replaced the former man-powered mowers in cutting the greens and tees. However, within the parks and sometimes between the parks, there was still a dependence upon horses. In fact, when the soil in the flower beds in Plymouth Park was replaced with fresh composted soil during 1949, horse-drawn dump wagons were used in bringing the soil from Genesee Valley Park to Plymouth Park. When the city-owned house in Highland Park, formerly the home of the Horsey family, was razed in 1950, gravel and soil was hauled in horse-drawn wagons from a site in Cobbs Hill Park for filling the depression left by the cellar. In the spring of 1953, Wilbur Wright, with help from the city manager, convinced city council that the time had come to replace the horses 100 percent with mechanical equipment. Funds were allocated for the purchase of said equipment, and eight teams of horses were sold at a public auction held at the stable in Genesee Valley Park. An additional team was sent to the zoo to become part of its animal inventory.

During the early 1950s, Wilbur Wright initiated a program of improvements at Seneca Park Zoo with very little expenditure of city funds. In 1952, by making use of manpower from the Forestry Division and other park units, an area for a children's zoo and for native animals was developed north of the zoo proper. In the late spring of that same year, Wilbur Wright and Alvan Grant, using the truck (van) from the greenhouse, drove to Cleveland, Ohio, to pick up a pair of emus and a pair of young bison from a small animal dealer. As part of this trip, they delivered a small donkey from Seneca Park to a Buffalo address. What both men specifically remembered from this trip is that every time the van was stopped for a traffic signal as they drove through Buffalo, the donkey would give out the loudest possible bray, attracting attention from every person within hearing distance. Interest in this zoo project was well demonstrated when several citizens donated small domestic animals that would make the children's zoo a reality.

During 1951, the City of Rochester purchased the Warner Castle property (5 Castle Park) for addition to Highland Park. After considerable redecorating and minor repairs in the building, the herbarium was moved to this site from the old wooden frame structure that had housed it for a number of years. This old building located off Pinetum Road in the park was in many ways a firetrap, certainly not suitable for storage of the valuable herbarium collection and other plant records of the parks, as well as the horticultural library. Wilbur Wright, who had been associated with the Garden Center of Rochester for a number of years, sought permission from city council for the Garden Center to use the old building for its headquarters.

A real innovation made under Wilbur Wright during the 1950s was the construction of two open-air, artificial ice-skating rinks. There were seven ice-skating rinks within the Rochester parks that relied upon natural freezing. During the winter season of 1948-49, there had been only one day of skating on these rinks, and then in the 1952-53 season there were only eight and a half days. Unfortunately, this lack of skating days was in no way a measure of the manpower and hours that had been required in attempting to prepare them for use by the public. At Cobbs Hill Park (Lake Riley), for example, during the 1948-49 season the payroll alone amounted to $9,969 and the public realized only four hours of skating. Wright had spent many hours in researching and observing artificial ice rinks and was able to convince city administration and city council of the desirability of artificial ice rinks as public-use facilities.

The first, at Genesee Valley Park, was opened to the public on Halloween night, 1954; the second, at Webster Avenue Park and playground, went into use for the first time on November 17, 1957. It is interesting to note that during the skating season of 1954-55, there were 80 days of skating on the artificial ice compared to 29 on natural ice. These artificial rinks were assigned under Alvan Grant's supervision, and he worked many nights with a small crew to make the ice sheet and in learning to operate the equipment used in chilling the brine. He was able to achieve a certain expertise in the care and maintenance of these rinks, which came to the attention of members of the American Institute of Park Executives, and he was asked to produce a paper for distribution to all members desiring such information.

In May 1954, after an eight-week study by city officials, a reorganization of the city's Bureau of Parks and Playgrounds was announced by Public Safety Commissioner Kenneth C. Townson. It was the most far-reaching in the bureau's history. It created four new superintendents, raising the number to six. It resulted in the promotion of twelve employees, with pay raises for some. The city was divided into four recreational districts, with a recreation supervisor for each. The shop buildings then maintained by the bureau were consolidated into a single structure, which would be built in Genesee Valley Park. Reasons given for this reorganization were to increase bureau efficiency, reduce operating costs, and provide special training for employees who qualified as replacements for those recreation leaders who were approaching retirement age. This plan was based upon recommendations made by Wilbur Wright and had the approval of City Manager Robert Aex.

Chester B. Leake, former Superintendent of Playgrounds and the Recreation Division, was assigned to a new post, Superintendent of Research and Development, and Raymond G. Slattery was promoted to succeed Leake as Superintendent of Playgrounds.

Calvin Reynolds, former Cemetery Supervisor, was promoted to City Forester. In promoting Reynolds, Commissioner Townson said that "the young man earned the substantial pay raise because of his excellent qualifications and his experience with the State Conservation Department and with private landscaping companies." Reynolds had been with the city for two years, starting as a tree trimmer, then being promoted to foreman and then to Cemetery Supervisor. This new position was provisional pending a Civil Service examination. He was a veteran of World War II and had graduated from Syracuse School of Forestry in 1951. His position entailed being in charge of every city-owned tree along the streets and in the parks and cemeteries, as well as the bureau's garages, shop, and new construction. At this time, Elmer Ingerick was asked to remain as an assistant to Reynolds while he was becoming fully cognizant of the duties and responsibilities of the position of City Forester.

William B. McMahon, who had been Superintendent of Cemeteries for many years, was retained in that position. However, for a period of several months while Wilbur Wright was hospitalized with a back condition, McMahon acted in a proxy capacity for him. McMahon would report to the park office for about four hours each workday to monitor phone calls and mail, which he would refer to other staff members for further action. He would also make daily visits to the hospital to keep Wilbur informed and to carry messages back and forth between staff members and Wilbur. During this period, many people never realized that Wilbur was absent from the office because park business was carried on as usual, with all staff members giving full cooperation.

Jacob J. Gerling, formerly an Assistant Superintendent of Parks, was made Superintendent of Building Maintenance in charge of all buildings for which the bureau had responsibility. As it turned out, this did not include the greenhouses and conservatory, several of the labor centers within the parks, and the skating rinks, natural and artificial.

Alvan Grant was promoted to the position of Superintendent of Parks, with all of the parks placed under his supervision. Serving under Grant would be the six park supervisors, the greenhouse foreman, the zoo curator, two greenskeepers (at Genesee Valley and Durand Eastman Parks), and the taxonomist. It soon became apparent that the "new construction" mentioned by Townson when speaking about Reynolds did not include any construction within the parks.

During the next few years, Wilbur Wright focused his efforts on developing a better recreation program for the city. Working closely with the Council of Social Agencies, he introduced an In-Service Training Program, which would be attended by both the old and the new activities leaders in the Recreation Division. He also coordinated the total program of his bureau by holding weekly staff meetings at the Castle, where there would be less disturbance than would be experienced in the office building downtown. When Raymond Slattery retired from his position as Superintendent of Recreation in 1956, Joseph M. Caverly was named to replace him.

In the spring of 1956, Congressman Ostertag, whose New York district included the Rochester area, arranged with Wilbur Wright to furnish a bouquet of Rochester lilacs for presentation to Mrs. (Mamie) Dwight D. Eisenhower. When the congressman, accompanied by Mrs. Ostertag, gave this bouquet to Mrs. Eisenhower, she commented that she was sorry that there were no lilacs on the White House grounds because lilacs, especially white ones, were among her favorite flowers. The congressman took this opportunity to pass this information to Wright, who agreed to take some bushes from Rochester to the White House in the fall when it was a good time for transplanting lilacs. Wilbur Wright and Robert Redman, the White House gardener, decided to plant the bushes taken to the White House in a group so that when in flower they would make a mass display. The varieties, bearing blue, white, purple, and pink blossoms, included three of John Dunbar's origination, 'President Lincoln,' 'President Roosevelt,' and 'General Grant.' On the same trip, Wright took three lilac bushes to the Eisenhower home in Gettysburg and planted them in a location on the grounds where Mrs. Eisenhower would be able to see them from her bedroom windows. "When I was a child, there was a lilac bush in the back yard," said Mamie. "I have a special feeling in my heart for lilacs. When they bloom, it is to me the beginning of spring."

A new policy for the management of Lilac Time went into effect in 1959 upon recommendations made by Park Director Wilbur E. Wright. Under this policy, the City of Rochester entered into an agreement with the Convention and Publicity Bureau, whereby that organization would be responsible for publicizing Lilac Time across the country. With the cooperation of the Gannett newspapers, an annual Rochester Parks Public Service Award was started whereby a specially engraved silver tray would be presented to a local citizen who had performed special service to the community in a field related to the parks. This program of making awards was added to in 1964 when the first annual Rochester Parks National Award for Parks Service was presented to Conrad Wirth of New York City, former Director of the National Park Service.

In 1959, the New York State Nurserymen's Association, in conference in Syracuse, presented Wilbur E. Wright with an award for "carrying on the selection of native trees for street planting and establishing a program of practical demonstration of tree values, at a time when replacement of many American Elms is required through aging and disease." In addition, the organization gave recognition to Wright's public relations "in the field of ornamentals through the recreation of parks in Rochester and through highlighting ornamental plants of seasonal interest and special appeal to the public as well as to plant specialists."

Beginning in the early 1950s, Wilbur E. Wright and Alvan Grant had both become members of the American Institute of Park Executives. Both men had served on several committees of the organization and also had presented papers relative to horticultural subjects at the annual conferences. In 1957, and again in 1958, they presented invitations to the organization to hold an annual conference in Rochester. With a policy whereby conference sites were selected three years in advance, Rochester was selected in 1958 to host the 1961 conference. Planning for this began in 1959. Although there were many rumors and also news stories floating around that changes were about to happen relative to the city parks, no one really expected in 1959 that in September 1961 it would be a newly formed Monroe County Department of Parks that would host this conference, along with the City Department of Recreation and Parks. Action was taken in June 1961 whereby five city-owned park areas would be brought together with the five county-owned parks to establish a new Monroe County Department of Parks with Wilbur E. Wright as Director. (More about this later.)

ALVAN ROGER GRANT

Alvan R. Grant, after serving in the armed forces for forty months during World War II (24 months in the ETO), began his career with the Rochester Park Bureau in November 1945. Although he was listed on payroll records as a skilled laborer, his specific duties were those of plant propagator. (Classification of park positions with titles for specific jobs had not yet been initiated, except for administrators.)

From the time he was seven years old until he graduated from high school in 1934, Alvan Grant lived in Youngstown, Ohio. He had lost his father in 1923, and his mother, with three sons, moved from New York State to Youngstown, where she had found employment as a social worker with the YWCA. While still in his pre-teen years, Al Grant became engrossed in gardening as he worked on the grounds of a home owned by his great aunts, who had a real penchant for plants of all kinds. As he grew into his teen years, he found part-time employment with a landscape gardener working on several Youngstown estates. While in high school, he had the good fortune to have as one of his teachers a woman who was especially interested in the preservation of trees and who had gained permission to establish a small arboretum on school grounds. Alvan became one of her most interested and willing volunteers. After his graduation from high school, Al Grant and his mother moved to Mumford, New York, where his maternal grandparents had lived for many years. Here, for two years, he did part-time gardening whenever he could find a "customer" and also worked as a mason's helper in the construction of new homes in the suburbs of Rochester.

In the fall of 1936, he entered Cornell University, where he majored in horticulture and ornamental floriculture. This was during the Depression years of the 1930s when money was a scarce item. Consequently, Alvan washed dishes for his meals and worked in the National Youth Administration (NYA) program to earn money for books and lodgings. In the NYA program, he worked in the greenhouses at the Plant Science Building and also at the departmental nursery or trial gardens area. For a few months during 1937, he acted as a foreman of a small crew of students planting the rock garden near Willard Straight Hall, and occasionally assisted an instructor who was making a special study of the genera *Erica, Calluna,* and *Saxifraga.* Not only did he learn from his academic program, but he also absorbed much about horticulture and plants from the practical experience in which he was engaged. During vacation periods away from campus, Grant worked for Hart and Vick Seed Company at its Stone Street store in Rochester and, upon several occasions, at its nursery on Mosley Road outside of Fairport, New York.

In 1940, he leased a small greenhouse range in Mumford from which he operated a florist, nursery, and landscape business. This was terminated in May 1942 when he received his draft notice and was immediately ordered to report for service in the army. While overseas with the 480th Engineer Maintenance Company, he went on detached service to several special service units, such as a water purification unit, a litter-bearing unit, a laundry unit, etc. He would spend several weeks with each unit learning as much as possible about them and their officers, and would then write biographical news releases about them that would be forwarded to the United States for publication within areas where these units may have originated. Whenever he could arrange some time away from his military duties, he would travel to Cambridge and spend a few hours in the botanic gardens in an attempt to keep himself familiar with the many plant specimens and thinking about the post-war days when he would return to some phase of horticulture.

In January 1945, he transferred to the Fourth Infantry Division for service on the European front. He suffered a concussion in late March from the nearby explosion of a German shell and was sent back to a hospital in England. He was released from the hospital in early May and rejoined his outfit just before the end of the war in Europe. The 4th Infantry Division returned to the United States early in July, and all members were granted 30-day furloughs, after which they were slated for special training prior to being sent to the Asian-Pacific area for the invasion of Japan. During this furlough period, Al (Roger to his family and friends) Grant married Mairian Sage, a young lady whom he had known since his arrival in Mumford in 1934. Fortunately, Japan officially surrendered on August 15, 1945 (the day that Grant was due back at Fort Dix) and the plans for more training were scuttled. It now became a matter of waiting for discharge, which occurred on October 20, 1945.

Without the necessary capital to finance a business, Grant decided to apply for work with the city park system and was offered a job with the condition that he establish a city address before he could begin work. This matter solved, he reported to the greenhouses in Highland Park on November 6, 1945. He introduced himself to Richard Horsey, who lived in the city-owned house just across Highland Avenue from these greenhouses, and his career with the parks was launched.

Mr. Horsey spent many hours with Al Grant, ushering him through the parks, especially Highland and Durand Eastman, pointing out the many different plant collections and indoctrinating him with some of the history of the parks and of the plantings displayed within them. Richard Horsey was constantly on the job, reviewing these plant collections and providing Grant with long lists of plants that he felt needed to be propagated and grown on for replacements within the parks. During his first four years with the park system, Grant, along with other duties, produced plants of 538 species and cultivars of deciduous trees and shrubs in 30 genera for future use in upgrading the collections. He also propagated hundreds of coniferous plants that would be used in future landscape plantings throughout the parks and on the grounds of other public buildings. (Note: The Bureau of Parks was part of the Department of Public Safety under the direction of the Commissioner of Public Safety. During the 1950s when the Fire College, several new fire stations, and some other public facilities were being constructed, the Park Bureau was involved in the landscaping for these facilities, with many plants furnished from the park nurseries.)

The combination of the Depression years of the 1930s and the war years of the 1940s had resulted in a curtailment in the maintenance of the park nurseries. The only park nursery still in operation in 1945 was the one located on the Disposal Plant property adjacent to Durand Eastman Park, and that had received very little care after Barney Slavin's retirement. Consequently, it was a "jungle" of overgrown trees and shrubs, weed plants, and "chance seedlings." Several beds of woody plant materials were still in existence in an area of Highland Park near the corner of Goodman Street South and Highland Avenue. These were also in bad shape and in need of a general clean-up and thinning out, a task Grant took on. He often put in many hours as an unpaid volunteer during evenings and on weekends, digging out weed plants and others not needed for replacements within the parks. He also undertook a program of corrective pruning, which was needed to properly shape overgrown or crowded plants into specimens worthy of moving into permanent locations.

During his first two years with the park system, Grant's assigned duties were interrupted upon two occasions for several weeks each time when he was called upon to assist in cleaning up storm-damaged trees from city streets.

In 1946, the Bureau of Parks entered into an agreement with St. John's Home to lease, for nursery purposes, vacant land that abutted Highland Park on the west. This former orchard had been neglected for a number of years and needed considerable clearing and fitting to prepare it for nursery use. Working with the assistance of a teamster with his team of horses, Grant had the area ready for planting during early fall and then began lining out many of the plants he had produced at the greenhouses. This nursery became a "way station" where plants propagated at the greenhouse could be grown and prepared for later planting in the parks or in other city areas.

Because of the reputation that the Rochester collection of lilacs had acquired, the propagation of this shrub was of prime importance. Mr. Horsey maintained special surveillance over the lilacs. Whenever he observed that a particular specimen was in danger of being lost because of insect infestation, vandalism, storm damage, or other reasons, he would notify Grant, who, in turn, would place it on the priority list for propagation. Upon occasion, information would be received about a lilac that had been introduced at another arboretum or by a commercial nursery. Inasmuch as Horsey was in constant correspondence with other horticultural institutions, he would request that a small plant or some propagating wood of the new cultivar be sent to Rochester so that the new variety eventually could be planted within the Rochester collection. In some cases, commercial nurseries would send new plant materials to Rochester in repayment for material (seeds or cuttings) that they might have received at a previous time from Rochester. All plants or propagating material would be turned over to Grant for further nurturing within the greenhouse or nursery and for subsequent planting within the parks.

During the late 1940s, Pat Slavin encouraged Grant to work on developing new varieties of lilacs. (Note: Pat always wanted to see a yellow lilac developed.) In the summer of 1947, Alvan Grant collected seeds from a fine double white variety, 'Edith Cavell,' a very showy cultivar that had been introduced by a French nursery, Lemoine, in 1916. He planted these seeds in flats in the greenhouse, where the resulting seedlings were potted and grown until 1949 when they were lined out in a special bed in the new Highland Park nursery.

Of some significance to this narrative, because Lilac Time at Highland Park each year became the goal when the park should be at its peak condition, is the following item that appeared in the March 12, 1948, issue of the *Democrat and Chronicle*: "Lilac named as official city flower—displaces the aster under ruling by City Council. The lilac whose name is firmly linked with that of Rochester became the City's official flower last night. Displacing the aster which had a tenuous standing, the lovely posy whose fame has been spread afar by the City's annual Lilac Day was designated by City Council."

At the same time, the city council provided that the "Mayor shall designate a Lilac Time dedicated to honor the new official bloom. Under the ordinance, the time, which shall be a full week, will vary as to time and will be fixed upon recommendation of the Director of Parks."

Although the lilacs had started drawing crowds to the park as early as 1898, it was not until 1905 that any declaration of Lilac Sunday was made by the officials in charge of the parks. The title "Director of Parks" did not appear on the park's roster until 1928. Calvin Laney, who had been appointed to the position of Commissioner of Parks after the retirement of William S. Riley in 1925, retired in 1928. (Note: Riley, after serving as Deputy Commissioner under Alexander Lamberton from 1915, had been appointed Commissioner in 1918 when Lamberton, then 79 years old, retired.) With the adoption of the city manager form of government in 1928, there was a major reorganization in the management of parks and playgrounds and the position of Park Director was created.

The designation of the lilac as the official flower for Rochester brought with it a campaign of promotion and consequently of pageantry such as had never been witnessed in the long history of Lilac Time. As a result of this, the park plantsmen were challenged to make significant changes each year—in other words, to furnish more bait that the promoters could use in attracting visitors.

Alvan Grant was promoted to Greenhouse Foreman effective January 1, 1949. This did not entail any real change in duties (or salary). It was simply adding the responsibilities of supervision and operation of the greenhouse and conservatory to those he already held.

Since its dedication in 1911, the Lamberton Conservatory had been a special attraction for city residents and out-of-town visitors. Grant initiated a change in the manner in which plants had been displayed by removing or lowering many of the raised benches. This made possible the arranging of plants in a more pleasing manner. With some encouragement from William Pitkin and Wilbur Wright, he completely overhauled the interior of the tropical house, constructing a small waterfall and a pool as a center feature surrounded by plants.

Almost as soon as Alvan Grant was appointed Greenhouse Foreman, he was asked by one of the many garden clubs in the area to conduct a tour of the greenhouses and conservatory. This was the beginning of a schedule of many talks to garden clubs and other groups, which continued throughout his entire career with the park system, and, in fact, has continued during his retirement. The subject matter has varied greatly. During the early years, most of his talks were concerned with some phase of plant culture. After he became Director of Parks in December 1965, most of his talks would be concerned with park policy, planning, and/or land acquisition. He also was a frequent contributor of horticultural articles for publication in the monthly bulletin of the Garden Center.

As Greenhouse Foreman and Propagator, Grant's responsibilities extended beyond Highland Park. He now had the added responsibility of embellishment of the various small city parks. Principal among these was Plymouth Park, where for many years (until urban development in the 1960s changed it entirely) 20,000 tulip bulbs were planted annually for spring display. After flowering in the spring, these bulbs were dug, stored, and subsequently planted out the following fall in new locations throughout the park system. The bulbs were replaced with annual plants that had been produced in the greenhouses, and these furnished colorful displays throughout the summer and early fall each year. As well as Plymouth Park, similar plantings were undertaken each year at Anderson Park, Ontario Beach Park, Bausch Park, and several lesser known areas. Another responsibility was the planting of several flower beds in Mt. Hope Cemetery and on many graves where perpetual care contracts had been purchased. During 1948 and 1949, Grant planted hundreds of deciduous and evergreen trees and shrubs in the Highland Park nursery. He also cooperated with Wilbur Wright in "cleaning up" the Disposal Plant nursery at Durand Eastman Park.

In January 1948, Bernard Harkness began employment with the park system, and in April 1950, Richard Fenicchia returned after fifteen years of absence. In March 1950, following a Civil Service examination, Alvan Grant was promoted to Assistant Superintendent of Parks. Consequently, with the assignment of many new duties, he could no longer focus his interest solely on the propagation and growing of plants. He had entered the field of horticulture because of a love for plants and the practice of working with them. He realized, however, that although he would have many new responsibilities, he would still be able to maintain a relationship with the career "roots" that he was giving up. One particular experience he would cherish from his "propagator days" was the propagation from seed of several dawn redwood trees. Botanical history had been made in 1946 when this plant was discovered in a remote area in Central China. As described in Andreas Feininger's book *Trees*, published in 1968, "This tree is a veritable 'living fossil' in so far as it is virtually identical with extinct trees that grew millions of years ago." Through the courtesy of Arnold Arboretum, the Rochester park system received six seeds from this tree in 1948. These were given to Al Grant for propagating and further growing on for eventual planting within Rochester parks. At the time of this writing, 45 years later, beautiful specimens of this plant can be found growing in Durand Eastman and Highland Parks.

Al Grant was pleased when Bernie Harkness and Dick Fenicchia exhibited interest in his seedling lilacs. All three men made routine observations of these seedlings and became especially interested in one seedling that, when it was still very small, showed some distinctly different characteristics from the other seedlings. When it first flowered in 1956, it became noticeable that this cultivar was really unique. More about this later.

It could be said that 1950 marked a new beginning in the Rochester Bureau of Parks. Calvin Laney, the first full-time employee of the park system, had retired in 1928, and the two real plantsmen who had been most responsible for "planting the parks," John Dunbar and Barney Slavin, had also retired—Dunbar in

1928 and Slavin in 1942. The last remaining "links" that might be classified as part of the original staff were Director of Parks Patrick Slavin and Botanist Richard Horsey. Pat Slavin, as mentioned earlier, began employment in 1890 as a water boy for one of the first planting crews and was active in the parks until his death on May 26, 1950. Richard Horsey, although he did not become a park employee until 1904, had been the first employee assigned full-time to the duties of taxonomist and curator of the herbarium. He retired in September 1949. Leadership in all phases of the park system would now pass to the next generation of park men. In 1950, the table of organization, from the viewpoint of the plantsmen, would read as follows:

- Wilbur E. Wright—Director of Parks;
- Alvan R. Grant—Assistant Superintendent of Parks;
- Jacob Gerling—Assistant Superintendent of Parks;
- Bernard Harkness—Taxonomist; and
- Richard Fenicchia—Plant Propagator and Nurseryman.

Dick Fenicchia was soon appointed Greenhouse Foreman while still keeping the duties and responsibilities of plant propagator. To a large degree Dick would become the "plantsman" of the park system from 1950 until his retirement in 1978, as he closely followed in the footsteps of John Dunbar and Barney Slavin.

Except for Richard Fenicchia and Bernard Harkness, the park careers of the men whose names appear in the table of organization have already been transcribed to some degree, and Fenicchia has been mentioned in his relationship with Barney Slavin during the years 1925 to 1935. (In fact, if one counts the volunteer time that he spends in propagating plants at his home and at the Highland Park greenhouses, he is, at the time of this writing, still producing for the park system.) Although the career of Harkness parallels the second period of Fenicchia's, it did not continue for as many years.

Although both men were outstanding plantsmen and horticulturists, their approaches to the plant world and to the parks were quite different. Fenicchia was a craftsman, working with his hands developing plants for use within the parks. He was also a student of horticulture, always trying to increase his knowledge of plants through correspondence, reading, and research. Harkness, on the other hand, was the consummate student with the plant world his laboratory. He was also a teacher, as he recorded his knowledge and shared it with others. He did not, however, confine his efforts to the "ivory tower" of books and study; he was also a "plain dirt gardener."

BERNARD E. HARKNESS

When Bernard E. Harkness joined the City of Rochester Park Bureau in January 1948, he brought with him a background of horticultural education and experience that had already earned him recognition as one of the country's leading horticulturists. His interest in plant materials started when he was still a student at Moravia (New York) High School. At that time he became friendly with Dr. Charles Atwood, whose career in medicine, at times, was almost overshadowed by his hobby of botany. Before he became interested in medicine, Dr. Atwood had earned a degree in botany at Cornell University. He had developed his own herbarium and botanical library and had done considerable plant collecting during the 1880s. He was responsible for much of the planting in Fillmore Glen, where a commemorative plaque cites his work in preserving the glen and working to make it a state park. Dr. Atwood took an interest in Bernard and permitted him to use his herbarium and library at will. At the same time Bernard was developing practical skills by working as a gardener on a local estate.

After graduating from high school in June 1924, Bernard secured a job at the horticultural greenhouses at Cornell University. In the fall of 1925, he registered as a student at Cornell, where he earned the lifetime friendship of Professor Ralph Curtis, a world-renowned expert on woody plant materials, who recognized Bernard as a true plantsman.

During his last summer as a Cornell student, Bernard worked at Hill House, the Long Island estate of Anton Hodenpyl, a Wall Street broker. Impressed with Bernard's work, Mr. Hodenpyl hired him as head gardener after his graduation from Cornell. This estate, with seven distinctly different garden areas, provided a laboratory where Bernard could more closely study plants and their usage in the landscape. In the fall of 1930, Bernard left Hill House to enroll in the Harvard School of Design to study landscape architecture.

In 1933, because he felt that he "was getting too far away from plants," Bernard changed his mind and became a landscape

111

supervisor for the Civilian Conservation Corps. His assignment was to help develop Palisades Interstate Park at Bear Mountain, New York. In this job, he directed a crew in the thinning out of native growth and in the planting of new materials.

In June 1937, he resigned to accept a position in Baraboo, Wisconsin, as manager of a nursery where he was involved in herb farming, landscape service, and flower growing. While in Wisconsin he also collected native plants, which he sent to Dr. Atwood for planting in Fillmore Glen, and he continued his preoccupation of corresponding with many of the leading horticulturists throughout the world.

In September 1942, Bernard was drafted and inducted into military service. Except for periods of boredom, his wartime experience was not too bad. He even found time during 1944 for an extension course on grasses offered by the University of South Dakota. Later that year, he was assigned to an Air Force weather cryptography station in China's Szechwan Province. He obtained permission to study at the University of West China during his off-duty hours and he made extensive use of the herbarium maintained by the university, where he became acquainted with Dr. Shui Ying Hu (a future Harvard Ph.D.). Dr. Hu was president of the International Women's Club and was responsible for much of the entertainment for the Air Corps community stationed in Chengtu. As Dr. Hu wrote in a testimonial letter to Bernard upon his retirement from the Park Department in 1967, "Your interest in Chinese horticulture already had led you to activities more serene and excitement more superb. You visited the flower fairs of the common people and the gardens and inner courts of the elite." Indeed, he made friends with several Chinese families, visited their gardens, and traveled throughout the countryside, studying the native and cultivated plants.

While in China, Bernard wrote many letters to his mother, Nellie Sturgis Harkness, in which he described his experiences and recorded his observations. It is fortunate that she saved these letters, because in 1975 Bernard, using excerpts from them, published a booklet entitled *Letters from Hsingching* (a small town near Chengtu). The contents of this booklet, while indicative of his intense interest in horticulture and plant materials, also reflect his deep concern for the people and their culture.

After the end of the war, Bernard was able to extend his travels in China for a month while he waited for orders to return home. He also spent three weeks in India, studying native plants.

After his discharge and his return home, where he experienced a brief period of illness, Bernard was hired in May 1946 by the State of New York as a landscape architect based in Albany. As he later stated, "I disliked being cooped up in an office where my only contact with plants was on paper." Consequently, when he heard through Professor Curtis that Richard Horsey was planning to retire after almost fifty years with the Rochester park system, Bernard immediately began efforts to become Horsey's replacement. It was a slow process, but on January 26, 1948, Bernard started his career with the Rochester Bureau of Parks, working closely with Richard Horsey until Horsey's retirement in September 1949. Although his starting position was listed as skilled laborer, Bernard was involved in the duties of plant taxonomist, a title that he was not given until 1951 when a general Civil Service classification of city employees was completed.

Because of his innate desire to learn as much as possible about plant materials, coupled with his habit of maintaining a continuing communication with other horticulturists, Bernard was well known in horticultural and botanical circles. These relationships would prove of benefit to the Rochester arboretum and parks and also to those around the world with whom he was in contact. An account of his duties, beginning in 1948, would read as follows:

1. He had direct responsibility for the herbarium with its collection of pressed and preserved plant specimens, numbering over 14,000 sheets. (In this capacity, Bernard reviewed the entire collection and, in many instances, collected and prepared replacements for those sheets that were not up to standard.)

2. He was responsible for the establishment of a library. (The Park Bureau had a rather loose collection of books stored on several shelves in the herbarium. These consisted of reference books on botanical and horticultural subjects, as well as several hundred bulletins, monographs, and journals. Over the next 19 years, with a small allowance from the park budget, $200 to $300 per year, and with substantial donations from his own pocket, he managed to build up the collection of printed material and organize it into a valuable horticultural library of approximately 1,600 volumes plus many more bulletins, monographs, and journals.)

3. He was also responsible for the proper identification and labeling of all plant materials within the collections located throughout all of the park areas. He initiated a new recording system for the location of all plant materials so that there would be permanent records within the herbarium files of all plants to be found within Rochester parks. (Richard Horsey had laid much of the groundwork for plant records; however, over the years with loss of labels due to vandalism and deterioration, as well as loss of some of the plant materials upon which others were keyed, updating the records was a challenging task.)

4. Bernard spent hours in the field, often accompanied by other staff members, observing and examining the trees and shrubs to determine the presence of diseases and insects and make specific recommendations relative to a program of control. (Upon many occasions he could be found in one of the parks manning a spray gun.)

5. Perhaps his most important duty was his activity as guardian of the plants within the arboretum. This required constant surveillance to determine the condition of the plants and the possible need for replacement. When replacements were indicated, he would follow through by referring the need to the superintendent of horticulture or, in some instances, he would make arrangements for replacement plants from other arboretums or, if necessary, from a commercial nursery. He was always reviewing articles and advertisements for announcements of new

species that could be added to the local plantings. This was especially important with the lilac collection, which, because of its use in the promotion of tourism, had to remain competitive in number of species and varieties with other areas with floral displays. (A large section of the nursery was always reserved for growing lilacs for eventual planting within Highland Park.)

When the Warner Castle in Highland Park was acquired late in 1951 and considerable renovation and redecorating had been completed, Bernard was faced with the problem of moving the herbarium from its former location in a small, fire-prone building off Pinetum Road within Highland Park to this new location. Although the heavy work of moving cabinets and the like was accomplished with help from park laborers, the more demanding job of carefully organizing the over 14,000 herbarium sheets and the 1,300-volume library (not including many botanical and horticultural monographs and journals) and the plant accession records was Bernard's responsibility.

Bernard's love of plants and his endless search for greater knowledge about them took him far beyond his routine responsibilities. The park system had, for many years, been involved in a program of plant exchange with other botanical gardens and arboretums. In 1948, Bernard initiated a more formal program of plant exchange, which each year required the collection, cleaning, and preparation of seeds of selected plants and the publishing of a "seed exchange list" that was sent to colleges, arboretums, and botanical gardens around the world.

The outreach of this seed exchange program can readily be appreciated by reading the herbarium reports that Bernard Harkness furnished each year for compilation within the annual reports of the Park Bureau. For example, the 1953 report states, "733 packets of seed from trees and shrubs within the parks were distributed to 28 connections within the United States, 5 in Canada, and to 36 more variously in Austria, Belgium, Canary Islands, Denmark, England, Finland, France, Germany, Ireland, Japan, Yugoslavia, Netherlands, Poland, Romania, Scotland,

Sweden, Switzerland and Turkey." Inasmuch as this program was reciprocal, Bernard perused seed lists published by sources around the world and requested shipment of seeds of many plants for trial within the Rochester parks.

In addition to the seed list that was sent out annually, Bernard maintained a constant flow of correspondence with leading horticulturists around the world and therefore kept abreast of all new plant introductions. As a result, he brought many new specimens to the Rochester arboretum. Included in these, during his career with the park system, he was responsible for receiving 163 new cultivars of lilacs for planting in the Highland Park collection.

Bernard even devoted his vacation time in search of plants in their native habitats and collected seeds, seedlings, and offshoots wherever possible for planting in trial beds in the nursery. An interesting account of one of these vacation trips appeared in the *Asa Gray Bulletin*, summer issue, 1953. Under the title, "A Trip to Tennessee for *Buckleya*," Bernard related details of his hunt for this semi-parasitic plant along the boundary between North Carolina and Tennessee. He concludes his article by writing, "My most persistent advocate of the *Buckleya* expedition was Mr. Kan Yashiroda, the Plant Acclimatization Garden, KagawaKen, Japan. In August, he wrote us, 'Will you not mind my asking you to spare for me a few fresh seeds of *Buckleya distichophylla*, if you go on the seed collecting trip to Tennessee and Kentucky this September? Last August I had prepared some potted trees (Hemlock) to be ready for the seeds and have still kept them. I am very anxious to try *Buckleya* a plant which I am so much interested in from C.S. Sargent's writings.'" Bernard was successful in this search, finding *Buckleya* growing at Wolf Creek in Tennessee and distributing it to 25 botanic gardens, including Mr. Yashiroda's.

The year 1953 also marked the start of a ten-year or longer project, the publication of a catalog of the trees and shrubs of the Rochester park collections. An intensive study was made of each plant so that it could be correctly stated and a search made for all of the information that could be found in the files concerning the association the local park system had with each specific plant. Selection was made of the most interesting facts to be presented. The first publication covered 37 species, alphabetically from *Abelia graebneriana* to *Aelanthus altissima*; the second covered 23 firs, the genus *Abies*.

For a few years, beginning in the mid-1950s, Eric Hans Krause, an artist with unusual and unique ability as a botanical artist, was employed by the Park Bureau. His assignment was to produce botanically correct drawings or paintings of plants for the herbarium under Bernard Harkness's direction and to build up a collection of slides that could be used by park employees giving lectures to local garden clubs and other organizations. The few examples of his work that were left with the park system when he resigned in 1958 were representative of the talent and skill of the artist. His work received national recognition for the exquisitely accurate botanical illustrations that he was invited to exhibit at the National Arboretum in Washington, D.C., from August 25 to October 8, 1975. He knew his plants—those that he used in illustrations—from the very inside of the plant. He painted with a exactness that showed every detail of the flower.

Protecting and improving the lilac collection, the symbol of the arboretum to the local public and a principal tourist attraction for the city, naturally required much attention from Bernard. He particularly enjoyed the academic and scientific interchange as a member of the 1953 Lilac Survey Team under the auspices of the American Association of Botanical Gardens and Arboretums (AABGA). This committee of six experts researched all lilac varieties growing in the American gardens, assigned color and flower form classifications, and developed a listing of the 100 best varieties for recommendation to collectors and commercial growers. The complete survey included over 900 varieties and was a complete lexicon of all known lilac varieties at that time. Bernard was especially interested in watching the development of the lilac seedlings that had been planted in the Highland Park nursery and was elated when one of these seedlings showed characteristics not found in other lilac cultivars. Bernard enjoyed his participation in the annual Lilac Time festival despite the fact that he had to replace hundreds of labels each year in preparing for the many visitors.

On July 19, 1954, a headline appeared in one of Betty Kieper's garden articles in the *Times-Union* that read, "Parks' Magnolia Wins Notice." The article stated:

> A Rochester-bred Magnolia makes its formal debut under a new name in the recent issue of the National Horticulture Magazine, journal of the American Horticultural Society. 'Slavin's Snowy' is the title bestowed on it in honor of Bernard Slavin, retired Superintendent of Parks who nurtured its unusual qualities back in 1917 when it first flowered in a park nursery and watched its development ever since. Bernard Harkness, Taxonomist at Highland Park, describes and names this Magnolia in an illustrated article in the journal. It is a hybrid of *Magnolia salicifolia* and its pollen parent is believed to be *M. soulangiana* in Highland Park near the seed bearing parent, natural hybrid. Slavin's Snowy is a vigorous growing small tree with flowers suggesting those of *M. soulangiana*, white with blush pink near the base. It blooms with the first warm spring weather and is recommended in regions where Star Magnolia (*M. stellata*) comes through without frost damage. According to Bernard Harkness, several other plants have been named for Bernard Slavin. *Cornus Slavini*, *Crataegus Slavini*, and *Robinia Slavini* were named in his honor by such noted authorities as Alfred Rehder of Harvard and Murray Hornbrook of London.

Bernard's technical writings can be found on the bookshelves of many scientific establishments. Among them are several articles that contained detailed information about plants within the Rochester parks. These were printed in the technical journal *Phytologia* and included in *Hortus Durobrivensis*, Parts I, II, and III, and "Checklist of the Cultivated Woody Plants of Rochester Parks."

In July 1961, when the City of Rochester and the County of Monroe entered into an agreement whereby the county took over the operation and maintenance of certain city-owned park areas, the office for the new Monroe County Department of Parks was established in the Castle in Highland Park. Along with many other employees, Bernard Harkness was transferred from city to county payroll and became Plant Taxonomist for the new department. The Castle proved to be inadequate as a park office, and within two years the office was moved into the former Nurse's Home at Iola (375 Westfall Road). This building had much more space for the expanding department and could also house the herbarium and departmental library. Once again Bernard was burdened with the reorganization of these two important components of the park system. During the next few years, Bernard spent many hours collecting and preserving many specimens in upgrading the herbarium collections.

Leading universities offering courses in plant science, botany, horticulture, and landscaping brought classes to Rochester to experience a field trip with "Bernie" Harkness. Those that planned annual trips included Cornell, Syracuse, and Alfred. Upon occasion, classes also came from Rutgers, Michigan State, and Farmingdale. The School of Gardening of the Niagara Falls, Ontario, Park System, en masse, frequently visited during Lilac Time. Many other visitors also appear on the visitor list: students working on advanced degrees, representatives from other botanical institutions, commercial nurserymen, leading educators, and governmental officials. All of these were interested in observing and studying selected plant materials under Bernard's guidance. Perhaps Herbert C. Barrett, Professor of Plant Breeding, University of Illinois, best expressed the esteem that all of these students and professors felt for Bernard in a letter he wrote at the time of Bernard's retirement: "I well remember my most pleasant and informative visits with you as we walked through Highland and Durand Eastman Parks discussing the various plantings and collections. Your comprehensive knowledge of plant materials and the historical background of the relationship to persons and places was most interesting and valuable to me in better understanding plants with which I was involved."

119

Throughout his tenure with the park system, Bernard devoted many hours to the Garden Center of Rochester as a consultant in the planning and operation of its horticultural programs. "Bernard Harkness, Horticulturist" appeared in the masthead of the Garden Center *Bulletin* for almost twenty years, and he contributed many articles to this publication. He also wrote articles for several of the leading garden magazines, including *Popular Gardening, Flower Grower, Horticulture*, and others. He was a featured speaker for many local garden clubs whose members appreciated the scientific knowledge of plants he could impart to them for use in their own gardens. He also conducted many tours through the local park areas for these clubs and, during Lilac Time, for the many visitors who were interested in learning more about the lilacs than what they could glean from a casual walkthrough by themselves.

Bernard's service at the Garden Center constituted much of his social life. It brought him into contact with the many volunteers who were greatly responsible for its program, and he particularly enjoyed the weekly luncheons with them. It was at the Garden Center that he met Mable Gleason Olney, a University of Rochester graduate and a long-time member of the Rochester Academy of Science. With many years of experience in library work as well as an interest in horticulture and gardening, she agreed in 1953 to develop a library for the Garden Center. Their mutual interests in horticulture, books, and the Garden Center brought Mable and Bernard together, and they were married at the Anabel Taylor Hall Chapel at Cornell on September 5, 1964. The importance of mentioning this relationship will become apparent later in this brief review of Bernard's career in horticulture.

Bernard demonstrated his gardening skills as he almost single-handedly developed and planted the gardens located on the grounds behind the Castle with plants he had acquired from many different sources around the world. These gardens, particularly the wall garden, the court garden, and the rock garden, are a living catalog of Bernard's special interest in rock garden plants.

Bernard Harkness received several professional honors while employed by the park system. These included his election as President of the American Association of Botanical Gardens and Arboretums, and also of the American Rock Garden Society. He served as Vice-President of the Rochester Academy of Science, and was made a Fellow of the Academy at the Civic Medal Award Convocation of the museum in November 1961. His citation made special note of his study of landscape architecture, his interest in tropical plants developed during his wartime assignments in China and India, and his field trips to Jamaica, Portugal, the Canadian Rockies, and Kentucky, as well as throughout the Rochester area.

Although he decided to leave the Monroe County Park Department in April 1967, he never really retired. With Mable, he moved to the cobblestone house they had purchased on Preemption Road near Geneva. Here they shared many interests, including the seed exchange of the American Rock Garden Society, a special project operated almost solely through their efforts. Lilacs also continued to be of interest to Bernard. In 1971, he was a founding member of the International Lilac Society and both he and Mable served as directors for several years.

At a retirement party given in his honor as he gave up his employment with the Park Department, he was presented with a portfolio of letters solicited from his friends and associates throughout the world. His friend and former classmate at Cornell, Ben Blackburn, Director of the Willowwood Arboretum, Gladstone, New Jersey, wrote that he sometimes had a feeling that his correspondence files must be put in order. "The 'H' file has been particularly resistant to reorganization. This file is all Harkness. During every attempt to reorganize, I become engrossed in re-reading letters, plant notes, etc. and end up with no change."

Russell J. Siebert, Director of Longwood Gardens, Kennett Square, Pennsylvania, wrote, "Your contributions to both American and international horticulture and botany will be long and significantly remembered. We have enjoyed your fruits and endeavor through the plant exchange program and do appreciate your active leadership in the affairs of the AABGA."

From the Royal Botanical Gardens, Hamilton, Canada, its Director, Leslie Laking (also then president of the AABGA) wrote, "The publication of the 'Check List of Woody Species in the Park System' has been exceedingly valuable to us. If you knew how frequently this is used at the Gardens here, you would know how worthwhile your efforts have been. The same applies to the dedicated attention you have given to the International Seed Exchange over the years."

David Leach of Brookville, Pennsylvania, and author of several books and other articles about rhododendrons and azaleas, remembered well his first meeting with Bernard: "You were tramping along on a trail, pack on back in the Blue Mountains ridges of Jamaica." Mr. Leach was making it the easy way, partly by car and then on mule-back to the mist forest of Morey's Gap. "After our momentary conversation," wrote Mr. Leach, "I made a chalk mark on my mental blackboard. I had met a man who loved the natural world . . . one who responded fully to the aesthetic appeal and the scientific fascination of plants."

There were many more letters that paid tribute to Bernard for his contributions in the field of horticulture. The name Bernard Harkness represents a source of knowledge and expertise in his professional world.

After his retirement from the park system, Bernard continued to study and to share his knowledge with others. His garden contained many rare and unusual plants. He devoted many hours to researching, compiling, and publishing the *Seedlist Handbook*, which lists over 9,000 plants, including habitat, height, outstanding characteristics, and country of origin.

Bernard Harkness was invited back to Highland Park during Lilac Time 1967 to receive the County of Monroe National Award for Public Service. His service in this field had gone far beyond the boundaries of the county. His expertise in botany and plant taxonomy was recognized worldwide, and he had often been called upon by fellow horticulturists to help in solving a problem, particularly in the identification of some special plant.

In the foreword to the third edition of this *Handbook* (Bellona, NY: Kashong, 1980), H. Lincoln Foster, author of *Rock Gardening* (Houghton Mifflin, 1968), stated as follows: "The updated and expanded third edition of the 'Seedlist Handbook' was readied for the publisher only a few days before Bernard Harkness died suddenly on September 18, 1980. This work and its predecessor editions will stand as a long-lived memorial to a man of importance in the world of horticulture. . . . The 'Seedlist Handbook' . . . is a remarkable document. . . . Unpretentious as it is, just as was its author, the 'Seedlist Handbook' is a veritable storehouse of dependable information based on the prodigious industry and immaculate scholarship of Bernard Harkness."

Before we move away from Bernard Harkness in this story of the plantsmen, we should include a summary of an article he wrote, entitled "What's in a Herbarium," which appeared in the February 1959 *Bulletin* of the Garden Center of Rochester. It may serve to give the reader a better understanding about the service a herbarium performs as part of the park system as well as about the duties of a taxonomist. Bernie stated that in the herbarium there are over 12,000 sheets of specimens as well as a great variety of pods, preserved cones, and fruits that can be dried without loss of their characteristics. In a strict sense, this collection constitutes a herbarium. These have to be indexed and arranged according to a scientific system to be of any use. He wrote:

> Their most extensive use comes when we ourselves are studying our living collections, perhaps one group of plants such as the maples. When this was done a while ago all the maple sheets were brought into use. Some of them were made years ago, some represented plants no longer living, some were taken from plants that proved to be not hardy when a severe winter came along, but all were of value for comparison with the plants under study. Studies such as this require all the manuals and other botanical references

that are available so that the library becomes an integral part of the herbarium and its work.

We are here to serve the public too. The public travels a lot and sees many plants to marvel at, especially as they travel south. So we sharpen our wits and try to determine Florida plants, Mexican plants, Hawaiian plants, and those from other places we have never been. Sometimes with all the aids mentioned above we are successful. More frequently, though, we can help the local gardener who runs up against an unknown in an ornamental plant, an unusual weed, or an exceptional wild flower. It is a very satisfactory proof to have a herbarium sheet which matches the plant in question.

Each specimen sheet has a printed label which is filled out giving its family, genus, and species names, the locality where this particular plant was found, the dates for its flowering or fruiting and by whom it was collected.

One outstanding contribution to the herbarium was made in 1954 when the Helen E. Rockwell collections, representing native flora of Monroe County, the Adirondacks, Florida, Georgia and Texas made in the first decade of this century, were given to us to be incorporated in the Highland Park Herbarium. Other collections of native plants have represented the interests of various members of the staff. Considerable scientific interest are sheets, mostly of woody plants, resulting from the travels just previous to World War I in Ohio and Kentucky of Richard E. Horsey who was working in these expeditions under the direction of Professor Charles S. Sargent of the Arnold Arboretum at the time he was preparing his monumental "Silvae of North America".

The herbarium is a continuing record of the growth of the Highland Park collections. Its great value comes from the fact that it was started almost as soon as the park system began. In no other way could as satisfactory a record have been kept of how the parks have grown, keeping pace with new knowledge of ornamental horticulture in this country. We confidently expect it will grow under many more guiding hands.

RICHARD A. FENICCHIA —
PROPAGATOR AND HYBRIDIZER

As the Rochester park system emerged into the 1950s and beyond, its rich botanical heritage, the result primarily of John Dunbar, Barney Slavin, and Richard Horsey, was added to by the achievements of Richard (Dick) Fenicchia. Other park employees made significant contributions to the routine operations of the parks. However, there would have been very little enhancement of this heritage without Bernie Harkness and Dick Fenicchia. Bernie, through his contacts with other horticulturists worldwide, quickly became aware of any new introductions in the plant world and, through the seed and plant exchange program, was successful in bringing many of these to Rochester, where they were given to Dick for further care. With his skill in propagation, Dick made good use of any seeds, scions, cuttings, or small plants, growing them into specimens for planting throughout the arboretum.

Inasmuch as a more complete profile of Bernard Harkness has been given earlier in this narrative, the words that follow will, to a large degree, be focused upon Dick Fenicchia, who furnished the continuity that was needed to bring the arboretum and horticultural programs into the last quarter of the 1900s. His introductory years with the park system (1925-1934) have already been mentioned, but in order to get a full assessment of his lifelong dedication to horticulture, it seems mandatory at this time to review these early years.

Dick's father, Louis Fenicchia, who immigrated to the United States from Italy in the early 1900s, had come directly to Rochester, where friends from his home area had preceded him. He brought with him skills in gardening and nursery work, which helped him in securing a position as a member of Barney Slavin's "gang" in the development of Seneca Park and Durand Eastman Park. After being in the Rochester area for about two years, Louis took a leave of absence to return to Italy to get married. Upon his return to Rochester with his wife, he went back to "work with Barney."

Americo (as Richard was originally named) Fenicchia was born in Rochester on December 19, 1908. His father worked for the park system for approximately two more years before he resigned to become a professional gardener working on several private estates throughout the Rochester area. Here he could earn a greater income with which to support his family. He also established a small nursery where he could propagate and grow plants to specimen size for planting on the estates for which he worked.

Dick's association with plant materials began very early in his life as he observed his father at work and later as a teenager while working with his father. As Dick has related about these early days, "After school, I would walk four or five miles to where my father was working. I did mostly gardening, cut grass and pruned. I always like plants, flowers, and trees, working with them was natural for me." During these learning years, Dick absorbed a feeling and love for plants that is inherent in the development of a true plantsman.

Dick's formal public school education came to an end in June 1925, when he received a vocational school certificate from Madison Junior High School, where he had received special training in electrical work. He thought about pursuing a career as an electrician but, still only 16 years of age, he had no luck in finding a permanent job in that profession. Consequently, in July 1925, he accepted a job with the park system under Barney Slavin, who assigned him to the greenhouses at Highland Park. One of his first tasks was propagating geraniums for planting in the flower beds throughout the parks. Dick observed that other greenhouse employees would strip the geranium cuttings of their lower leaves before setting them into the propagating medium. He decided to do as little trimming as possible and, as a result, he produced healthier and stockier plants. Records for 1926 show that he propagated over 17,000 geraniums, which he potted in four-inch pots. These were later planted in flower beds throughout the various parks.

The next nine years might well be considered a period of advanced education for Richard. He was in a position where he could observe firsthand the work that was being accomplished by Dunbar and Barney Slavin. Highland Park, with its richness of botanical specimens, was a library of living plants that were readily available for study, and Dick spent many hours before and after the workday and during his lunch hour roaming through the park, learning the names and the characteristics of the various plant materials. In Dick's own words:

> When I started as an employee of the park system, I worked directly for Barney Slavin in the greenhouses at Highland Park. Here I started growing greenhouse plants and nursery stock. Because of the interest which was generated in me when I was about 14 years old by reading the autobiography of Luther Burbank, I was vitally interested in the search for new and different plants, and I could now experiment a little in hybridizing plants in the greenhouse. One of the first that I had any success with was cross-breeding some begonias. The result of this breeding was a tiny seedling which developed into a white flowered begonia that grew to a height of 15 to 18 inches. At that time white begonias were rare. I named this Fenicchia's White. One day, just for something to do, I crossbred some azaleas. When Barney noticed these, I thought that he was going to yell at me, but instead he said, "grow them on, we'll see what they develop into." I soon worked my way into grafting hardy plant materials, principally new plants discovered by Barney in his nurseries at Durand Eastman and during his explorations. I also worked directly with Barney in a program of hybridization of Rhododendrons and Azaleas, Viburnum, Magnolias, Lilacs, and many other genera. One of my first experiments with Azalea began on December 3, 1927 when I sowed seeds of 'Azalea Professor Walters', a clone which belongs to the so-called Indian Azaleas. Several selections were made when the seedlings came into flower, the first flower appearing on January 7, 1930. I also sowed seed collected from *Azalea macranthum*, commonly known as *Indica alba*, in 1929. In 1932, two

seedlings designated as No. 18 RAF and No. 17 RAF were selected for further propagation. About twenty plants from these selections are still (1993) used in the floral display in the conservatory. During the years 1930 and 1934, I made many crosses between native Rhododendrons and Asiatic forms, approximately 189 crosses. I also made several bigeneric crosses in 1933, *Enkianthus campanulata* crossed with *Rhododendron calendulaceum* (No. 175), the same *Enkianthus* with *Kalmia latifolia* (No. 176), and with *Rhododendron japonica* (No. 177). [Note: Numbers are identification numbers assigned to his crosses by Dick. Sometimes they will appear in combination with his initials, "RAF." He also used them on seedlings that show variation from the parent.] In 1934, I made several other bigeneric crosses using *Kalmia latifolia* crossed with several Rhododendrons. Seeds of these bigeneric crosses germinated but after I was forced to give up my job in 1934, I lost track of these seedlings. During my absence from the park system, about 50,000 plants were lost, including about 95 percent of the hybrid azaleas and rhododendrons that I had developed with Barney's encouragement. There wasn't anybody there with the interest to take care of the plants the way I did. For a while after I left, I would go in anyway to the greenhouse to water the rare plant materials, but I could see that the new guys that they had hired didn't like my being there, so I stopped. I had been doing some very extensive hybridizing of plants. When I came back to the park system in 1950, I found very few of those plants still there.

The following list of the cuttings that Dick made of woody plants just during the months of June and July 1931 provides a good example of the amount of plant propagation that Dick accomplished during this first period of employment with the park system:
- 21 species and varieties of *Hydrangea*;
- 83 species and varieties of *Berberis*;
- 51 species and varieties of *Deutzia*;
- 40 species and varieties of maple;

- 6 species and varieties of *Lespedeza*;
- 7 species and varieties of *Indigofera*;
- 2 species and varieties of *Coronilla*;
- 5 species and varieties of *Campsis*;
- 26 species and varieties of *Hibiscus*;
- 350 species and varieties of lilac (over 2,100 cuttings);
- 31 species and varieties of *Diervilla*;
- 11 species and varieties of *Potentilla*;
- 8 species and varieties of *Sorbaria*;
- 83 species and varieties of *Philadelphus*;
- 44 species and varieties of *Viburnum*;
- 78 species and varieties of azalea;
- 20 species and varieties of *Rhododendron*;
- 15 species and varieties of *Magnolia*;
- 17 species and varieties of *Euonymus*;
- 7 species and varieties of *Catalpa*; and
- 4 species of *Cornus*.

The above list shows plant production at a very high level, especially when one considers the various steps that must be taken: the collection of cuttings or scions, preparation of the media used in propagation, preparation of the cuttings, care while rooting is taking place, transplanting rooted cuttings into pots and/or into nursery frames, eventual planting into the nursery, and, of course, the careful labeling and recording that must accompany all stages in the process. Dick tells of using a motorcycle while collecting cuttings and scions for propagation, especially within Durand Eastman Park and Highland Park. Several plants of each of those listed were propagated, some for replacement or upgrading of the plantings already within the arboretum collections, many for new plantings throughout the park system and on other public areas, and still others for shipping to other arboretums and parks throughout the United States.

During this first period of employment with the park system, Dick completed his high school education by attending night school. With encouragement from Barney, he also attended short courses and seminars on horticultural subjects at Cornell University. He also took a correspondence course in horticulture and the landscape use of plants that was offered by the American Landscape School located in California, and he followed the example set by Barney Slavin of reading every article and publication about plants that he could get his hands on. He not only read, but actually digested the material. His retention of what he read and studied has proven to be a lasting strength in his day-to-day work. Whenever possible he also spent time in the herbarium, where he made good use of the library and the herbarium sheets.

When Dick was terminated on April 14, 1934, he was well versed in the science of horticulture and better prepared for a career in park and arboretum work than when he started in 1925. His departure from the park system would prove to be a real setback as far as the production of plants for the parks was concerned. The new employees did not have the special skills or the interest so vital for the job of perpetuating the plant collections. Although Barney Slavin failed to convince Dick to stay with the parks, he was still interested enough in him to assist him in getting a job on the Lindsay estate. Here, although the salary was low, Dick worked in a "share-crop" arrangement where one-half of the plants he grew were his. The remainder were used to landscape the estate. With his share of the plants, Dick started a small nursery on land that he had acquired.

Barney permitted Dick to collect propagating material from some of the plantings within the park system. Consequently, many of the plants he propagated and grew were not those ordinarily common to commercial nurseries. During this time, Dick made several crosses of hardy rhododendron. Some of the resulting hybrids, as well as many other plants propagated by Dick, were planted on the estate by a small crew of men who also worked with Dick in his private landscaping and nursery ventures.

Many more plants were propagated than were needed to satisfy both partners in this "share-crop" arrangement. Many of the surplus plants were sent to three of the county parks—Ellison, Webster, and Mendon Ponds—which at that time were in the early stages of development. After about five years of working with the

131

Lindsay family, Dick went to work for the County of Monroe park system (originated in 1926, still in the process of acquiring land and early development), where Park Director Robert Cochran assigned him to the development of a small nursery in Mendon Ponds Park. He continued working in county parks until late May 1943.

On June 1, 1943, he was drafted into the U.S. Army. After receiving his basic training at Camp Siebert in Alabama, he, along with other trainees, was sent to Australia, where he was assigned to an army ship. He was soon promoted to the rank of sergeant and placed in charge of the ship's engine. He spent most of his time aboard ship located near Australia and New Guinea. However, whenever he had an opportunity to leave ship for one or more days, he would go exploring for plants on the nearby islands, some of which were still partly occupied by stragglers from the Japanese army. The story is best told in Dick's own words:

> During the war our army transport ship landed at Hollandia in New Guinea, General Douglas MacArthur's headquarters. Well, there were known to be 15 or 20 varieties of Rhododendron on that island which had never been described. So every chance there was, I'd go off into the countryside to find them. The guys all thought that I was nuts because I wouldn't take a gun, but there were a lot of Japanese around and I was afraid they'd kill me if they saw a gun. There wasn't much to collect. It was the wrong time of year and there weren't any seeds. But there was eggplant, two and a half to three feet in diameter, and hot pepper, three feet tall amongst the mahogany trees.

Dick's account exhibits the regard that he has for plants of all kinds. Although he failed to find the rhododendrons that he was looking for, he observed with interest the other plants he found growing on the islands. He preferred exploring for tropical plants over the more mundane activities of many of his fellow soldiers. As he remarked, "When the guys would go to the pub, I'd go to the parks and countryside and collect seeds."

After the war ended, while waiting orders to return to the United States, he was able to extend his explorations. Late in 1945 he returned to the United States and, upon discharge, to Rochester. Here, as well as doing some landscaping, he worked as a carpenter.

During the 1930s, Dick had been active in a social club known as the Rochester Argonauts. He contributed to its newsletter, *The Reflector*, in which can be found several writings by Richard A. Fenicchia. These display his intense interest in the environment at that time. In fact, the following words from one of his short articles sound much like those of some of the leaders in the environmental movements of the past thirty years:

> The contaminated air is tortuous to the inhaler;
> The germs, gases and explosives have done their work well.
> Throughout the whole world they have permeated,
> Bringing death in its path
> And, behold, the extinction of mankind has been achieved.

It was during his association with the social club that he met Margaret (Marge) Orlando. This was the beginning of a relationship that resulted in their wedding shortly after Dick's discharge from the Army. As Marge would later say, "We had two nurseries. His was in the parks with his plants, and mine was home with the children."

It was fortunate for the park system that in April 1950, Pat Slavin made a real effort to contact Dick Fenicchia to persuade him to return to the park system. (Pat died in May 1950). Alvan Grant had been promoted to the position of Assistant Superintendent, and the plant propagation program was at a standstill except for the routine growing of plants for use in the conservatory and the annual flower beds scattered throughout the city. Richard Fenicchia, with his inherent interest in plants and with the skills and experience he had accumulated, was the ideal choice to take over the plant propagation program.

Dick has often commented that if Pat had not contacted him, he might never have returned to the parks. In his words, "I would read in the newspapers about those new men in the parks, Wright and Grant, and I would say to myself, 'What do they know about our parks.' I didn't ever think about going to work with them. As far as I was concerned, Barney Slavin was 'Mr. Parks' and these new men were interlopers and newcomers who probably didn't know much about parks."

It was not long, however, before a mutual respect developed between Dick the veteran from the days of Barney Slavin and the newcomers, Wright and Grant. Dick, of course, was soon working in cooperation with Bernard Harkness, whom he recognized as an outstanding botanist and horticulturist.

Within a few months after he rejoined the park system as its plant propagator, Dick was appointed Greenhouse Foreman. This added to his duties the responsibility of supervising the operation and maintenance of the conservatory, the greenhouse, and the nurseries. Shortly after that Highland Park was added to the list.

During his first few weeks in 1950, Dick spent many hours reviewing the rhododendron collection, which was of special interest to him because of the hybridization work he had undertaken while working for Barney Slavin. He was also immediately involved in maintaining the Highland Park nursery on St. John's Home property, which had been started by Al Grant. He soon became acquainted with the various seedlings and small plants that were growing there. In 1950, Dick moved the 300 lilac seedlings that Grant had started to this nursery. With Bernie Harkness and Al Grant, Dick made routine surveys of these lilac seedlings, which were beginning to blossom in 1952 and 1953.

Dick well remembers the day when he first noticed one particular seedling, a plant somewhat smaller than the others, "about two feet in height with two branches about the size of a man's finger. Two little flowers were showing on the thyrse. Upon investigating these thick yellowish flowers more closely, I found one corolla had 20 petals on it. I thought this is a break in the genes! I quickly notified Grant and Harkness so that they could see for themselves." All three men continued to watch the development of this particular plant, which Dick moved to a protected area in the nursery where he could give it the special care it needed. His efforts paid off. He was able to obtain several cuttings from this plant, which he rooted, thereby ensuring perpetuation of this new cultivar. (Note: For reasons that I am sure the reader will agree with, the full story of this lilac and the part it will play in the future will not be told until this narrative proceeds into the decade of the 1960s.)

In the fall of 1950, development of a new municipal rose garden at Maplewood Park was started at the site originally planted by John Dunbar. Dunbar's garden had contained many old-fashioned roses in species and varieties no longer commonly grown in home gardens. Members of the Rochester Rose Society had been petitioning the city government to build a garden featuring modern and improved rose cultivars. When they were successful in their mission, they staged bake sales, paper drives, and other projects to raise money for the purchase of plants. Much credit must be given to this group for its support, which enabled the Park Bureau to develop a "living catalog of modern varieties of roses where people could observe and make decisions relative to the varieties that they might like in their own home gardens."

The landscaping preparation and planting of this garden was under the direct supervision of Al Grant, using a plan that had been prepared by Tom Carey. Tom had formerly worked for Chase Brothers Nursery, where he prepared planting plans for customers. Tom was employed by the Park Bureau for about ten years, beginning in 1950. He later supervised the crew that was doing minor construction jobs throughout the parks. Many evergreen and deciduous trees and shrubs used in framing the garden area and in furnishing background were dug at the park nurseries and replanted at Maplewood Park by Dick Fenicchia and his crew. Dick was also responsible for removing many of the old roses and transplanting them in the Highland Park nursery, where they could be preserved, probably for replanting in the

Highland Park Rose Garden, where many species and "old-fashioned" roses were on display.

This new rose garden, which was dedicated in June 1951, covered over 1.9 acres and contained 3,500 rose bushes, 78 varieties of hybrid tea roses, and 16 varieties of floribundas. This garden was expanded each year and by 1960 covered over three acres and displayed 7,200 plants representing 200 varieties. Many of these were purchased from several different commercial growers, some of whom would annually furnish new varieties for testing (at no cost to the city) within the Maplewood Garden, which was accredited as an All-American Rose Garden and cooperated in making reports relative to the performance of these new varieties.

With two skilled laborers who were transferred from Genesee Valley Park—Bill Balco, a former nurseryman, and Bill Dunbar, no relation to John—Al Grant gave personal attention to the rose garden, maintaining the records of all plantings and supervising the many changes that were necessary as some varieties proved not to be desirable for this area. Grant assisted in the planting as well as supervising the routine care of this garden.

Barney Slavin had instilled in Dick the importance of maintaining constant observation of plants wherever they are found, whether in someone's garden or by the side of the road. "Look for variations in the plants in your own garden; that's how you discover new plants." Dick took this advice to heart, and one day while making a routine inspection of the plants in Barney's original nursery in Durand Eastman Park, he discovered a seedling crabapple tree with a beautiful double pink blossom entirely unlike any already named. Bernard Harkness was also impressed with this plant and named it 'Margaret' in honor of Dick's wife. Margaret Fenicchia did not really want a crab(apple) named after her. However, when she saw this tree in full bloom, she was pleased. Dick propagated several plants of this crabapple by grafting, and a fine specimen can still (as of 1993) be found in the landscaping at the War Memorial.

In 1950, Dick Fenicchia had begun a new program of hybridizing rhododendrons and azaleas that he would continue throughout his tenure with the park system. Seeds resulting from the crosses he made were sown in flats in the greenhouse. As seedlings developed, they were potted and, when of proper size, they were planted out in specially prepared beds near the greenhouse. In later years, when discussing his work with rhododendrons, Dick commented:

> It was Barney Slavin who started me hybridizing rhododendrons. I had just come to work for the park system and had crossed a native viburnum with a Chinese viburnum, then grew the first generation from seedlings. Barney happened to see the plant and asked me to hybridize rhododendrons and azaleas. . . . Probably there are 50 new varieties of rhododendrons and azaleas, we've been watching for 20 years, some lilacs and evergreens, and the flowering crabapple named after my wife Margaret. The purpose of making these crosses was to develop hybrids which would be best suited to our climate disregarding color of bloom. I consider hardiness to be more important than the color of the flowers. During the period between 1950 and 1973, many hybrids came into bloom and many selections were made and kept under number. Most of these were planted in the park nursery.

> Site or location of planting plays a major role in growing rhododendrons as far as permanence is concerned. The site should offer shade or partial shade and protection from wind in varying degrees. The texture of the soil should be somewhat organic and have an acid reaction. One good indication is moss, lichens, sphagnum moss and evergreen moss. These should show that the soil may be capable of growing rhododendrons, regardless of the exposure.

> Many rhododendrons have thrived fairly well exposed to winds and full sun and have developed into magnificent plants. Some rhododendrons, *maximum* forms and *brachycarpum* forms and many others, are shade-loving

plants. Basically, protection from winds and sun is beneficial to all rhododendrons and azaleas.

At Willowbrook Farm in Webster, owned by the Fenicchias, Dick grows rhododendrons as a hobby. These were grouped and planted in a cultivated area, then the sod and mosses were allowed to grow around them. For more than twenty years, no fertilizer was added. Little spraying was done. No water was applied during those twenty years due to the subsoil retaining water throughout the summer. Hybridizing and crossing of rhododendrons have, in the opinion of Dick, many drawbacks as well as advantages. Some things to strive for would be "to try to make some tender rhododendrons that have unusual characteristics a little bit hardier."

Dick continued his conversation about hybridizing:

I know of no evidence that supports that it is possible to develop hardiness by crossing. I do not like to bastardize plants. I prefer the natural hybrids as they exist in nature because of their remarkable constitution and vigor due to natural selection and the compatible environment that they've been growing in for many years. I have nothing against hybridizing plants and I realize much fine plant material has come into being through hybridizing. Perhaps there are too many named clones and forms already in existence.

I am very interested in the new species discovered in New Guinea within the last few years even though most are of tender nature. I have a few forms that have been growing in the greenhouse. The remarkable thing is the propagation—they root as easily as ivy, and come into bloom without rest or a cold period. Having made several explorations in New Guinea, my only regret is that I wasn't able to find this new species for myself.

Throughout the entire process of hybridization, from selection of seed parents, dates when crosses were made, collection of seed, seed sowing, potting of seedlings, planting into outdoor growing frames, recording of first bloom, and selection and labeling of desirable cultivars, a careful history was recorded by Dick. When they attained sufficient size, most of these hybrids would be planted in a new nursery that Dick would be developing on new parkland, yet to be acquired.

Although Dick is an expert in plant breeding, he has a preference for plants in their original state. According to Dick, "They're hardier and much more resistant—whenever you hybridize, you sacrifice something." Despite this feeling for plants in the wild, Dick had a definite affection for his own creations. "Sometimes people will steal plants from the nursery or greenhouse," Dick said. "One time I missed from a nursery bed in Highland Park a special hybrid rhododendron that was very important. After that, everywhere I went as I drove around in the city and suburbs, I kept my eyes open for that rhododendron. After two years, I saw it growing in someone's front yard. I immediately parked the truck, jumped out, ran up to the plant and started digging. The woman in the house yelled, 'What do you think you're doing?' 'You know what I'm doing,' I said and kept on digging. She knew—she could see Park Department painted on the door of the truck."

Dick had a somewhat humorous experience while working within the rhododendron beds in Highland Park. The plants were in full bloom, and he was inspecting some of the blooms and making notes for future reference. He noticed a man slowly approaching in his direction, stopping occasionally and raising up some of the branches and thoroughly examining the plants in some detail. When the man got close enough for Dick to converse with him, he said, "Are you interested in rhododendrons?" The man answered, "No, what are they? I'm looking for the golden key." It seems that a local radio station was involved in a promotion whereby the station was releasing a new clue each day that would eventually lead someone to find a hidden key. The finder would be given an automobile. Dick learned that interest in an object (or a plant) varies according to the observer.

When a group of plant propagators from several leading nurseries as well as from horticultural institutions throughout the United States and Canada convened in Cleveland, Ohio, in December 1952, Richard Fenicchia was there and became one of the charter members of the International Plant Propagators Society, which was formed at this meeting. The objectives of this organization, as stated in its constitution, were "to secure recognition for the plant propagator as a craftsman to provide for the dissemination of knowledge through the proper channels, and to provide helpful guidance and assistance to plant propagators." In a summary about the Rochester park system that Dick prepared for the society, he listed the following as arboretums maintained by this park system:

- Highland Park—the major arboretum with over 3,900 kinds of trees, shrubs, and perennials, including the conifer collection. These plants were gathered from all parts of the world and have proved to be hardy in this climate. The principal collections are oak, maple, linden, ash, lilac, magnolia, sorbus, crabapple, cherry, poplar, willow, hawthorn, rhododendron and azaleas, and peonies.
- Durand Eastman Park—over 50,000 trees and shrubs were planted in this park. Included were Japanese cherries, crabapples, rhododendrons and azaleas, magnolias, viburnums, hawthorn, oaks, hickories, tupelos, and many other choice trees and shrubs. Also a large pinetum with pine, fir, spruce, yew, juniper, and others.
- Seneca and Maplewood Parks—many choice trees, native and introduced.
- Cobbs Hill Park—collection of lilacs and many choice trees and shrubs, native and introduced.
- Genesee Valley Park—large hawthorn collection, a large oak collection, and other choice trees and shrubs, native and introduced.

There were over 5,000 different species, varieties, and forms of trees and shrubs in the city park system. Dick always spoke of the parks as having five different arboretums. However, other staff members considered the aggregate of these five areas, although in different locations, as comprising the Rochester arboretum.

He became very active in this organization, serving on its board of directors for several years, and at various times on special-purpose committees. The fact that Dick was asked to present papers relative to plants and plant breeding and propagation at many of the annual meetings speaks well of the reputation he had earned within this group of his peers. Dick's wife, Marge, accompanied him to many of these annual meetings, and because of her skill in the secretarial field, the organization often put her to work recording minutes and performing other related tasks.

Dick's paper presented at a session of this society in November 1957 covered many plants of distinct and unusual habits of growth that were growing within the Rochester parks and gave information relative to their propagation. Many of these were plants that had been discovered and developed by Barney Slavin. Others were plants developed by Dick. This paper attracted much attention to the Rochester parks and established Dick as one of the outstanding propagators within the society. Commercial nurserymen as well as college professors and botanists from leading arboretums would write to Dick for information regarding specific plants. Many of these professionals also made it a priority to come to Rochester to observe these plants under their growing conditions with Dick as their guide.

With some help from Al Grant, who enjoyed "keeping his hand in the dirt," Dick made some changes in the large display house (dome) at the conservatory, which resulted in improving the seasonal floral displays. (As many as 10,000 visitors were clocked entering the conservatory on Easter Sunday in 1954.) One of Dick's responsibilities as greenhouse foreman was the growing of more than 40,000 plants that were used each year in the conservatory displays as well as in the various flower beds throughout the parks. Under his supervision, two and a half million spent blooms were clipped each year from the lilacs following Lilac Time and another 250,000 from the rhododendrons.

To a large degree, this was a "housekeeping" chore, but it also assisted in maintaining the health of the plants by voiding for them the formation of seed, and perhaps assisted in the control of some insects and disease.

Beginning in 1951, after the purchase of the Castle in Highland Park, Dick had a new area to plant. In describing the plantings he accomplished in this area, Dick had this to say: "The Castle gardens contain many different forms of plants, over 14 different species of conifers, 18 different deciduous shrubs, about 70 rhododendrons, many of which are unnamed hybrids, and several rare plants such as *Torreya nucifera* which I had raised from a cutting, and *Magnolia ashei*, a large-leaved Magnolia not known to survive this far north: also two large evergreen viburnum hybrids which resulted from a cross I made of *V. lantana* and *V. rhytidiphylum* in 1928. Many of these plants had been under test for over 25 years."

Beginning very early in the 1950s and during his entire career with the park system, Dick Fenicchia was approached by garden clubs as well as by his professional organizations to present talks on many different horticultural subjects. He also led many tours throughout the greenhouse and conservatory, Highland Park, and Durand Eastman Park for groups ranging from Cub Scouts to groups of students from various colleges and universities (Cornell, Syracuse, Alfred, etc.) and students from the School of Gardeners at Niagara Falls, Ontario. He wrote many short articles for the Garden Center *Bulletin* and for local neighborhood newspapers, as well as for the professional organizations to which he belonged.

The January 16, 1956, *Rochester Times-Union* carried a story that was headed by the phrase "Lilacs Bloom at the War Memorial in Welcome to Horticulturists." The occasion was the beginning of the second century of meetings of the New York State Horticultural Society, which was staging its annual meeting at the War Memorial. The Park Department had been asked to install two gardens that would fill the north end of the main arena with spring flowers in full bloom, creating a warm atmosphere during mid-winter. Dick Fenicchia and his crew dug fourteen large lilac bushes from the nursery on December 17, 1955. These plants, which had been balled and burlapped, were taken inside and placed in an airtight compartment where they were subjected to ether gas for a period of ninety-six hours. This treatment served to break the dormancy, and the lilacs were then forced into bloom in seventeen days. They became the "stars" in this display, which also contained many conifers, some easy-to-force woody plants, and several hundred pots of tulips, narcissus, and hyacinths in full bloom. Many Rochesterians visited the War Memorial to see this display and to get an early glimpse of spring. The many horticultural experts attending the meeting were surprised that this forcing of lilacs could be timed to produce flowers at the time they were needed, a real triumph for Richard Fenicchia and his crew. As a result of this display, the Park Department received many other requests for similar participation in special events where public attendance was encouraged. This involvement was sanctioned by the city administration, which considered it to be an act of good public relations for the city.

In the late 1950s, after occupying land leased from St. John's Home for nursery purposes for about ten years, the Park Bureau received notice that the home was planning to expand its facilities and that the nursery would have to be moved. Fortunately, at about the same time, the county decided to quit using the land at the penitentiary site (at the corner of South Avenue and Highland Avenue) for farm use. This freed up about 15 acres of land, which the Park Bureau got permission to use for nursery purposes. The digging and moving of many small trees and shrubs from the St. John's Home property placed a burden upon Dick Fenicchia and his crew. Although he was also maintaining part of Barney Slavin's old nursery at the Disposal Plant property next to Durand Eastman Park, retention of an area close to Highland Park was very important, particularly because of the lilac collection. The move of specimens from nursery to permanent locations in the park could be undertaken in less time and with less threat to the plants from damage in transit, such as foliage burn and drying out of roots.

During 1959, Dick Fenicchia was asked to present a paper relative to municipal nursery management at the annual conference of the American Institute of Park Executives, which was held in Philadelphia. In this paper he stated:

The problem of operating a municipal nursery has been a controversial subject for many years between park men and budget directors of city administration. When most cities inaugurated their park systems, the park nursery had an important place in the picture. As parks were planted and land became scarcer and labor more expensive, the problem arose as to the practice of maintaining these nurseries.

In Rochester, the wide variety of plant materials contained within our parks is a strong argument for maintaining our own nursery. The conifers, deciduous and broad-leaved plant collections of the Rochester parks contain plants of distinct and unusual habits of growth. The maintenance, perpetuation and expansion of our lilac collection, for example, is of prime importance. Throughout our park system which is, in effect an arboretum, are many plant materials of tremendous botanical value. These are to a great extent plants which cannot be replaced from commercial sources. It is necessary, therefore, that our park department maintain its own nursery as a source for replacement of choice specimen plants.

Management of its own nursery by a park department enables it to carry out an experimental program which can lead to future benefits in the use of plant materials. At the present time in Rochester, we are conducting a program of hybridization with lilacs and various forms and species of rhododendrons and viburnums. Another phase of nursery operations that has come to the forefront is the growing of suitable trees for street planting. The Rochester Park Bureau for many years has been one of the pioneers in the growing and planting of street trees of various species and forms. At the present time, our Park Director is conducting an experiment of great importance, planting trees to

144

determine those best suited for street tree planting under various conditions of soil and location within the city. This experiment is concerned not only with species and varieties but with trees of various size within the same species to determine which will respond the best under test conditions. The nursery plays a very important role in all of these activities which have just been mentioned.

Dick's speech continued with a discussion of nursery procedures and layouts, soil preparation, types of plants grown, nursery cultivation and weed control, mulching of nursery rows, pruning, insect control, and digging of trees readying them for removal from the nursery.

As he concluded his paper, Dick pointed out that municipal nursery management differs in many ways from commercial management. The greatest difference, perhaps, lies in the fact that the municipality needs to grow a large number of plant species and varieties but in small quantities. Coupled with efficient nursery management should be an active planting program throughout the park system. This would tend to keep the nursery from becoming overgrown because plants would be removed as they reached desired sizes. Areas should be reserved in the nursery for the storage of leaves for mulching and dirt for filling in holes left when plants are removed. He stated:

> Several of the advantages of a municipality maintaining its own nursery are: the perpetuation of plants of particular value which might not be available commercially; it furnishes an area where plants, however procured, can be grown to a size safe for planting in a park area; special pruning or tailoring can be done to develop plants for special locations; plants of the type desired will be available when wanted; the time gap between digging and planted can be kept to a minimum; plants will be available at any time for any special purpose; and perhaps the greatest advantage is that the park system will have a crew of capable trained plantsmen who will be available as needed for any special landscaping or other planting project.

Elsewhere in his paper, Dick stressed that all plants should be kept carefully labeled and accurate nursery records should be maintained showing the original source of the particular plants as well as size and quantity:

Perhaps the most important step in the management of the park nursery is the development of a good workable plan which leads to the proper organization of plant materials in nursery blocks. One procedure is to plant nursery blocks according to anticipated needs in calendar years; for example, a block can be designated for digging in 1960, another in 1961, etc. This procedure has distinct advantages:

1. Plants can all be handled in the same way during the growing program;

2. The entire block can be cleared at one time permitting the area to be cover cropped for a season before putting it back into use; and this method facilitates the keeping of the nursery records.

This writer has thought it expedient to quote the above material extracted from Dick's paper. It provides an insight into Dick's understanding of what his job was all about. He also is indirectly making mention of the work that was accomplished by the plantsmen who preceded him, not by name, but by referring to the pioneers in the park system who had been responsible for the growing and planting of street trees of various species and types. He also indirectly refers to the importance of maintaining a herbarium when he mentions the need for accurate labeling and careful records of the plant materials. By citing from his experience with the Rochester park system, Dick was able to generate much interest within this group of park professionals and he received many follow-up inquiries relative to the establishment of municipal nurseries.

Dick's paper presented at this conference, combined with one by Al Grant relative to artificial ice-skating rinks, contributed to Rochester being designated as the conference city for 1961. Interest had been aroused, and conferees wanted to see for themselves what Rochester was all about.

In 1960, Richard Fenicchia became a member of the Great Lakes Chapter of the American Rhododendron Society. In later years he would serve one term as president as well as several terms as a member of the board of directors. Dick especially enjoyed the competition with other hybridizers. Annual meetings of this organization were held at various locations near the Great Lakes during the blooming season each year. Hybridizers would take their cut blooms or small plants to be displayed and judged against those of other members.

Dick Fenicchia was responsible for the production of thousands of plants during the years 1959 to 1961. Some of these had been used in the seasonal displays at the conservatory and in the flower beds in the small parks and nursery squares throughout the city. Dick moved many more to the park nurseries, where they would be grown to specimen size for later planting within the parks. Some were also used in landscaping various public buildings throughout the city. In later years, Dick would find many living memorials to his career with the park system as he moved throughout the community.

Another group of plants that presented a challenge to Dick Fenicchia was the taxon magnolia, which each year furnished major displays of bloom prior to the lilacs. In fact, some of the "old timers" among the park employees would remark that "it always snows at least one more time after the magnolias come into bloom." In deciding to become involved in a program of hybridizing magnolias, Dick was influenced by the fact that Barney Slavin had planted large collections of these in Highland and Durand Eastman Parks and in the center mall of Oxford Street, which attracted much visitation each year. In order to be kept informed about developments with magnolias, Dick became a member of the Magnolia Society of America. During the 1950s, Dick made many crosses of magnolias, which he would keep under close scrutiny for many years as they grew into specimen plants, a measure of the curiosity and the patience of a true plantsman.

In order to maintain some chronological order in this narrative, the story of Richard Fenicchia will be interrupted to permit some mention of the changes that transferred the maintenance and operation of the major plantings within the Rochester park system, to a large degree, to the County of Monroe. The continuing story of Richard Fenicchia and his contributions to the park system will be woven into the overall story as the parks with the many plant collections move toward the twenty-first century.

THE PARK MERGER AND
THE GRANT-IN-AID PROGRAMS

Beginning in the 1940s and continuing to the present, Monroe County and the City of Rochester experienced a period of much growth, with all of the complexities of new roads, urban sprawl, extensive development of shopping malls, movement from city to suburbs, and consequent consumption of open space. The city, in particular, had reached a point in its history where much of its infrastructure needed upgrading or replacement, and it was faced with serious budgetary problems that caused it to impose a strict "hold-the-line" policy on its departments. This, of course, had a great impact upon the park system, one that was especially felt by the older park areas, which were located close to the most densely populated sections of the county where they were subjected to heavy usage by residents of the outlying towns as well as by the city residents who carried the burden of financing the operation and maintenance of these areas.

In 1960, a special Parks and Recreation Study Committee authorized by the county proposed a merger of the city and county park systems under full county management and support, thereby spreading the costs of the parks over the larger tax base of the whole county rather than having this remain strictly a burden for property owners in the city.

Consolidation of city and county functions as a means of alleviating some of the city's financial problems had been on the agenda for several years. In the February 27, 1957, *Rochester Times-Union*, there appeared an article entitled "Consolidation for Parks? Pros, Cons Stir Questions." In the article, arguments for and against consolidation were discussed. "Officially, the joint city-county committee of councilmen and supervisors has placed 'Parks' as no. 8 on its agenda of subjects to study." A park subcommittee of this joint group had been named in June 1955, but no meeting of this subcommittee had taken place in the 21 months since it was appointed (as quoted from the February 1957 article). This matter of consolidation of parks made headlines again on March 20, 1958, with "City-County Parks Merger Gains Favor—Wright Seen Heading New Setup . . . within the next few months."

On August 1, 1958, the *Times-Union* announced, "County Creates Park Department." This article stated, "Parks is believed to be one of the next major consolidations planned to be affected between the city and county and the action today would be a necessary step in that direction." Until this time, the county parks had been a separate entity under the administration of the Welfare Department. Robert Cochrane, who had been Director of County Parks under the old system, now became Director of a full-fledged Park Department reporting directly to the county manager.

In mid-1960, Robert Cochrane decided to retire effective October 1, 1960, and at that time, George Herrick, a veteran of 31 years with the county, was appointed to head the Monroe County park system with the understanding that he would probably serve until the arrangements between the county and city were finalized.

In 1961, the state legislature passed an amendment to the General Municipal Law of the State of New York providing "that any county may undertake to operate, maintain and improve public park and recreational facilities theretofore established by a municipal corporation within its boundaries on land owned by such municipal corporation. Such county and any municipal corporation located therein when authorized by majority vote of its governing body may enter into an agreement for the aforesaid purpose for a term not to exceed thirty years." Subsequent to the passing of this state legislation, the city council and the county board of supervisors authorized an agreement to be entered into between themselves for such purposes, and on the sixth day of June 1961, such contract was executed to become effective July 13, 1961.

This agreement between the city and county brought together into the county park system 1,613 acres of city-owned parkland and 3,140 acres of county-owned parkland for a total of 4,753 acres. For benefit of the reader, the city-owned areas were as follows: Durand Eastman Park, that section of Genesee Valley Park east of the Genesee River, Highland Park, Seneca Park and Zoo, and Ontario Beach Park. The five county-owned areas were Churchville Park, Ellison Park, Mendon Ponds Park, Powder Mill Park, and Webster Park.

This park merger, as it was commonly entitled, called for the transfer of 124 year-round city park employees and 100 seasonal employees to the county. Among the seasonal employees were the lifeguards, bath-house attendants, and seasonal park laborers assigned to general park work.

Wilbur E. Wright was appointed as the new Director of County Parks by County Manager Gordon A. Howe. George Herrick stepped down to the position of Deputy Director. Alvan Grant transferred to the county as Superintendent of County Parks. Also included in the transfer were those employees most responsible for the arboretum and the horticultural work performed within the former city parks, Richard Fenicchia, who would become Nursery Foreman, and Bernard Harkness, Taxonomist. At this time, the administrative offices of this new department were moved to the Warner Castle at 5 Castle Park (within Highland Park).

Inasmuch as the trees along the city's streets were strictly a city responsibility, Calvin Reynolds remained with the city as City Forester, along with his entire staff of tree trimmers, truck drivers, and associated employees. For administrative purposes, the Street Tree Division was placed within the Department of Public Works. All of Maplewood Park was excluded from the transfer. Consequently, the Rose Garden became a responsibility of the city's Department of Recreation, which inherited all remnants of the former Rochester park system. At a later date, when the city reorganized, some of its functions, such as the street trees and cemeteries, were placed within a new Department of Parks, Recreation and Human Services.

Although the city retained on its payroll some employees skilled in horticultural work, this task was definitely one of maintenance as compared to the more innovative opportunities that would be available to some of the county employees. In many ways, the changes wrought by the enactment of the park operating agreement between the city and county had little effect upon the horticultural program as previously conducted within the former Rochester park system. There was no actual movement of plantsmen involved or of the plant collections. All of the plant breeding and propagation previously performed at the Highland Park greenhouses and at the park nurseries would continue in the same locations that had served the Rochester park system.

Several events of great significance to the park system occurred prior to the enactment of the park agreement in July 1961, and although these events may not be considered horticultural or botanical by nature, they certainly would have a lasting impact upon the park system. These were:

1. In the 1960 election, the voters of New York State approved the $75 million Park and Recreation Land Acquisition Bond Issue, which would be further augmented by a supplementary bond issue of $25 million approved in the 1963 election. In January 1961, the Rochester Bureau of Parks applied to the state for grant-in-aid under this program for addition of land to Durand Eastman, Genesee Valley, and Seneca Parks. After the city-county operating agreement went into effect, legislation was approved whereby the county could use funds in the bond issue reserved for upstate cities in the acquisition of the land for these parks, which had been transferred to county jurisdiction.

2. Another important factor that would contribute greatly to the program of land acquisition by Monroe County was the study made by the Eckberg Committee regarding the need for more recreational and park land in Monroe County. In its 1960 report, the committee proposed the purchase of land for four new parks and the addition of land to the five already established county parks.

3. A third event was the approval by the U.S. Congress in June 1961 of Title VII of the Housing Act of 1961, which

provided financial aid to communities for acquiring urban open-space lands.

4. Then, just a year after the operating agreement went into effect, the Monroe County Board of Supervisors, on November 1, 1962, adopted Resolution No. 363 of 1962, which authorized the county manager to execute a contract with Carl Crandall, Consulting Engineer, to study and prepare a report relative to the future development of the Irondequoit Bay area.

5. In May 1962, the U.S. Congress enacted Public Law 88-69, which created within the Department of the Interior the Bureau of Outdoor Recreation, which was charged with the responsibility of assuring to all Americans adequate outdoor recreation. The Land and Water Conservation Fund Act of 1963 implemented the program of this bureau by providing federal funds to be used on a matching basis for grants-in-aid for the acquisition of park and recreation lands.

6. In the November 1966 election, the voters of New York State approved the Next Step program, which established a $200 million Park Development Bond Issue to provide matching funds for state and local governmental agencies for acquisition and development of park areas.

7. By means of the Food and Agriculture Act of 1965, the federal government authorized the Secretary of Agriculture to make grants to public agencies for acquiring cropland for the preservation of open space, natural beauty, the development of wildlife, recreational facilities, or the prevention of air or water pollution. This program was called Greenspan.

The seven factors listed above, although they did not all come into existence, as this writer stated, prior to the enactment of the operating agreement, are so interrelated that it was easier to list them in this section of this story. They would, to a large degree, determine the workload for both Wilbur Wright and Alvan Grant during the early 1960s and beyond. Several hundred parcels of land were listed for acquisition, applications had to be prepared, site inspection had to be made, negotiations with owners were necessary, and many conferences with U.S. and New York governmental officials had to be scheduled and undertaken. There was also the necessary screening by members of the board of supervisors, and later the county legislature and the administration, which required hours of conference and site examination. The legislators and the county administration, especially County Manager Gordon A. Howe, until succeeded by equally cooperative County Executive Lucian Morin, took an active part in the overall program of acquisition of new lands for the county parks, but more significantly, for the people of the county.

The inclusion of this section in this history of the plantsmen may seem to be out of order. However, the acquisition of new land will become of great significance in all aspects or phases of the work of county parks as these parks move into the future. These new lands will have a lasting impact upon the park system, an impact that will bring about new challenges and new opportunities for the horticulturists and plantsmen in the department, as well as for all others associated with the Monroe County park system.

THE HORTICULTURE PROGRAM
MOVES TO THE COUNTY

In June 1961, just a month before the park merger took effect, Alvan Grant wrote an article for the Garden Center *Bulletin* in which he summarized the eleven years that had intervened since the Maplewood Rose Garden was redesigned and the new planting had been accomplished. Over 450 varieties of roses had appeared in the garden, some for but a single season, others for the entire eleven years. In 1961, there were 200 varieties to be found in this garden. Among these were forty-two varieties out of the fifty-nine that had been chosen as All American selections since that program was initiated in 1938.

Mr. Grant, in this article, listed the roses that he would not recommend because of susceptibility to black spot and mildew, as well as some that did not respond favorably to our growing conditions. He also listed those to which he gave high ratings on their performance at the Maplewood Garden. This information was provided to members of the Rochester Rose Society as well as to representatives of the City Department of Recreation and Parks, who possibly would refer to it in planning the maintenance program of this garden after the operating agreement between the city and county became a reality.

The new Monroe County Park Department had been in operation for less than three months when it was host to the 63rd annual conference of the American Institute of Park Executives and the American Association of Zoological Parks and Aquariums. Wilbur Wright, Director of Parks, had enlisted the assistance of many Rochester leaders who served on the executive committee for this conference and their part in this conference drew much praise from the conferees. It might be said, however, that it was the plantsmen of the park system and the "fruits of their labor" that made this conference a special one in the memories of those who attended it.

As was recorded in the Conference Report, Rochester, known nationally as the "Flower City," proved its reputation with flowers everywhere along the streets, at the hotels, and in the meeting rooms. "Special commendation goes to fellow member Alvan R. Grant, Superintendent of Parks for bringing flowers, shrubs and even trees into conference decorations," the report stated.

A special social event was held at Eastman Theater. The program at this event was centered around "The Rochester Park Story," a color slide presentation making use of three projectors and three twelve-by-twelve-foot screens. This presentation resulted from the efforts of Donald Yeager, a botanist with the park system who had spent ten months photographing and writing this show, assisted in this work by technical staff of Eastman Kodak Company. The program also included live music provided by the Park Band and by area choirs. The entire program was presented in a park setting that had been placed on the theater stage.

While the program was being presented, park employees directed by Al Grant and Richard Fenicchia, working in the dark and behind curtains, were creating a park scene that would be part of the grand finale to this program. When the elevator stage decorated with hundreds of chrysanthemums in full bloom as well as with small trees and shrubs was raised to blend in with the landscape scene already in place on the stationary stage, the audience, many with tears in their eyes, rose to their feet and cheered.

Perhaps a greater challenge to the "decorators" was preparing the War Memorial for the final banquet. They met the challenge once again, converting the somewhat bleak, large arena of the War Memorial into a well-decorated banquet room, which again won the acclaim of the conferees. The planning necessary in producing the plant materials for use during this entire conference had been assigned to Al Grant by Park Director Wright. Grant continued to work with Dick Fenicchia and his greenhouse and nursery crew during the many months that it took to grow and prepare the many plants used during this conference.

156

The fact that all plants reached their peak condition for display during the week of the conference is a reflection of the skill with which these two men met the challenge given to them and earned for them the words expressed in a letter from Mr. M. Foss Narum, Park Manager from Northampton, Massachusetts, and General Program Chairman of this conference: "Just a special word of thanks for all you did to make the AIPE conference a success. The 'landscaping' of the War Memorial was excellent and the transformation of the big arena for the banquet was outstanding. The Eastman Theater stage was one of the most beautiful settings that I have ever seen." Also mentioned in the Conference Report had been the manner in which the main arena of the War Memorial was landscaped "with the stage arranged with a park setting."

A central feature of this "park setting" was an easy-to-erect log cabin that had been displayed by one of the vendors of park equipment. An arrangement to purchase this building with a considerable discount was made, and it was then dismantled and taken to Mendon Ponds Park, where it was erected to become the Nature Center.

Donald Yeager, who had worked for a short time with Bernard Harkness in the labeling and recording of plant materials, was appointed to the position of Park Naturalist with the above-mentioned building serving as his headquarters as soon as it was ready for use in the early winter of 1961. Don had received an associate degree in horticulture from the State University College at Alfred and later earned his bachelor's degree from the University of Rochester. He became very enthused about his program of nature study and soon set up a program of special classes as well as a schedule of guided tours through Mendon Ponds Park. A group of interested citizens soon organized a Mendon Ponds Natural History Association to work with Don and to promote the programs.

Because of the amount of time involved in plant breeding, many crosses made within the park system during the decade of the 1950s would not prove their worth until the 1960s and 1970s after the "merger" of the city and county parks. Relative to the time involved in plant breeding, Dick Fenicchia made the following comment: "Barney H. Slavin, former Park Superintendent, was of the opinion that it would take 25 years or more to test a new plant. Richard is of the same opinion. I realize it would take many lifetimes for me to evaluate some of the selected hybrids we have in Highland Park, so Richard will do the best he can with describing and ascertaining the hardiness factors of these selections."

Although the lilac cultivar 'Rochester' resulted from open pollination rather than from a controlled cross made by a plant breeder, it can still be used as an example of the time spent in the development of a new plant. The Rochester strain or family of lilacs had its start in 1947 when Alvan Grant, then plant propagator for the Rochester park system, gathered seed from 'Edith Cavell,' a double white lilac that was growing in Highland Park. The 300 seedlings that resulted from the planting of these seeds were lined out in the Highland Park nursery during the 1950s, where they were nurtured by Dick Fenicchia. During the early 1950s, one particular seedling in this group began to show some unique characteristics and it was then transplanted in a special area in the nursery where it could be more carefully cared for. In fact, Dick Fenicchia, who had become responsible for the maintenance of this nursery in mid-1950, succeeded in rooting several cuttings from this plant, thus insuring against the possible loss of this selection in case something happened to the original plant. In 1962, after this seedling had been evaluated for ten years and it was determined that the unique characteristics were permanent in nature, Alvan Grant named it 'Rochester' in honor of the city.

On May 24, 1962, Dick Fenicchia unveiled this new white lilac 'Rochester' to the Lilac Week Committee of the Real Estate Board, who visited the nursery. Dick was honored by that committee for 22 years of service in the parks, and special notice was made for the care he had provided for the Rochester lilac collection. It is of interest to note that Richard Horsey, who had retired in May 1950, sent the following letter to Dick:

May 25, 1962

Dear Dick,

Congratulations on your award by the Rochester Real Estate Board for your work with the lilacs. It is well deserved.

The new Rochester lilac must be very fine. I look forward to seeing it in bloom next year.

With many pleasant memories of our associations from the time you came to work in the greenhouse propagation. At times you came to the Herbarium to study the books on horticulture and you were real in your interest.

Wishing you as long a service with the parks as I had and when retirement comes that it will be enjoyed as much as my retirement has been.

Yours Sincerely,
/s/ Richard E. Horsey

In his letter, Mr. Horsey is referring to Dick's first period of employment with the Rochester park system, 1925-1934. This letter documents the fact that Dick, during those years, devoted time to the study as well as to the practice of horticulture.

During Lilac Time, 1963 (May 15-23), 'Rochester' was placed on public display for the first time as a potted plant in the Lamberton Conservatory. The discovery of this new lilac was destined to become of real importance because of the great influence it would have in any program of hybridizing lilacs by Fenicchia and also by other plant breeders. Beginning in the mid-1960s, this seedling was of sufficient size and had flowering capacity enough so that Dick could use it in a somewhat extensive breeding program, one that proved to be very rewarding in the number and quality of the new cultivars that were produced.

159

On Lilac Sunday, May 20, 1962, Mr. Richard E. Horsey was presented with the fourth annual Parks Public Service Award. In his long service with the park system, Mr. Horsey had made voluminous notes on the lilacs, notes that have been used extensively by botanists and horticulturists from all over this country and in several foreign countries as well. His vast knowledge of lilacs had been recognized when he was selected to serve on the 1941 Lilac Survey Committee of the American Association of Botanical Gardens and Arboretums. His service to parks and people extended far beyond the workday limits inasmuch as he was always willing to share his knowledge of plants and birds with any who requested it.

Despite his habitual shunning of publicity, Mr. Horsey was recognized locally in 1943 when he was made a Fellow of the Rochester Museum of Arts and Sciences. The late Patrick Slavin, Director of Parks for the city, said of Mr. Horsey, "He was of the greatest assistance in building up the city's park system." During Lilac Time in 1963, a special program was held at Midtown Plaza to commemorate the 75th anniversary of Highland Park. Miss Helen Ellwanger and Peter Barry, descendants of the two men who donated the original acreage that formed the nucleus of that park, were honorary co-chairmen of this program. Several distinguished horticulturists were present at this program to show the respect they had for this park and the park men who had created it. Among these were:

- Mr. George Avery from the Brooklyn Botanic Garden;
- Maxim Gray, General Manager, Niagara Falls Park, Ontario, Canada;
- Leslie Laking, Director, Royal Botanic Garden, Hamilton, Canada;
- Ralph W. Curtis, Professor Emeritus, School of Horticulture, Cornell University;
- M. S. Pridham, Professor of Floriculture and Ornamental Horticulture, Cornell University;
- Thomas M. Thompson, Metropolitan Parks Commission, Toronto, Ontario, Canada;

- John G. Seeley, Professor of Floriculture and Head of the Department of Floriculture and Ornamental Horticulture, Cornell University;
- Dr. Henry Skinner, Director, National Arboretum, Washington, D.C.;
- Dr. John Wister, Arthur Hoyt Scott Horticultural Foundation, Swarthmore College and author of the book *Lilac Culture*;
- Dr. Donald Wyman, Horticulturist, Arnold Arboretum, Harvard University;
- Leonard L. Huttleson, Director, New York Division of Parks;
- And many others representing various park systems and botanic gardens that had maintained a relationship with the Rochester park system over a period of many years, primarily through contacts with the plantsmen of the system.

Although the location in Highland Park seemed ideal as the site of the main office of the County Park Department, the Castle building itself was not satisfactory for this ever-changing department. The building was in a historic preservation district, and major renovations or changes that were needed to convert it into a workable office building would result in spoiling its historic character. When the former Nurse's Home in the Iola complex became available for other county purposes, Wilbur Wright gained permission to move the park office into this much more accommodating building, which would adequately shelter all of the administrative functions of the department. It was decided that the herbarium with its collection of preserved specimens and its horticultural library would also move to this new site. Bernard Harkness was once again burdened with reestablishing these two important functions in a new site.

Concurrently with the move of the office to the Iola site, Wilbur Wright convinced the county administration that the Garden Center of Rochester would be a logical tenant at the castle. He, as well as Bernard Harkness and Alvan Grant, had been associated with the Garden Center in some manner during their

161

entire careers with the park system. This organization, which had been occupying the old herbarium building on Pinetum Road in Highland Park since 1952, despite the fact that it was an independent nonprofit organization, was providing a public service as an educational extension of the Park Department.

In July 1963, George Herrick, who had been Deputy Director of County Parks since July 1961, retired and Alvan Grant was appointed to succeed him. At this same time, Richard Fenicchia was appointed Superintendent of Horticulture for Monroe County Parks.

For several years, Professor Pridham from Cornell University was in charge of the Horticulture Building at the State Fair in Syracuse. In 1963, feeling that the annual displays "lacked luster," he appealed to Wilbur Wright to send a display from the Monroe County Department of Parks, which he hoped would set a pattern for others to emulate. Wright agreed and turned to the team of Fenicchia and Grant to produce a "quality display." This would be a change from the simple moving of plants from the greenhouse and nursery to a display area within the Rochester community.

Consequently, "the team" carefully planned the garden they proposed to create in Syracuse so that they knew exactly what plant or landscape accessory would be used in each square foot of the display area. After the plants were selected and, in some cases, specially groomed for the display, they were carefully loaded onto two park trucks for a trip down I-90 to Syracuse, where they were assembled into a colorful and educational exhibit in the Horticultural Building. Every plant in this exhibit was carefully labeled in a manner that made the exhibit "self-guided."

This 1963 Monroe County display was so well received by visitors that the State Fair authorities issued invitations for "repeat performances" in 1964 and 1965. Special awards were given to the Park Department in appreciation for its involvement. In fact, in 1963, some much-needed nursery equipment (for which there was no funding in the budget) was donated to the department by State Fair authorities. Also, Grant and Fenicchia were asked to consider preparing a plan for the entire horticultural show for use in the future. However, despite the fact that these exhibits had attracted much attention and had performed a real public relations function for the County of Monroe, they had to be discontinued after 1965 because of the expense in time and money.

In his 1963 budget submission, Wilbur Wright, anticipating the need for a staff member who could devote himself full time to the study and planning of park areas, requested the creation of the position of Park Planner. This request was approved by County Manager Gordon Howe and by the County Board of Supervisors. Early in 1963, Wilbur was successful in recruiting Ed Mika, a young man from Livonia, Michigan, who had gained considerable experience in park planning in the vicinity of Detroit. Unfortunately, Ed, finding it difficult to adjust to the move to Rochester, resigned early in 1965 to return to his home state of Michigan. Wilbur was then successful in bringing Calvin Reynolds from his position as City Forester to the Park Planner position in the Monroe County park system, where he would work closely with Wilbur and Al Grant in the land acquisition program and with the various park supervisors in planning changes and improvements in the parks for which they were responsible.

Introduced and on public display for the first time during Lilac Week 1964 (May 17-24) was the new rhododendron hybrid, 'President Kennedy,' which had won the Great Lakes Chapter of the American Rhododendron Society Award for the best new hybrid seedling never before shown, at the 1963 Rhododendron Show held in Cleveland, Ohio. This hybrid developed by Dick Fenicchia was an especially fine white-flowered cultivar that was enthusiastically received in England.

Another innovation during Lilac Week 1964 was the awarding of the first annual National Award for Parks Service, an engraved silver tray presented to Conrad L. Wirth of New York City, former Director of the National Park Service. It was planned that presentation of a similar award from the Monroe County Park Department would be given each year at Lilac Time to someone of national stature who had made a notable contribution to the park movement across the country. All expenses (cost of the engraved tray and transportation and temporary housing cost of the awardee) involved in this award were shared by the Convention and Publicity Bureau and the Gannett Newspapers.

Wilbur E. Wright continued to serve in the position of Director of Parks for Monroe County until December 1965, when he resigned to accept appointment as Director of State Parks. From July 13, 1961, to December 1965, he had successfully merged the park systems from two separate governmental entities (county and city) into a well-operating county park system. With full support from County Manager Gordon A. Howe and the County Board of Supervisors, he had prepared and forwarded to state and federal agencies applications for grants-in-aid in the acquisition of new parkland, which included additional areas for four of the five county-owned parks and two of the city-owned parks as well as total acquisition of three new parks for the county park system.

When Wright resigned in December 1965 to accept his appointment to the position with the State of New York, Alvan Grant was appointed as Director of Monroe County Parks. In appointing Grant to this position, County Manager Gordon A. Howe stated, "The County of Monroe is fortunate to have a team of high caliber people who can keep our parks program moving forward and maintain the exceptionally high standards that have given the County Park system a nationwide reputation for excellence. Mr. Grant has many assets, including an educational background in his chosen field of horticulture and an intimate knowledge of the County Park system. He has worked closely with Mr. Wright and I am confident that we could not find a more qualified man for this important position." Privately, Mr. Howe's challenge to Al Grant was to "keep the parkland acquisition program moving."

At the time of his resignation, Wilbur Wright could take credit for the completed acquisition of 1,336 acres of new parkland and approved contracts with the state and federal governments for some 2,000 additional acres.

Inasmuch as Alvan Grant had worked closely with Wilbur Wright in the program of land acquisition since the inception of that program in 1961, he had very little adjustment to make in keeping this program moving. During the eleven years that followed his appointment to the position of Director of County Parks until his retirement in 1977, Grant monitored the acquisition of over 5,000 acres of new parkland.

Applications for federal and/or state aid in the acquisition of approximately one-half of this acreage had been processed prior to Wright's departure from the county park system. The remaining acreage was comprised almost entirely of land for three new parks: Greece Canal Park in the Town of Greece, Black Creek Park in the Towns of Chili and Riga, and Irondequoit Bay Park East in the Town of Penfield. This latter area was of particular interest. In late 1967, Mr. John Brush offered a gift of 14.055 acres of land on the east side of Irondequoit Bay to the County of Monroe. County Manager Gordon Howe, before recommending acceptance of this gift, suggested to Al Grant that he try to "put together a larger package" that would more adequately serve as a county park.

By making personal contact with several adjacent owners, Grant was able to bring the total acreage to 177 acres. With 4,000 feet of frontage along the bay, this acreage was comprised of steep, forested slopes extending 100 to 150 feet above the water to a flat plateau. Approximately twelve acres of this flat area was included in the county's acquisition. While making an inspection of this area, Grant and Fenicchia discovered that the top soil that covered this twelve acres was a rich, sandy loam with a depth of over twelve inches, ideal for nursery purposes. There also was a paved road leading off of Bay Road into the property, which made it easily accessible for vehicles and equipment for use in nursery maintenance and in moving plants to other park areas. Establishment of a nursery in this area would also guarantee some maintenance of the area in a manner that would not be objectionable to neighboring property owners. Dick immediately started work on developing this area as a nursery, bringing many of the new plants he was developing at Highland Park to this area

165

for growing to specimen plants for eventual planting in selected areas throughout the park system.

With the acquisition of Irondequoit Bay Park East, Richard Fenicchia now had three sites available to him for nursery purposes. Principal use made by Dick of the Highland Park nursery (on County Penitentiary land) was the growing on of named varieties of lilacs, which, after reaching a size of three to four feet, were used for replacements in the lilac collection as well as for expansion of the collection. He also used this area for growing some of the named varieties and new forms of conifers for later planting within Highland Park. Some of this land was used for trial beds for perennials, trees, and shrubs, some of which he was acquiring through the seed and plant exchange program.

At Mendon Ponds Park (the largest county park, with approximately 2,500 acres), Dick planted blocks of oak trees: red, English fastigiate, Turkey, scarlet, chestnut, and white species. He used some of this area in a program of preserving the American chestnut (*Castanea dentata*), which he grew from seeds gathered from second-growth trees at Durand Eastman Park. Some of these have reached a height of fifteen to thirty feet and most have borne fruit. Some have died back due to the chestnut blight, but are sprouting new growth from the roots that remained in the ground. Dick believes that, through natural selection, trees immune to the blight may eventually be found—consequently the urge to keep some growing. Otherwise the American chestnut could be lost forever. Also, in this nursery, Dick planted many named evergreens and species of many rare and unusual deciduous trees, including a collection of named flowering cherries.

The nursery area at Irondequoit Bay Park East very quickly became a somewhat special area. It was here that Dick planted hundreds of newly propagated lilacs in named varieties as well as seedlings from his hybridization program using 'Rochester' as one of the parents. This latter group would be kept under close observation. When any proved to be unique in some characteristic, they would be selected for growing on to specimen size, and at a future date might be named and added to the Highland Park

166

collection. In fact, several have been placed in this collection while still under Fenicchia's number. Many rare varieties and forms of conifers, rhododendrons, azaleas, crabapples, and many other plants that Dick had earmarked for further selection and testing were also transferred to this nursery. Some of these were plants that had resulted from selections made by Barney Slavin during his career with the park system. Because of the example that Barney furnished during his tenure in the park system in the production of new plants, Dick Fenicchia, with a deep admiration for Barney, has proposed that the test area at Irondequoit Bay be dedicated as the Barney Slavin Arboretum.

In 1967, the county Park Department submitted a proposal to the Agricultural Stabilization and Conservation Service Bureau of the U.S. Department of Agriculture for a grant-in-aid under the Greenspan program for the purchase of approximately 1,400 acres of land in the Towns of Chili and Riga. (This would become Black Creek Park.) Also included in this submittal were 110 acres for addition to Churchville Park and 150 acres for Mendon Ponds Park. With the approval of this request, Monroe County was credited with the largest Greenspan project in the country. Black Creek Park was also Monroe County's largest land acquisition project measured by acreage.

As well as furnishing funds for the purchase of land, the Greenspan program also provided funds for assistance in approved development of the acquired land. These funds helped in the creation of a small lake and an entrance road into the property. An existing house on this property was immediately put to use as a park facility that could be reserved by small groups or families for picnics and parties.

Despite the success that Richard (Dick) Fenicchia was experiencing in his lilac-breeding program, he still preferred working with rhododendrons, azaleas, magnolias, and selected trees and shrubs. The number of crosses he made of rhododendron and azaleas from 1950 until his retirement in 1978 exceeded 300.

In 1966, when Dick was serving as President of the Great Lakes Chapter of the American Rhododendron Society, he helped negotiate an agreement with the Ohio Agricultural Research and Development Center to establish an official Rhododendron Test and Display Garden in the Center's Secrest Arboretum in Wooster, Ohio. This garden was expected to attract thousands of visitors to the Research Center from throughout the northeast, according to its director, Dr. Roy M. Kottman. The ultimate goal was to build a collection of all of the rhododendrons and azaleas that would grow satisfactorily and become one of the outstanding floricultural displays in the Great Lakes region. This location was selected from among several that had applied for the honor. The garden would have at least one specimen of each species grown in the region, and new and improved cultivars would be added as they became available. These would be evaluated annually for national awards, and some would probably become commercially available. Dick took fourteen of his numbered hybrids to Wooster, five of which were mentioned in a letter from the curator of the arboretum in June 1978 as having excellent blooms. In this letter, he also inquired if any of these cultivars had been named and whether any were commercially available.

In 1967, Donald Yeager, Chief Park Naturalist in charge of the nature center at Mendon Ponds Park, was given the new title of Supervisor of Interpretive Services. This change of title reflected a change of emphasis from a specific aspect of what the parks have to offer to an appeal to many interests. Don had become a member of the International Association of Interpretive Naturalists' board of directors. He believed that his role had become one of "provoking visitors into wanting to broaden their horizons of understanding not only their natural but also their social and historical environment with an introduction to the geological, anthropological and archaeological background of the area as well as its flora and fauna."

In five years, visitation to the center in Mendon Ponds Park had grown from less than 10,000 visitors to more than 100,000 each year. Don and his assistants had a somewhat different approach to horticulture and plant materials than some of the other plantsmen already mentioned, in that they were interested in bringing to the public a knowledge and understanding of the native plants that were growing within our parks. Many visitors came to view the wildflowers as they were guided along park trails either by a person or by the self-guiding brochures prepared by Don and his staff.

Don Yeager recognized that Mendon Ponds Park had all the attributes needed to qualify it as worthy of being on the National Registry of Natural History Landmarks. It had a wealth of flora and fauna that could be observed from the trails that led visitors into and throughout the more than 2,000 acres of interesting terrain. It was recognition of the value and high quality of its dramatic geological features that led the park to be named to the National Registry in November 1969. In granting registry status to this park, the National Parks Advisory Board noted the park's "significant and unique complex of glacial features."

Don prepared an interesting and informative brochure about the special geology of this park. Being on the National Registry has given this park a certain amount of protection from encroachment of many kinds on its natural features. From a pure horticultural viewpoint, this park contains many native plant materials, which perhaps make it the most ecologically unique area in Monroe County as well as one of the most fragile. Kennedy's Bog, located in a low-lying area near the south entrance (off Clover Street) of this park, is home to many plant species that are rare in this area, including Virginia chain fern, fringed gentians, sundews, rose pogonia, cotton grass, black spruce, and bog rosemary. A local teacher who has led many classes into the park to study the plant materials states that there are sixty-one species of protected plants to be listed within this park. Another writer visiting the park in the spring writes, "Entwined among the sphagnum moss are thousands of marble sized red berries, bog cranberries, that are sweeter than the store bought variety, but still possessing the unmistakable cranberry tartness."

Certainly Don Yeager, with his emphasis on the native flora that adorn several areas in the park, qualifies as one of the park

169

system's plantsmen. Although he was not a plant breeder or a nurseryman, he labored to protect what nature had created and to bring these features to the attention of the park visitors.

The Center for Interpretive Services (a new title for the Nature Center) was relocated to its present location after a parcel of land (100.24 acres) was added to the park in the summer of 1964. Located on this property were several buildings, including the home of the former owners and a small guesthouse. The home was easily converted into a headquarters, or center, for Don and his staff (seasonal or part-time as well as volunteer), where they could exhibit displays depicting the geological and historic background of the area as well as the flora and fauna native to the area. The guesthouse became a small lecture room where classes were held for groups interested in learning about some aspect of the program. This property not only furnished more commodious accommodations for Don and his program, but also, because of its location, provided good access to the nature trails.

Shortly after Bernard Harkness retired in April 1967, Robert Clark was appointed to succeed him as Plant Taxonomist. Mr. Clark had been active in the horticultural world for several years, having served in the following positions: Senior Curator of the Liberty Hyde Bailey Hortorium of Cornell University; Assistant Director of the Bayard Cutting Arboretum in Oakdale, Long Island; and Assistant Professor of Ornamental Horticulture in the College of Agriculture, Rutgers University. He had contributed articles to many different horticultural publications and was co-author of *Trees for New Jersey Streets*, a handbook published by the New Jersey Federation of Shade Tree Commissions. He was also the author of a book, *Flowering Trees*, published by D. Van Nostrand Company, Inc. Bob's memberships included the American Association of Botanical Gardens and Arboretums, the American Institute of Botanical Sciences, the American Institute of Plant Taxonomists, and several other special plant societies.

Inasmuch as Bernard Harkness and Bob Clark were already good friends through their association in many of the same professional societies, Bernard made the transfer an easy one for Bob, often driving up from Geneva for visits during which he would discuss the operation of the herbarium, arboretum records, labeling plants, and other horticultural duties with Bob. Bob also took an interest in the plant and seed exchange program that Bernie had promoted so successfully. An example of Bob's interest in this program can easily be seen in the statistics compiled during one of his years with the county park system. In 1973, 1,454 packets of seeds, 1,273 scions and cuttings, and 844 small plants were sent to 284 arboretums and botanical gardens throughout the world. The majority of the scions and cuttings were lilac, which were sent to the National Arboretum in Washington, D.C., and to Morton Arboretum in Lisle, Illinois.

After lilac festivities were over in 1967, Dick began an extensive program of pruning to rejuvenate many of the lilacs. "We took out all the larger branches and we lowered maybe 79 to 80 percent of the bushes," he said. "Cut them down so that when they are in bloom the flower clusters will be more easily visible from a person's eye level. We probably sacrificed a few blooms for the following year but everything will look better. We also planted a collection of 24 new Rochester hybrids in the western end of the lilac collection along the main path through the park."

Several plantsmen associated with the Niagara Falls, Ontario, Parks Commission School of Horticulture had become acquainted with Dick Fenicchia through their affiliation with the International Plant Propagators Society. When they were preparing for the 21st annual Horticultural Convention of the Alumni Association of this remarkable school, to be held January 18, 19, and 20, 1968, they contacted Dick to be their principal speaker. He responded by presenting a slide-supported lecture on the many plants of distinct and unusual habit of growth that can be found in the Monroe County park system, practically all of which were selections of Barney Slavin or of Dick himself.

Starting in the late 1960s, with encouragement from the director of parks, Dick Fenicchia expanded the rhododendron collection at Highland Park, with the largest planting established

171

in the conifer collections north of Pinetum Road. Through the years, pine needles and tiny branches had fallen from the trees planted in this valley and had created a rich acid mulch favorable to rhododendrons. The method of planting in this area differed enough from the original planting of rhododendrons in Highland Park, where two and a half to three feet of native soil had been replaced by peat hauled in from a nearby deposit, to make it of interest to the reader.

At this new planting of several hundred rhododendrons, the "pine needle mulch" and native soil were dug out to a depth of one foot, with each planting hole four feet in diameter. Two parts of sphagnum peat moss were mixed with each part of the native soil. Before planting, a quarter pound of fine sulphur was scattered in each planting hole and worked in with a fork to a depth of three to four inches. The balled and burlapped rhododendrons were brought in from the park nurseries and placed in the planting holes. The soil mix was then put into the holes and firmly tamped by foot around each plant until the proper level was reached (ground level at the top of the root ball). A mulch of pure sphagnum moss was put around each newly planted rhododendron to a depth of two to two and a half inches.

Throughout the summer, when conditions demanded, the newly planted rhododendrons were given soakings of water, using the spray truck in absence of any nearby water line. These rhododendrons have made remarkable growth and have greatly added to the Highland Park display. This planting in Pinetum Valley now gives an appearance resembling that of native rhododendrons growing naturally as underplantings in the coniferous forests throughout southern Pennsylvania and areas farther south.

The plants used as described above were crosses made by Dick Fenicchia beginning in the 1950s. One of these crosses he had named 'Mrs. Alvan Grant,' and he planted it in the foundation planting just outside Al's office window at 375 Westfall Road, where, according to Dick, "she can keep an eye on you." After Al Grant's retirement, Dick moved this plant into the pinetum plantings at Highland Park, where it has produced a good display of bloom each year.

In late April 1969, acting upon arrangements made by Congressman Frank Horton, Richard Fenicchia and Alvan Grant took a carefully selected plant of Fenicchia's hybrid lilac 'Dwight D. Eisenhower' to Washington for planting on the grounds at the White House to join the group of lilacs that had been planted in 1956 by Wilbur Wright and Bernie Harkness. Dick had wanted to name this lilac 'General Ike,' but the Eisenhower family preferred 'Dwight D. Eisenhower,' and Dick concurred with their wishes. In describing this plant, Dick said:

> We have been developing this cultivar for 12 years. This is what is called a controlled hybrid. It was created by cross pollinating two plants—in this case the 'Rochester' lilac and 'Madame Souchet.' [Note: He is referring to 'Mme. Charles Souchet.'] It takes four to five years for a new plant to bloom for the first time and then you watch it to make sure that the characteristics are constant. This new lilac has a dwarf compact habit of growth and the bloom is bigger than that of either parent. Also, most varieties have four petals per floret; this one has up to 18, which is unusual. The basic color of the large thyrse is blue. Lilac gardeners must be patient. One of our greatest American growers of lilacs once stated that "the quality of the variety should not be judged until ten year old plants were to be seen."

Although by March 1971 Bernard Harkness had been retired for four years, he kept in close contact with the Park Department. He made many trips from Geneva to use the herbarium library and to observe many plants that he had brought to the park system through the seed and plant exchange. He also maintained his interest in the Garden Center, making regular visits there to assist in solving many problems of identification or culture of plants, problems that were constantly being brought to the Garden Center by home gardeners in search of more information about plants that they had growing in their gardens or that they had observed when visiting a botanic garden such as Longwood.

It was no great surprise to anyone when Bernie issued an invitation through the Garden Center *Bulletin* to all interested parties to attend a meeting at the Garden Center on March 21, 1971, for the purpose of forming a rhododendron club in Rochester. To attract a nucleus of potential members to this meeting, he had arranged for Professor Arthur Lieberman of Cornell University to speak about the culture of rhododendrons. After Professor Lieberman's lecture, the audience of rhododendron fanciers organized itself into a local branch of the Great Lakes Chapter of the American Rhododendron Society, which would be of great assistance to Dick Fenicchia when he hosted the Twelfth Annual Rhododendron Show in the Holiday Inn Downtown on May 29 and 30, 1971.

The conference floor of the Holiday Inn was practically paved with rhododendrons and azaleas in thirty-two different classes grown by members of the Great Lakes Chapter. Local members of the newly formed branch of this chapter were also invited to display their prize blooms. A beautiful rhododendron garden with background planting of coniferous plants was built under Dick's supervision using several hundred plants that he had been grooming for this purpose over a two-year period. The aim of this show, besides bringing members of the society together to discuss and compare their plants, was to "create a better understanding and appreciation of rhododendrons in Rochester and Monroe County," according to Dick. At this time he pointed out that the Ellwanger and Barry Nursery, in its 1875 catalogue, had stated, "The Rhododendrons are the most magnificent flowering shrubs that we raise." That this show was a big success was attested to by the many members of the Great Lakes Chapter who attended and displayed cut blooms from their favorite plants, as well as by the hundreds of local plant enthusiasts who visited this colorful exhibit.

As well as bringing in a new taxonomist for Dick to work with, Bernie Harkness's retirement also resulted in an addition to

Dick's responsibilities. Dick now became responsible for supervising and implementing a plant protection program, which included the spraying of many trees and shrubs throughout the county parks in an effort to prevent and to combat the infestations by plant disease and insects. Each year, 20,000 to 30,000 gallons of spray materials were used in the operation of this program, depending upon seasonal differences in insect and disease population. Inasmuch as the taxonomist was constantly involved in the surveillance of the many plant collections, he assisted in this program and often brought to Dick's attention any plants in need of spraying.

During the next few years, as well as fulfilling his duties as taxonomist, Bob Clark acted as a consultant to the Garden Center and wrote several articles for the *Bulletin*. He also maintained constant correspondence with botanists and horticulturists worldwide. In mid-1971, he received notice that a group of lilac enthusiasts were planning to meet at the Bayard Cutting Arboretum in Oakdale, Long Island, to form a lilac society. He attended this meeting, carrying an invitation from Alvan Grant for the group to hold the first annual meeting in Rochester. The invitation was accepted by the horticulturists present at the meeting, and Bob Clark was asked to serve as chairman of the first convention. The pressure was on Bob to provide a convention that would set a pattern for other years. In his words:

> What shall we show them? Highland Park contains one of the most complete collections of lilacs in the world, extending over 22 acres along Highland Avenue. It contains several specimens of any given variety. The Highland Park collection is distinctive because of the lilacs which John Dunbar grew from seed in the early 1900s, but even more so because of Alvan Grant's 'Rochester' and the cultivars which have resulted from Richard Fenicchia's hybridization work with 'Rochester' as a parent. These flowers have never been seen by the public. Are they distinctive? "Yes," says Reverend John L. Fiala of Medina, Ohio (one of the founding members of the Lilac Society). "They are far superior to any lilacs available from nurseries today."

One of the first steps that Bob Clark took in preparing for this first conference was to organize the Rochester Chapter of the International Lilac Society. This took place at an open meeting at the Garden Center on January 19, 1972. At the meeting, Bob Clark was elected Director of the Rochester Chapter. Richard Fenicchia, Bernard Harkness, and Alvan Grant were also members of this local chapter as well as of the parent society.

The first meeting of the International Lilac Society was held in Rochester on May 19, 20, and 21, 1972, to coincide with the local lilac season. Members of the local chapter devoted many hours in helping Bob provide a successful convention. Robert Clark, Bernard Harkness, and Mabel Harkness from the local chapter were elected to serve as directors of the International Society. Alvan Grant was presented with an "Award of Merit" for outstanding work in promoting the lilac and as originator of the 'Rochester' lilac. Richard Fenicchia was awarded the Director's Award of the International Lilac Society "for improving the Lilac through hybridization, scientific selection and selective research." This is the highest scientific horticultural award given by the society, and everyone agreed that Dick was most deserving of this recognition.

At this point in this narrative, it seems that some special space should be devoted to the 'Rochester' lilac and the Rochester strain or family of lilacs that resulted from Dick Fenicchia's hybridization program.

'Rochester' is a single lilac that displays florets with a varying number of petals mixed throughout the thyrse (flowering cluster or panicle). The majority of the florets are four- or five-petalled. However, scattered throughout many of the thyrses, one may find florets with as many as fifteen to twenty-one petals. There is no set pattern, but the variation in the petallage is one characteristic of this cultivar. Dick often refers to the multi-petalled florets as "daisies," and they do resemble the flowers of the common field daisy. Fr. Fiala, in his book entitled *Lilacs, the Genus Syringa*, published in 1988, refers to this multi-petalled characteristic as "primula-flowered." Other characteristics of

'Rochester' are as follows: the cupping of the petals of the florets; the creamy appearance of the thyrses, which is especially noticeable before it is in full bloom; the lower growing, more compact form of the overall plant; and the distinct fragrance that it offers. 'Rochester' is one of the lilacs featured in Fr. Fiala's book with a full-page, color plate. The descriptive caption that accompanies this plate reads as follows:

> *S. vulgaris,* 'Rochester' (1971). Preeminent among white flowering lilacs. Perhaps one of the finest white cultivars ever produced, but a very slow grower and difficult to propagate. This magnificent multi-petalled white seedling of 'Edith Cavell' is the work of Alvan Grant. It is a hybridizer's dream that has ushered in a whole new race of heavy textured multi-petalled lilacs called the Rochester Strain.

Fr. Fiala gives the date 1971 in his description. This was the date when it was introduced to members of the International Lilac Society, not the date when it was named (1962). In another place in his book, Fr. Fiala makes these remarks about 'Rochester':

> It turned out to be an amazing plant indeed! The florets were single yet multi-petalled, wax-like and magnificent in bloom with long well filled spikes (thyrses). As Grant's single contribution to lilacdom, it established a new plateau from which whole new races of lilacs have emerged. 'Rochester' has never been introduced into general commerce because it is difficult to propagate and grows too slowly to suit most gardeners. It remains a small plant after several years. However, once established on its own roots, it is truly a most outstanding lilac. I think it is the most outstanding lilac ever produced, both for its intrinsic beauty and also its extraordinary genetic make-up for hybridizing. Its value was immediately recognized by the International Lilac Society with a special Award of Merit. Today Rochester and its hybrids are being heavily used by hybridizers. It is the foundation of the Rochester Strain of hybrids of Richard Fenicchia and also is the center of much

177

hybridizing done by Dr. Don Egolf at the U.S. National Arboretum and my own work.

Fr. Fiala wrote the following about the part Richard Fenicchia played in the cultivation of the Rochester lilac:

> Much of the credit of bringing 'Rochester' to public notice was due to Richard Fenicchia who recognized the possibilities for its use in hybridizing. Although Dick had been involved with new plants and plant selection all of his life, hybridizing lilacs was a new venture for him. In the Highland Park greenhouses, he successfully pollinated 'Rochester' with several cultivars which he selected. From the resultant seed he raised a whole new generation of new lilacs. When these were first seen in blossom by several lilac fanciers, Dick was urged to name the best and to exhibit them at the International Lilac Society Convention held in Rochester in May, 1972 and, indeed, an outstanding feature of the convention was the introduction of six new lilac cultivars, all the result of Dick's hybridization program using Rochester as a seed parent. These six lilacs which had been growing in a park nursery as unnamed seedlings were now named to honor the memory of once prominent Rochesterians.

Chosen to receive posthumous recognition were:
- Dr. Edward Mott Moore (1814-1908)—the first president of the Park Commission. This lilac was described by Fr. Fiala as single, violet, multi-petalled, showy, and excellent.
- Bernard H. Slavin (1873-1960)—Superintendent of Parks who expanded Highland Park lilac collection, developed Durand Eastman Park, and was a plantsman extraordinaire. Fr. Fiala's description: single, white, multi-petalled, very good.
- John Dunbar (1859-1927)—Assistant Superintendent of Parks who introduced over 30 lilac cultivars. Single, light-violet, multi-petalled, good.
- Bishop Bernard J. McQuaid (1823-1909)—founder of the Roman Catholic diocese of Rochester and member of the

Board of Park Commissioners. Single, multi-petalled, purple, very fine to excellent.

- Frederick Douglas (1817-1895)—editor of the *North Star* and an early abolitionist. Single, magenta, multi-petalled, very fine.
- George Ellwanger (1816-1902)—partner of Ellwanger and Barry Mt. Hope Nursery and a co-donor of the first parcel of land for Highland Park, and also of many plants, including about 50 lilacs. Single, moderate purple, very fine.

Also included in this introduction was a seventh lilac named for Dwight D. Eisenhower (1890-1969), 34th President of the United States—single, multi-petalled lilac, pale blue, brushed lavender, heavy bloomer, very showy, excellent.

At the same time (1972), a dozen or more of Dick's lilac seedlings were set aside for future introduction. Fr. Fiala has this to say about 'Flower City,' which was named in 1983: "exceptionally outstanding, one of the finest in a special class, excellent." 'Flower City' is a single, deep purple violet, a landmark in lilac breeding. Dick continued to work in the hybridizing and raising of lilacs throughout his entire career in the park system. In his book, Fr. Fiala wrote, "The lasting tribute to Fenicchia is that he first recognized and used 'Rochester' in hybridizing and opened the way for others to follow. Meanwhile, other hybridizers, taking their cue from Fenicchia's genius, have begun to use 'Rochester', as difficult as it is to obtain, in various other crossings with equal success and with outstanding variations. New hybrids are being introduced yearly."

Fr. Fiala also mentions the first and second generation from Fenicchia's crosses showing amazing color variations, from pale pastels to pearled colors not seen before in lilacs, as well as the number of dwarf and low-growing forms excellent for rock gardens and Japanese gardens. Again quoting from Fr. Fiala's book, "For his work Richard Fenicchia received the highest award from the International Lilac Society, a richly deserved recognition! There are still many seedlings among those raised by Dick that are well worth naming."

In developing the Rochester strain of lilac cultivars, some of which were named in Fr. Fiala's book, Dick crossed the following five named varieties with 'Rochester' serving as the pistillate or seed parent:

- 'Mme. Charles Souchet'—single bluish;
- 'Dusk'—single purple;
- 'Edward J. Gardner'—silvery pink, double;
- 'Sensation'—single purple bicolor (florets bordered with white); and
- 'Glory'—single magenta.

The plants used had been potted in the fall of 1959 and were forced into bloom in the greenhouse, with the actual crossing taking place in mid-January 1960. The resulting lilacs are all considered first-generation hybrids.

In an interview that Richard Fenicchia had with Bill Beeny, a reporter for the Rochester *Democrat and Chronicle*, in May 1974, he pointed out, "The care and breeding of lilacs is only about 10 percent of our work. When the lilac blooms are gone, no one cares about lilacs. We're doing all sorts of other things." What Dick really meant was that the general public quickly loses interest in lilacs after they stop their annual blooming, but there is still much work to be done with them to get ready for the year that follows, the next period of bloom. Dick said:

> In perpetuating the lilac collection, there are four principal ways to create new bushes: by using cuttings, by division, by grafting, and by hybridizing which involves the manual pollination of a selected plant and the gathering and planting of the seeds which result.
>
> Cuttings are simply small branches cut from an existing bush. They are planted in pure sand where they should develop roots after a period of several weeks.
>
> Divisions are shoots (suckers) which spread at the base of a bush and have small root structures. They are planted in pots where they develop a larger root system and are later

planted outside. [Note: Often suckers are planted directly in the soil, outside where the planter wants them to be.]

As for grafting, we usually do this during the winter by using some pencil size twigs from existing bushes and placing them on privet root stock. After they have gained some growth, in a year or two or three, we replant the resulting plants in the nursery. The three methods that I have mentioned so far all reproduce the true plant from which the branches (twigs) have been taken. In three or four years more you have a pretty good bush.

Hybridizing is the way you create new varieties or cultivars. It is also a process which calls for plenty of patience. It's a long process. For example, on January 14, 1960, in the greenhouse, we cross-pollinated the 'Rochester' lilac with Mme. Charles Souchet lilac. We used a small camel hair brush to take some of the pollen from Mme. Souchet and put it on the stigma of a 'Rochester' blossom after first removing the male parts from the 'Rochester' blossom. We did this to about twenty blossoms. When the seeds formed, we collected the seed pods before they had opened. We dried them for a few days and then opened them. You get four to five seeds from each pod about 40 to 80 seeds from the 20 blossoms. Then you plant the seeds in flats in the greenhouse. After the seedlings have grown for about a year you put them into little pots. Two or three years later, when they have grown to eight or more inches tall, you move them to the nursery. They stay in the nursery anywhere from two to four years before they bloom. So that process takes up to seven or eight years from the time you planted the seeds. When the resultant seedlings have grown sufficiently large in size, they are ready for transplanting into permanent locations. While in the nursery, they are carefully nurtured and observed at regular intervals until they first bloom. You don't really know what you have until that happens. Incidentally, throughout this whole period of time, we haven't pruned or fertilized very much because you might build up to a plant that isn't true, isn't natural. We can have 2000 plants in the nursery. We select about 100 of these for further examination. Then we re-select the next year and hope to come up with six or more varieties that are worthy of naming. It's a long process. You don't do this just for the fun of it. We try to perpetuate the collection and to develop improved varieties. With the 'Rochester' lilac we were hoping to get the desired traits of this lilac into new varieties with different coloring. The Rochester strain has these characteristics: dwarf, compact grower, blooms little later than most of the French Lilacs, flower has from 4 to 21 petals in some of its florets, bloom stands straight up like a candle and doesn't fade in the sun. 'Rochester' itself is a creamy white with cupped florets.

In this interview, Dick omitted to mention open pollination, where seeds are collected from selected plants and planted in flats in the greenhouse. The resultant seedlings are grown on as Dick has stated. If variations from the parent seed-bearing plant are discovered, you may have a new cultivar. This was the history with 'Rochester.'

Robert Clark continued as Taxonomist with the Monroe County Department of Parks until his resignation in late 1973. Upon leaving the park system, he returned to his family home in Meredith, New Hampshire, where he maintains his own private arboretum with its own collection of lilacs. Bob has stayed very active in the International Lilac Society and worked closely with Fr. Fiala as he prepared his book *Lilacs, the Genus Syringa*. Bob also served as editor of the quarterly *Journal of the International Lilac Society* until the last quarter of 1993.

Appointed to succeed Robert Clark as Plant Taxonomist for the Park Department was James Kelly. Jim was born in Rochester on December 25, 1939. At the age of seven he developed an interest in plants and the following year he had his first garden and also a collection of houseplants. Two years later he joined the Rochester Garden Club and was their youngest member. While in high school he became interested in chemistry and majored in it at the

University of Toronto, from which he graduated in 1962. He later realized that his true interest was botany, but he had only taken classes in it for two semesters while at the university. He then attended the University of Rochester and Geneseo State College at night and on Saturdays to build up a suitable background in the biological sciences. He attended graduate school at Geneseo from 1967 to 1969 and graduated in 1973 upon completing his thesis. He worked with Dr. Herman S. Forest of Geneseo College in floristic studies of the Conesus Lake Inlet Swamp and the slopes of Irondequoit Bay, and assisted him on field trips to the Fallbrook area of Geneseo.

Jim had been working as an analytical chemist at Fine Organics Corporation in Sayreville, New Jersey, until he received the appointment as Taxonomist with the county park system. Jim continued with the duties that had formerly been performed by Robert Clark, and by Bernard Harkness and Richard Horsey, duties that had been considered vital to the proper operation of the Rochester arboretum for over 80 years of its existence.

Upon several occasions during the late 1960s and early 1970s, the Monroe County Park Department participated in the annual Home and Garden Show held in the War Memorial. A typical example of these exhibits arranged by Dick and his crew would be the transformation in the spring of 1973 of a 3,000-square-foot area in the basement of the War Memorial into a lovely display of evergreens interspersed with colorful spring flowers.

"All of the material was grown in the Highland Park greenhouses and will be planted in the parks after they are removed from the show," said Dick. "There are a few particularly unusual plants. See this shrub; it's a pendulous American Yew 'invented' many years ago by Barney Slavin, the father of the Rochester Park system. There are only two of them in the parks."

Dick himself is responsible for these spruce, which grow naturally in a beautiful global fashion. There were also other spruce, Douglas fir, yew, and arborvitae, as well as crabapples and a Pacific Coast dogwood, azaleas, tulips, hyacinths, daffodils, primroses, calceolarias, and cinerarias in full bloom. The city administrators and councilmen had considered participation in events such as this as an act of good public relations for city government. The same feeling now prevailed among the county leaders, and each year the Park Department was encouraged to set up another display.

With the retirement of Art Blensinger in June 1973, the park system lost one of its most dedicated employees. An expert woodsman, unparalleled in his concern for "his Durand Eastman Park," Art spent Sundays (his day off) roaming through the park looking for tree seedlings that he could move to other locations, where they would eventually add to the beauty of the park. He always carried sharp pruning shears with which he would trim out any undesirable growth that might "catch his eye." At the age of ninety in 1993, Art can occasionally be found looking over the landscape that he helped to build in this park.

Beginning in the late 1960s, it became common knowledge that the County Penitentiary, the Department of Social Services of Monroe County, and other county agencies would be vacating the buildings they had occupied for a number of years. These buildings were located on thirty-nine acres of land owned by the county. This land extended from Highland Avenue to Elmwood Avenue, with approximately 1,500 feet of frontage along South Avenue beginning north of the area occupied by Al Sigl Center and extending to Highland Avenue.

As early as 1966, Park Director Alvan Grant had gone on record requesting the dedication of the penitentiary land (the entire thirty-nine acres) for park purposes, specifically as an annex to Highland Park. Inasmuch as some of the plants in the park collections were at mature size, they were becoming overcrowded and there was no room for the planting of new species and varieties as they were introduced. The penitentiary land, because of its proximity to Highland Park, would be an ideal location for the expansion of the collections. Also at this time, a real interest in the tourism value of the lilac collection was beginning. This created a demand for more parking space and for concessions to accommodate the many visitors. Dedication of the penitentiary property for park purposes would provide the necessary space to take much of the "wear and tear" away from the park proper.

As the word spread that this land was being vacated by the county agencies, requests for the use of the land came from several sources, specific among which were the city school district, Al Sigl Center, St. John's Home, and also several entrepreneurs interested in using the site for townhouses, high-rise apartments, condominiums, professional office buildings, and motels.

Beginning in 1970, the struggle to gain use of this land began in earnest. Many meetings were held with members of the county legislature and neighborhood groups (who supported park use) and the various other parties seeking use of the land. In January 1974, a special task force of citizens, to be known as the Penitentiary Landsite Committee, was appointed by County Manager Lucien Morin, who had succeeded Gordon Howe in January 1972, to study and recommend how this county land should be used. In November 1974, this committee submitted a summary of its study, which stated, "After a comprehensive review of input received by this committee, it is the opinion of the Penitentiary Landsite Committee that the acreage under consideration be utilized as parkland along the lines suggested by the County Park Department."

Among the major considerations were naturalistic landscape plantings, display gardens, educational plantings, and a nursery. After the Park and Recreation Committee of the County Legislature had reviewed the study summary, it unanimously recommended that the land be dedicated as parkland, and at its meeting on November 29, 1974, the county legislature adopted a resolution formally dedicating the former penitentiary land as parkland.

A report on the soils found within this area had been made for the Landsite Committee by Robert L. Hafner, Conservationist of the Soil and Water Conservation District. This report stated, "This site has a wide variety of soils for such a small area! Soils on

185

the site are so widely varied in their characteristics that they are well suited to a wide variety of plants."

Dick Fenicchia put this implied endorsement of the soil for nursery purposes to immediate test by expanding the small nursery that he had previously established on part of this land. He also initiated a long-range program of landscaping this area by immediately preparing and planting much of the area to lawn for the purpose of easy maintenance until other plantings could be put into place. Dick also planted some special fastigiate English oaks along the South Avenue frontage of the property. Several acres of the property with entrance from South Avenue could be used for parking during Lilac Time and for special events at Highland Bowl. Major development of the site would have to be postponed until funding was made available.

In December 1974, Mrs. John C. Trahey made a gift of twenty acres of land to be added to Webster Park. This land abuts the northwesterly wooded section of the park and has 600 feet of frontage on Lake Road. In making this gift, Mrs. Trahey stated, "It is a pleasure to make a gift of my property fronting on the Lake Road and adjoining the west side of Webster Park to the County of Monroe to be used for additional park purposes. I am familiar with the outstanding work which has been performed for years by Alvan R. Grant, Director of Monroe County Parks, in improving our splendid park system. In making this gift, I wish to honor my mother, Mrs. William B. Hale, and my aunt, Miss Kate B. Andrews, who conveyed the property to me many years ago."

The agreement between the County of Monroe and the City of Rochester whereby the county took over the operation of certain city-owned park areas, which had taken effect on July 13, 1961, was for a period of thirty years. Beginning in 1971, the agreement became the cause of some problems for a park director who was in favor of initiating a program of capital improvements within the park system. It was brought to Al Grant's attention that it is not legally possible for the county to borrow funds for capital development on property that it would not have jurisdiction over for the full life of the bonds. Most municipal bonds for park development were for a period of twenty years. After July 13, 1971, the county's jurisdiction over the city park areas dropped below the twenty-year period. After many meetings with the county legislature, the county administration, and representatives of the city, a solution was worked out, and in July 1975 the county legislature approved amending the original agreement to a period of ninety-nine years and also added three more city-owned areas: the Rose Garden area at Maplewood Park, Lower Falls Park, and Tryon Park, east of the Sea Breeze Expressway.

After the original agreement went into effect in 1961, the City Recreation and Park Bureau had been responsible for the care of the Rose Garden. Because that bureau was primarily responsible for the recreation program within the city and had limited funds for operation of its total program, it was understandable that it had allowed the maintenance of the Rose Garden to slip. For a few years after the amending of the agreement, the County Park Department was able to restore the garden to an acceptable state. Charles Grande, a young man with considerable landscaping and gardening experience, was hired as foreman of this garden under the supervision of Dick Fenicchia. The Rochester Rose Society cooperated by staging workshops at the garden and through volunteering assistance upon many occasions.

Early in 1976, Lucien A. Morin, then County Executive of Monroe County (succeeding Gordon Howe, who retired on December 31, 1971), sent out a news release that stated, "Not only is 1976 an important year for the United States as it celebrates its Bicentennial, it is also an extremely significant year for the Monroe County Park system which is celebrating its 50th year, for it was on October 2, 1926 that the Monroe County Parks Commission held its organizational meeting. At its meeting on December 15, 1926, this Commission accepted a gift of 210 acres of land by the Ellison family. That land became the first Monroe County Park."

In this news release, while outlining the various features of the park system, Mr. Morin made a special mention of Springdale

Farm in Northampton Park, which had become a new feature in the county park system during 1975, when he stated that "in effect, this farm and the program which it will offer, will serve as a lasting memorial to the Bicentennial of the Country." This new park located in the Towns of Ogden and Sweden resulted from successful negotiations with 40 different owners. These negotiations began in 1964 and extended into December 1966. The last parcel to be acquired was, at the time, an operating farm of 132+ acres complete with house, barns, and several small sheds. Al Grant proposed that, with very little renovation work, this parcel be maintained as a farm dedicated to the youth of Monroe County, an area where children and adults (it became very popular with senior citizens) could come to view farm animals and learn something about farm procedures. They might have an opportunity to milk a cow, bottle-feed a small pig, participate in some small farm chore, or perhaps enjoy a ride in a horse-drawn wagon.

At about the same time, a committee of volunteers working with the Association of Retarded Citizens of the Al Sigl complex of social agencies was searching for an area where some of the constituent citizens could become involved in a work therapy program. With approval from the county manager and the legislature, an opportunity was given whereby selected members of this group were permitted to participate in some horticultural activities at Springdale Farm. In fact, they were assigned a garden area where they grew vegetables, which were sold at a small market area back at Al Sigl Center. The participants in this program were transported to and from the farm by vehicles furnished by the Al Sigl Center and were accompanied by an employee of the center. This proved to be a worthwhile program for the center inasmuch as the participants learned how to do some horticultural chores that prepared them for programs that were later made available to them throughout the community.

At Lilac Time 1976, Richard Fenicchia was presented with the annual Lilac Time Award for his many contributions in the field of horticulture and in the breeding of new plants, including the Rochester strain of lilacs. One of these was named 'Bicentennial' during the 1976 festivities in honor of the 200th birthday of the United States. At the same ceremony, on May 27, Professor Donald Egolf, botanist and hybridizer from the National Arboretum in Washington, D.C., was given the National Award for his contributions in the field of horticulture and plant breeding.

Richard Fenicchia's broad interest in plants and their perpetuation is apparent in an interview that Bill Beany, a former reporter with the Rochester *Democrat and Chronicle*, had with him in October 1976. The following is taken from that interview:

> Just as there will always be an England, there will always be American Chestnut trees. There are presently more than 150 genuine American Chestnut trees in the Monroe County Park system. The life span of the American Chestnut is not great, probably a twenty year maximum. The blight which struck down thousands of these trees in the 1930s was a fungus disease that came to the United States from Asia. It spread through windblown spores and within two years every Chestnut tree in the east was killed. The blight destroys the tree from the ground up. It doesn't kill the roots. New shoots come up and the tree is reborn. The unfortunate thing is that the new tree is still subject to the blight. Eventually it too will die. Some trees, the ones which grow from the new shoots, are stronger than others. They are more resistant to the blight and may live 20 years. However, none of the American Chestnuts are immune; some are disease resistant. There always are the new shoots to live and last as long as they can. That's why I say there will always be an American Chestnut.

Dick began his program to try to restore the American chestnut in 1951 when he found two trees growing in Durand Eastman Park. According to Dick:

> They were in bad shape, puny and as crooked as a dog's hind leg. I took them to the nursery in Highland Park and brought them back to health. They grew to about 40 feet tall after I set them out in the park. But after about 22 years they got the blight and died. Not without contributing

something, however. Some trees matured enough to set seed. I harvested enough seed from those trees to grow 200 new trees in the nursery. Mendon Ponds Park has about 100 trees, some over 30 feet tall. Highland Park has 40 and Churchville Park about twelve. I deliberately scattered these in different locations. But you have to remember this—none are immune to the disease, but some are resistant to a certain extent. The tree doesn't die until the trunk is girdled, which explains how sometimes a blighted tree will heal over and will survive for several years until the disease hits again. After seedlings are started in the nursery, they form a tap root in the spring and the tree grows to a height of three to four feet in two years. Then it is set in the field.

A lot of people are working on chestnut propagation, but I doubt that any of them have as many plants as we have in our nursery. . . . The significance of the whole program really is to try and save some trees and thereby possibly learn ways to control the diseases that strike other trees and crops. Some of the maples and oaks are getting attacked by a form of blight. We want to know more about ways to stop this on all trees.

Through the several horticultural organizations with which he was affiliated, Dick Fenicchia was in contact with most of the leading horticulturists in the United States and Canada. There was a natural overlap of these organizations. Consequently, any special skill or knowledge that a person might possess became known to his peers and would be "tapped" by the others upon occasion. Dick's work in Rochester in the hybridization and propagation of plants, his knowledge of the work of Dunbar and Slavin, and the wide range of plants to which he was exposed in the local park system established him as a real source of information.

Dick willingly complied with any request for information, and his correspondence with other professionals as well as with the average homeowner was often equal to that of the taxonomist.

An example of one of Dick's letters, dated September 12, 1978, in answer to a questionnaire sent to him by Dr. L. C. Chadwick, Professor Emeritus in Horticulture at Ohio State University and author of several books about trees, shrubs, and other plant materials, can be found in the Appendix.

On December 14, 1976, in recognition of the first 200 years in the history of this country, the Real Estate Board of Rochester, New York, hosted a special dinner, a Bicentennial Salute, during which it cited five individuals, seven organizations, and the City of Rochester. One of the individuals was Alvan R. Grant. This citation, mounted on a beautiful wooden plaque, read as follows:

A BICENTENNIAL SALUTE TO
Alvan R. Grant
for distinguished abilities and unselfish service
given to the greater Rochester Community
AND IN PARTICULAR FOR
Monroe County Parks Development
December 14, 1976
Presented by Make America Beautiful Committee of the
Real Estate Board of Rochester, N.Y., Inc.

After 32 years of service with the park systems of the City of Rochester and the County of Monroe, Alvan Grant resigned from the position of Monroe County Parks Director, effective March 12, 1977. In accepting his resignation, County Manager Lucien Morin stated in part as follows:

> Your many years of faithful productive services to this community and more particularly your notable contribution to the Monroe County Parks system are gratefully recognized and appreciated by all of us.

> The accomplishments and innovated development of the parks and recreational facilities which occurred under your tenure will stand as a lasting tribute to you and those who worked with you during your 32 years of loyal service to our community.

I know there have been some frustrating times and also realize that some of your plans and ideas may not have been fully realized. You may gain some measure of satisfaction in knowing you leave a goal for those who will continue your work and those of us who appreciate the meaning of your wish for our parks.

I shall miss your wise counsel, your support, loyalty, understanding, and most of all, your friendship.

In Mr. Morin's message there was a hint at the reason for Al Grant's resignation when he stated, "there have been some frustrating times and some of your plans and ideas may not have been fully realized." The years of the mid-1970s were very frustrating. The Park Department had been the victim of a "hold-the-line" policy. Budget cuts had resulted in reductions in manpower at a time when there was considerable pressure for development of some of the new areas. The key word in Mr. Morin's message was "frustration," which, coupled with a period of poor health, had influenced Alvan Grant to retire.

Evidence of Dick Fenicchia's widespread interest in the hybridization of plants was on display at the retirement party for Alvan Grant on March 18, 1977. This writer remembers with pleasure the outstanding amaryllis that decorated the podium and the speaker's table. Those huge, red, orange, and yellow lily-like blooms on strong stems resulted from hybridization undertaken by Dick.

Beginning in the 1940s and throughout his tenure with the park system, Al Grant had been associated with the Garden Center of Rochester. On many occasions he had conducted classes and given lectures on horticultural subjects, and also had prepared articles for the *Bulletin*. In the roster of officers that was printed in the *Bulletin* for several years, he was listed as "Consultant." In the years when the Garden Center was housed in the old herbarium building in Highland Park, "Consultant" meant that he was the person who was called whenever there was an emergency of some kind. Upon several occasions, the emergency was "a skunk under the building." By use of a hose attached to the exhaust pipe of a park vehicle, the skunk could be persuaded to leave the premises.

During the years when he was Director of Parks for the city, and then with the county, Wilbur Wright had served as president of the Garden Center's board of trustees. After Wright resigned from employment with the county in 1965 to move to employment with the state, Alvan Grant was elected to the position of President of the Board to succeed Wright, and he continued to serve in that capacity until 1988. During his last two years as president, new bylaws were prepared for the Garden Center and a change of policy resulted in the introduction of a salaried director for this not-for-profit organization.

With full cooperation from the board of trustees, the Garden Center director coordinates the activities of the volunteers and has initiated many new programs. The emphasis of the Garden Center is focused on horticulture and its relationship to the community. Although the Garden Center is completely independent from the Park Department, it supplements the program of that department through the programs it offers. Al Grant continues to serve on the board of trustees of this outstanding community institution at the time of this writing. After his retirement from the Park Department in December 1978, Richard Fenicchia would become a volunteer at the Garden Center, serving as a horticultural advisor. In this capacity, he devotes several hours each week to visiting the Garden Center and responding to questions on gardening and plant culture as they are called in by people seeking help in solving their garden problems.

On March 14, 1977, County Executive Lucien Morin announced the appointment of Calvin Reynolds to the position of Monroe County Park Director. In his announcement, Mr. Morin stated, "As Deputy Parks Director, a position he attained in August, 1976, Reynolds worked closely with the Park Director, helping formulate policy and operation procedures."

Very early in Cal Reynolds's tenure as Director of Parks, county government was reorganized in an effort to reduce the

193

number of county bureaucrats who were reporting directly to the county executive. As a result of this reorganization, the Park Department was placed under the administrative supervision of the commissioner of public works. As Director of Parks, Cal was still responsible for the operation and programs of the department. However, his contacts with the county administration and the legislature were now channeled through the commissioner. This relieved Cal from having to attend many meetings with the county administration, but, at the same time, it may have taken away from him the opportunity to present new projects that had been in the department's plans for several years. (Alvan Grant had prepared a long-range plan for park development, which he presented to the county executive and legislature in 1966. This served as a guide for the five-year capital program that departments were required to submit each year to the administration for approval before submission to the legislature.)

Unfortunately, much of the frustration that Al Grant felt during the mid-1970s carried over into Cal Reynolds's tenure as Park Director. The county was involved in several major and costly programs: sewer improvements, construction of a new terminal at the airport, and other upgrading of infrastructure. These programs, coupled with the ever-increasing cost of social and medical services, created a situation that mandated the curbing of many other desirable new programs of capital improvement, including those proposed by the Park Department, and also resulted in a cutback in the manpower assigned to the department. One program in particular that suffered from this cutback was the Maplewood Rose Garden, which was no longer assigned any full-time employees. Consequently, the lack of adequate maintenance soon became apparent. The city then agreed to take back the responsibility of caring for this garden with a promise of some volunteer assistance from the Rochester Rose Society.

It was during Cal Reynolds's tenure as Director of Parks that a nonprofit corporation known as Monroe County People for Parks Inc. was formed. Despite its name, this organization is entirely independent from Monroe County government and from the Park Department. It also was formed without any input from

Calvin Reynolds. It does, however, seem relevant to mention it at this time.

When he was Director of Parks, Alvan Grant had attended all meetings of the county legislature. In fact, it was a mandate of the county manager that all department heads be present at these meetings. Of special interest and concern were the annual budget hearings held prior to the legislators' voting on the budget as proposed by the administration. At these hearings, Grant had observed that many citizens, often as members of organized groups, appeared to support their special interests (Veterans' Bureau, day care, museum, art gallery, etc.). It seemed that there was never anyone present speaking out in favor of the park system or some of its programs that were under threat of being cut back or eliminated.

As a result of his observations, in 1976 Grant was able to recruit several local citizens who had special interest in the parks to work with him in establishing a support group to be known as People for Parks. Working closely with him was Richard Fenicchia, who was deeply concerned about the future of the park arboretums and the plant collections. In October 1979, with the assistance of an attorney whom Fenicchia had counseled in the landscaping of his property, this organization became incorporated as Monroe County People for Parks, Inc. under Section 402 of the Not-for-Profit Corporation Law of New York State.

The purpose of People for Parks (as it is commonly known), as stated in its certificate of incorporation, is as follows:

a. to provide support for the state, county, town, village, and city parks in Monroe County so that these parks will effectively serve the diverse needs of the public for leisure time activities and still maintain the essential characteristics of a "sanctuary for people"—a place to escape the harried pace of modern living and to participate in such activities that are in harmony with the environment and with each other.

195

b. to focus public and governmental attention, not only on the uses and benefits of the present park system, but also on the importance of continued growth and expansion of the park system.

c. to serve as a communication link between the parks, the public and governmental representatives.

d. to assist and cooperate with the county of Monroe, the city of Rochester, and the towns and villages of the county in the planning, evaluation, and implementation of capital improvements and recreational activities.

e. to foster and promote the preservation of open spaces and natural resources and to educate the public and government as to their significance.

During the years that have followed the founding of People for Parks, members have been attending many meetings throughout the county in carrying out the purposes as expressed above. Although at times it may seem adversarial to some governmental officials, the aim of People for Parks is to ensure that the public is heard and that the parks will best serve the people who use them. Perhaps the preservation of natural areas and of the arboretum is the greatest challenge that lies before this organization. These two fundamental parts of the park heritage must be protected for the use, education, and enjoyment of the residents of this county at the present, and for the generations of the future.

Twenty months after Cal Reynolds became Director of Parks, Dick Fenicchia, having reached the age of 70, retired in December 1978. At one time in park history, the retirement of an employee with the responsibilities such as those assigned to Dick would have been a matter of great concern to the park director. However, although Cal realized the great contribution that Dick was still capable of making, conditions of employment within local government had changed greatly since the 1930s when Dick had been forced to leave the park system because of a change in the politics of municipal government.

Beginning with the introduction of Civil Service and the employee unions in the late 1940s, employees had gained some guarantee of longevity with the city or county. As a result, more young people began to consider long-term employment by municipalities as a viable career. This really worked to the advantage of the County Park Department and its horticultural program during the 1960s.

Robert Hoepfl, who was appointed to succeed Dick as Superintendent of Horticulture, had worked with him since the early 1960s. Bob had begun his career with the park system while still in high school, working during summer vacations, a procedure he continued after enrolling at Farmingdale Agricultural and Technical College, where he majored in horticultural studies. After completing his courses in 1964, he became a permanent employee assigned to Highland Park under Dick's supervision.

In 1970, Bob was joined by Louis Fenicchia, a nephew of Dick's, who came from a family of down-to-earth gardeners and horticulturists. Louis proved to be a valuable member of Dick's group of "young men," with his practical experience greatly supplementing the academic background the others had attained.

A third member of this group is John Stewart, who joined the Monroe County Parks Department in 1970 after completing his horticultural studies at Alfred Agricultural and Technical College.

In 1975, Kent Millham, who had graduated from Cornell University, where he majored in floriculture and ornamental horticulture, became an employee of the County Parks Department. Dick's group that he "was leaving behind" was almost complete.

A new member, definitely not a "young man," was a young lady named Noelle Nagel, who had majored in botanical studies at the State University College at Geneseo.

For several years after Dick retired there was one other member in this group who had an important role in maintaining the reputation of Highland Park (plus other park areas) as a leading arboretum. This employee was the Taxonomist, James Kelly, who, following the example set by Richard Horsey and Bernard Harkness, took a real interest in keeping the many plants throughout the parks correctly named and labeled. During the 1980s, Jim developed a new checklist of all of the woody plants and entered this information on a computer, listing the plants in alphabetical order. Jim also guided the firm of Dole and Dole, which was under contract with the Park Department, in the computer mapping of some of the park areas. He was also involved in the propagation of some special plants, which was underway in the greenhouses.

During 1993, Jim was removed from the county payroll as a result of what this author considers ill-advised orders issued by County Executive Robert King and Park Director Dean Spong. The position of Taxonomist and Curator of the Herbarium (not always listed as such, but embracing the same duties) had existed within the park system for almost 100 years, and was responsible to a large degree for the park system receiving worldwide recognition as an arboretum. This is a level of prestige earned by very few public park systems. The termination of Jim Kelly has placed an additional burden upon the other members of this group of horticulturists, and this at a time when their workload has been increased due to the reduction of several subordinate positions with the department.

At the time of his retirement, Dick Fenicchia had stated, "It's now time to give the young men whom I am leaving behind in the parks a chance to do what I have done." He, of course, was referring to the cadre of young people described in the several paragraphs preceding this one. His statement was, in reality, a challenge to these young people, one that they accepted and began immediately to meet. Bob Hoepfl has furnished the necessary supervision and has the responsibility for making assignments to the others. He also has been attempting to ensure that some of the duties of the taxonomist—record keeping, labeling, etc.—are continued. The propagation and growing of the many plants for conservatory display and for decorative planting throughout the park system became the responsibility of Louis Fenicchia, who now had the title of Horticulturist. He was ably assisted by Kent Millham, Greenhouse Person. They have also been producing thousands of plants under contract with the City of Rochester for planting within city areas. John Stewart, while serving as Assistant Superintendent of Horticulture, also has as a basic assignment the operation and maintenance of Highland Park. Noelle Nagel, whose title is Horticultural Interpreter, has as her direct responsibility the care and maintenance of the displays at the conservatory. Despite their individual assignments, the group works as a team, complementing each other in the care of Highland Park and the conservatory and in the total horticultural program of the Park Department.

In the early 1980s, the Monroe County Planning Department initiated a program of long-range planning for park and recreation development in Monroe County—this, of course, with the cooperation of the director of parks. One proposal in this program was the establishment of hiking and biking trails throughout the county. Teams of volunteers were assigned the tasks of thoroughly inspecting selected locations to determine the feasibility as well as the features of proposed trails, most of which were along small creeks and abandoned railroad rights-of-way. One trail that was acquired as a result of this program was the former Lehigh RR course through the Towns of Rush and Mendon from the Genesee River to the Ontario County line. This trail is now under the jurisdiction of the Park Department.

Don Yeager resigned in June 1983, and Karen Riggs, a young lady who had joined the park staff in January 1976 as a horticultural aide, was put in charge of the interpretive program. Karen was responsible for the preparation of several informational brochures that would assist the public in becoming better acquainted with their county parks. Also, under Karen's direction, special attention was given to the establishment of an interpretive program at Springdale Farm in Northampton Park. This area soon became a favorite with many family groups, schoolchildren, and senior citizens. Don Hammond, who had been an assistant to Don Yeager in the nature program in Mendon Ponds Park, was placed in charge of the Interpretation Center and the nature program in that park. Karen later was appointed Superintendent of Recreation and Education, but resigned in January 1990 to return to her home state of Ohio.

During the last years of Cal Reynolds's tenure as Park Director, there was a change in the attitude toward park improvements. From a viewpoint of horticulture, plans were underway for the development of the former penitentiary property at Highland Park and for conservatory renovation. Renovation of Ontario Beach Park had also been started. Completion of these projects, however, would take place after Cal's successor was appointed. Also during Reynolds's tenure, considerable reorganization of departmental staff was undertaken. This had perhaps the greatest effect at Genesee Valley and Durand Eastman Parks, where instead of having two employees with supervisory responsibilities in each park, a greenskeeper in charge of the golf course and a park supervisor in charge of the park, one supervisor (the greenskeeper) would have the overall responsibility. The effects of this change would show up in the future, especially at Durand Eastman Park.

When Calvin Reynolds retired in August 1985, Dean David Spong was appointed to succeed him as Director of Parks. Dean, a graduate from Michigan State University, where he majored in landscape architecture, had served as assistant to Cal when he was Park Planner. With Cal's promotion to Director of Parks, Dean had been promoted to Park Planner and while in that capacity had also served in the capacity of Assistant to the Director.

Although Dick Fenicchia had retired in 1978, he found it to be difficult to completely leave the park system and the plants with which he had been involved while on the payroll. He was not content in "puttering around" on the land that he owns in the Town of Webster, where he maintains a small nursery. He has spent many hours worrying about the future of the Monroe County parks, particularly those owned by the city but under county jurisdiction. According to Dick:

> This is something that I am very concerned about. We have tremendous arboretums here. Highland Park is known worldwide for its plants. We would get calls from as far away as Italy wanting seeds we have developed here. We sent seeds out, and we also got hundreds of packets of seeds from every country including Russia, except for China. What I'm concerned about is the maintenance of the collections at Highland Park of Rhododendrons, Azaleas, Maples, Oaks, Lindens, Magnolias, Conifers, and, of course, the Lilacs and the arboretums in Durand Eastman, Seneca and Genesee Valley Parks, although they are on a smaller scale.

In 1988, the results of Dick's work with lilacs were still making horticultural history. On May 20th of that year, the first 'George Eastman' lilac was planted in the grounds of the International Museum of Photography at the George Eastman House on East Avenue. This lilac originated from a natural seedling of *Syringa julianae* discovered by Dick in Durand Eastman Park in 1965. (Note: *Syringa julianae* is now classified as *Syringa pubescens* subsp. *julianae*.) He had propagated several bushes using cuttings taken from that bush. These had been evaluated by Robert Clark, former Taxonomist of the Monroe County park system, and by Fr. John Fiala, a lilac fancier and breeder from Cleveland, Ohio, during several visits they made to Rochester during the 1970s. After several years of observing this lilac, they determined that the habit of growth and the color of the bloom warranted it to be named. The 'George Eastman' lilac has reddish buds that open into magenta-reddish flowers. It comes into bloom somewhat later than the average lilac in the Highland Park collection. It was named and registered in 1981 by Fr. Fiala, giving credit to Dick Fenicchia as the originator.

The naming of this lilac was followed in 1990 by the naming of still another lilac from Dick's family of 'Rochester' lilacs. This one was the result of some cross-pollinating that Dick had done using 'Rochester' as the seed parent and was named 'Frederick Law Olmsted' in honor of Olmsted, who had developed landscape plans for Highland Park during the 1890s. 'Frederick Law Olmsted' is a magnificent white lilac with very large thryses. It was judged the "best in Highland Park" during the 1992 and 1993 Lilac Time by Dick Fenicchia and Al Grant as they made their annual inspection of the lilac collection.

In November 1989, Alvan Grant was chosen to receive the Hugh E. Cummings Environmental Quality Award, presented annually by the Center for Environmental Information, Inc. In presenting this award, Rudolph C. Gabel, chairman of the awards committee, cited among Grant's contributions the following: "Expansion of Monroe County park lands from about 5,000 acres to more than 11,000 acres. Efforts in promoting nature education. Development of a lilac bearing the city's name." In response, Grant urged those present at the award dinner to keep themselves aware of the county parks and to speak out for them whenever they are threatened in any way. County Executive Tom Frey, in submitting his budget for 1990, had proposed a $2 million cut in the park budget.

In September 1991, Dick made a scouting trip through Durand Eastman Park to assess the damage that had resulted from the ice storm of March of that year. In Pine Valley he found that some of the pines with long, protruding branches had taken a real beating and these had to be cut close to the trunks. Also, several trees, both deciduous and coniferous, had been uprooted. Dick's overall assessment was that Durand Eastman Park was in need of a vigorous renovation program, which would include clearing out brush that had been allowed to develop to the extent that it was crowding out specimen plants that need some room to survive, control of the deer and beaver population that have wreaked damage in certain areas of the park, careful selective pruning on many specimen plants, replanting, and, of course, following through on storm-related problems. He definitely feels that Durand Eastman Park is too valuable an asset to the park system and the county to allow it to continue to deteriorate.

In 1991, as a member of the Town of Webster Conservation Board, Dick Fenicchia prepared a brochure relative to various trees and shrubs that should be considered for planting throughout the town. The primary purpose of this publication was to present a list of those cultivated trees and shrubs that were of proven hardiness in this area. To assist in the selection of the right plants for various locations, his brochure listed plants in three categories, with all plants being identified by both botanical and common name along with their mature height and spread and some additional description and comment.

There were four of the charter members of the International Plant Propagators Society still alive when the society held its 40th annual meeting in Cleveland, Ohio, in December 1991. Dick Fenicchia was one of these. All four had received special invitations to attend this meeting, where they were honored for their achievements in plant propagation and for their loyalty and service to the organization. Receiving special attention and honored for her contribution to the society by serving as volunteer secretary at several of the early conventions was Margaret (Marge) Fenicchia. Dick appreciated this honoring of his wife Marge more than the honors he received.

Fifteen years after his retirement, Dick is still propagating plants for the parks. He has been given the privilege of maintaining a propagating bench in the greenhouses at Highland Park, where he propagates some of the more difficult plants for the parks. He visits the Smith Road nursery (Irondequoit Bay Park East) at regular intervals from mid-April until November to check up on the many lilac seedlings and other rare plants that he planted there. Dick feels strongly that this area should be named "The Barney Slavin Arboretum" (or Test Garden) in honor of that former plantsman and park superintendent whom he considers to be one of the best horticulturists of all time. In recent years, Dick has given many plants from his private nursery to the park system for planting within Highland Park. Principally among these were several dozen fairly large rhododendrons and azaleas, which would cost hundreds of dollars if purchased from commercial nurseries.

On Saturday, May 15, 1993, during the annual Lilac Time celebration, the Garden Center of Rochester held a special ceremony during which a hybrid magnolia was named in honor of Richard A. Fenicchia. Alvan Grant had been asked to speak about Dick and his career. Here are some remarks from that brief talk:

> How often we look in far off places to find our heroes and skip over those who are close at hand. We give plaudits to someone whom we don't even know for a somewhat mundane accomplishment, but fail to recognize the many accomplishments of one whom we see at frequent intervals. . . . I am speaking of Richard A. Fenicchia. During his tenure with the park system, Dick made over three hundred crosses of Rhododendrons and Azaleas. His white flowered Rhododendron, President Kennedy, which he named about 30 years ago, received much acclaim in England. He also hybridized many other plants, trees, shrubs, perennials, and even some bulbous materials. . . . He propagated thousands of trees which have been planted along the streets throughout the city and in city and county parks. . . . Many of these were special forms of trees which had been selected from seedling lots by Barney Slavin with whom Dick worked from 1925 to 1934. Many of the shrubs which adorn our park areas today were originally started by Dick and then were grown to specimen size in the park nurseries for which he was responsible. Some of these various plant materials were shipped to other arboretums and parks in scattered locations across the United States. It is impossible in any brief period of time to recount all of the achievements of Richard A. Fenicchia or to enumerate his accomplishments. He is recognized as one of the world's outstanding propagators by the organizations with which he has been associated: the International Plant Propagators Society, the Magnolia Society, the Rhododendron Society, the International Lilac Society, and there are others.
>
> In recognition of his work in developing the Rochester family of lilacs, Dick received the highest hybridizing award given by the International Lilac Society, a richly deserved

recognition. In his book entitled *Lilacs, the Genus Syringa*, Fr. John L. Fiala wrote, "All who love lilacs will ever be grateful for the hours of work, insight and genius that have given us a whole new race of 'Rochester' strain Lilacs," and of course he was referring to Dick.

I was approached to suggest a plant which would be named in Dick's honor. In a somewhat foxy manner, I asked Dick if he was to have one of the plants which he had hybridized named for him, what it would be. I was somewhat surprised and maybe a little taken aback, considering that it was Lilac Time, that without hesitation he said, "The Magnolia hybrid which resulted from a cross that I made in 1953, *Magnolia soulangeana* forma *lennei* with *M. liliflora* var. *nigra*." This cultivar is now located in the Magnolia collection in Highland Park. The flowers are numerous, appearing before and also with the leaves. The flower is deep purple on the outside and light purple on the inside. It is a superior hybrid in many respects and has great potential as an ornamental shrub. Unlike many *M. soulangeana* hybrids it maintains its symmetry and appears not to become infested with carpenter ants as do many others. The flowers appear later which has value in that they usually escape the severe frosts which damage earlier blooming magnolias. It surpasses its parents in flower size and vigor. Dick, during Lilac Time 1993, it is my pleasure to inform you that the Magnolia cultivar that resulted from your cross of *M. soulangeana* forma *lennei* with *M. lilflora* var. *nigra* will henceforth be known as 'Fenicchia's Magnolia.'

A full description of this Magnolia cultivar, as named, is being prepared for filing with the International Registrar of Magnolia cultivars. The dedication and naming of this Magnolia, a product of his creativeness, will serve as a fitting memorial to the horticultural genius of this plantsman, Richard A. Fenicchia, who devoted most of his life to the science and art of growing plants.

205

Several projects of much significance to the park system have been in the process of development during Dean Spong's tenure as Director of Parks. Perhaps outstanding among these have been the beginning development of Greece Canal Park, improvements or new development of Ontario Beach, Ellison, and Mendon Ponds Parks, historic restoration of Genesee Valley Park, the completed renovation of Lamberton Conservatory, and the development of much of the former penitentiary property as an extension of Highland Park. There has also been a beginning in the long-range development program at Seneca Park Zoo. Plans are also being made for development in other park areas, including Highland Park.

Many of these projects had been included in proposed capital development programs for many years, but funding had never been made available. Except for the projects at Highland Park, these developments had little immediate impact upon the horticultural aspect of the park program. However, this will change in the future as new areas are in need of landscaping and planned planting.

During the fall and early winter of 1993, Dick Fenicchia was working with the Town of Webster as a volunteer in developing a small arboretum on town property. He donated many of the plants, which were dug from his nursery, and collected others through contacts he made with nurserymen and other horticulturists whom he knew from mutual membership in the plant societies to which he belonged. He has also donated many oak seedlings for planting throughout the town. He had grown several hundred of these from acorns that he had collected while on a plant exploratory trip in Arkansas in November 1982. There are plans for a plaque to be placed in the Webster arboretum in memory of Dick's wife, Margaret, who died in August 1993.

"The chance to do what I have done," as stated by Dick Fenicchia, remains a viable option for the present plantsmen within the department. All of the facilities available to Dick are still available for use by his successors, and Dick himself through the weekly visits he makes to Highland Park, as a resource of knowledge about plants and propagation of plant materials. Highland Park remains an "open-air laboratory" filled with plants for use in horticultural projects. The real challenge to the present plantsmen is not to continue to produce new cultivars, but to conduct a program of propagation that will guarantee that valuable species and cultivars of plants already in the collections will not be lost.

Highland and Durand Eastman Parks have, for many years, been among this country's leading repositories for many plants of great horticultural value. As well as subverting the heritage of the Rochester/Monroe County community, which has been enriched by these parks, it would be a real disservice to the horticultural world if these parks were permitted to be downgraded and the plant collections neglected. The present cadre of plantsmen have proven that they have the abilities to meet this challenge, but they must be given support by the county administration, the legislature, and especially the residents of this county.

ADDENDUM PART I

It has been my intent in this manuscript to tell the story of the men most responsible for the planting of the park system. They led the way by directing many other employees in the actual work of turning acquired acres of land into an outstanding system of parks.

It must be acknowledged that their accomplishments were made possible by the support they received from many other sources. In a speech made during the mid-1920s (see Appendix II), John Dunbar described the development and growth of the Rochester park system, giving due credit to the Ellwanger and Barry families for their many contributions of plants and to the park commissioners for their support. He also recognized Dr. Charles S. Sargent as a major contributor because of the many trees and shrubs that he arranged to be sent from Arnold Arboretum for planting within the Rochester parks. Dunbar stated that, as a result of the combination of support, "Every part of Highland Park, and also sections of the large parks (Genesee Valley, Seneca, Durand Eastman, and Cobbs Hill), are occupied with genera and species, and with different family groups so that, in reality, a large and comprehensive arboretum is spread throughout the park system, although it does not have that official title. These are the features that have made Rochester's parks notable in this country and many parts of Europe."

The combination of support, as mentioned by John Dunbar, although somewhat subjected to historical changes, has continued to the present. The Ellwanger and Barry nursery went out of business in 1918; however, the interest in the park system by members of the Ellwanger and Barry families continued well into the 1970s. I remember the occasional phone calls from Helen Ellwanger as well as the many conversations with Peter Barry relative to the parks. Because of his stature within the city, Peter Barry was able to generate much support for the parks from both private and governmental sources. I remember the daily visits that Frederick Barry, as long as he was physically able, made from the homestead on Mt. Hope Avenue to Highland Park. He never failed to express his "likes" or "dislikes" regarding how the park was being maintained.

The relationship between the Rochester park system and Arnold Arboretum was continued after Dr. Sargent was no longer active. As new plants were discovered by its plant explorers throughout the world or developed by its plantsmen, Arnold Arboretum sent specimens for planting and testing within the Rochester park system. I well remember receiving from Arnold Arboretum six seeds of the dawn redwood (*Metasequoia*) during 1946. This ancient tree had been discovered in China by plant explorers of the Arnold Arboretum. Plants raised from these seeds are presently flourishing within Highland and Durand Eastman Parks.

The Rochester park system became an active member of the plant and seed exchange program that had been developed between the various arboretums and botanical gardens throughout the world. Through its involvement in this program, the Rochester park system shared not only in the distribution of new plants but also in the furnishing of plants discovered or developed within the park system.

The new city charter that went into effect in 1928 brought changes in the administration of the park system. The park system was placed as a Bureau of Parks under the commissioner of public safety. Although established as another level of government that exercised some control over park operations, it actually had little effect upon the park system. The commissioner of public safety had direct access to the city manager and the city council and could forward referrals from the park director directly to the decision makers. To a degree, the city councilmen took the place of the former park commissioners, especially when "pet projects" were offered for action.

In 1961, when the agreement between the city and county concerning operation of certain city parks by the county became effective, the park system became a department of county government reporting directly to the county manager (now county executive). The organization of the county legislature, with its committee structure, provided the Park Department with a "sounding board" for its plans and projects. Legislators from both political parties, especially those serving on the Park and Recreation Committee and the Park Land Acquisition Committee, carefully reviewed park projects and gave support to those that they thought would benefit the community. Both Gordon Howe, while County Manager, and Lucien Morin, while serving as County Manager and later as County Executive, were fully supportive of the Park Department. Each of these men encouraged the Park Department in its program of land acquisition and were of great assistance in securing approval by the legislators. Members of the legal staff of the county were of special assistance in the land acquisition program. Much support was also provided by many volunteers from the community at large who gave many hours of time serving on special committees to which they had been appointed by the county manager.

To quote from John Dunbar's speech, "It is this combination of support that has made Rochester's (and Monroe County's) parks notable in this country."

ADDENDUM PART II—
A RAMBLING UPDATE

More than a year has passed since this manuscript was considered complete and set aside by the author; consequently, some updating is in order. It is necessary to give some review of the past in order to understand what is happening at the present time to the legacy of horticultural wealth that is now the responsibility of the park plantsmen of the 1990s.

During the overlapping careers of John Dunbar (1890-1926) and Barney Slavin (1890-1942), many areas throughout the parks were being planted with trees and shrubs, many of which had been grown to specimen size in the park nurseries. These were the formative years for the park landscapes, years when the early plantsmen could proceed at their own free will and when a real emphasis was given to horticultural development of the park areas. As a result, Highland and Durand Eastman Parks became known as arboretums. From some of the early payrolls, we learn that it was not unusual to have 30 to 40 men working in one of these parks under the supervision of Dunbar or Slavin. With this manpower and their affinity for plants, they created parks that became known throughout the world.

By the late 1930s, the planting of Highland and Durand Eastman Parks was completed, although, upon occasion, space could be found for a new species or cultivar of lilac or of some other plant of special interest. The primary responsibility of the park plantsmen became one of maintaining the many plant collections.

During the economic troubles of the 1930s and the wartime demands for men during the early 1940s, the horticultural activities of the park system were greatly limited. At the end of the war in 1945, interest in the parks was renewed. In anticipation of the need to replace overgrown, mature, and diseased and dying plants, attention was directed to the old nurseries that had been neglected during the war years. They were carefully screened for any specimen plants that might be worthy of planting within the parks. Much effort was devoted to renovating these nurseries to prepare them for the growing of the many plants that would be needed. This interest in the nurseries was bolstered by the invasion of Dutch elm disease into the Rochester area. With the return of Dick Fenicchia to the park payroll in 1950, the park system gained an employee well versed in nursery work and the propagation of plants.

During the next 25 years, much was accomplished in the renovation of many plantings throughout all of the parks, with special attention being given to Highland and Durand Eastman Parks. A new nursery was established in 1954 on the old penitentiary property adjacent to Highland Park. It was here that many trees and shrubs were grown to specimen size for planting within the park. After the park operating agreement between the county and city became effective in July 1961, an area in Mendon Ponds Park was selected for the establishment of a tree nursery. Many seedling trees that were propagated at the Highland Park greenhouses were moved to this area for growing on to the proper size for planting throughout the entire park system. In 1971, approximately ten acres of the newly acquired area east of Irondequoit Bay were selected for the establishment of another nursery. Because this area had ideal soil for nursery purposes and was also easily accessible for equipment, Dick Fenicchia supervised the moving of hundreds of plants propagated at the Highland Park greenhouses to this area. Included among these were hundreds of lilacs that were the result of a hybridization program using 'Rochester' as one of the parent plants. Many of these have been selected for naming and have since been planted in Highland Park and at several other locations throughout the community, including the George Eastman House and the Strong Museum. Also planted in this nursery were many special plants, some of which were discovered by Barney Slavin or were the results of his special propagation practices. It is this area that Dick Fenicchia feels should be dedicated as the Barney Slavin Arboretum. The nurseries have, for many years, been a strong factor in the overall park program. With parks such as Highland and Durand Eastman where there are many plants that are not readily available from commercial nurseries or other sources (other arboretums or botanical gardens), a nursery is a necessity.

Unfortunately, during the past two decades, while the capital program of the park system has been moving ahead, there have been reductions in the operational budgets and in the manpower allotted to parks. These reductions have been felt in all of the parks. However, it is the horticultural program that has suffered the most. Although it is often concluded by some that horticulture has been limited to Highland and Durand Eastman Parks, with some spillover to Genesee Valley and Seneca Parks, this is a misconception. The horticulture program of the park system consists of more than the planting and maintenance of plant collections in a few choice areas. It includes the care and maintenance of plants throughout the whole park system—for example:

- spraying of trees and shrubs to protect them from disease and insect infestation;
- surveillance over all vegetation, native and exotic (in reality, a preservation program that will guarantee that future generations will still have the opportunity to enjoy the natural and man-created areas as they exist at present);
- trimming of trees and shrubs to remove broken or diseased branches;
- thinning out where plants are crowded, selecting the desired plants, and removing the undesirable or the weed trees and shrubs;
- feeding or fertilizing, if needed, to keep plants in healthy condition; and
- cleanup of storm-damaged trees and branches.

Dick Fenicchia and this author have made many visits to our Monroe County parks during the past few years. We have discovered that, despite the capital projects that have been undertaken or that are underway, there are many areas within the parks that are suffering from lack of care. At Durand Eastman Park, for example, many plants of horticultural value have been lost. To be fair to park personnel, it must be stated that much of this can be attributed to several factors over which the park employees have no control, including:

- the change in eating habits of the large deer population;

213

- the introduction or immigration of beaver into this park;
- damage sustained during storms (for example, the ice storm of March 1991); and
- lack of sufficient help to undertake all the tasks that are necessary.

There are also instances where proper forestry practices, which could have prevented the loss of some specimen trees, have not been possible because of reductions in manpower.

At Highland Park, it is evident that several plant collections are no longer represented as in the past. Plants are no longer being replaced "in kind." There is a trend toward landscaping the park areas as opposed to maintaining them as part of an arboretum. This may not be wrong; however, careful study must be given to maintaining many of the valuable plant collections for which the park has received its worldwide reputation. There is not sufficient staff to maintain the arboretum areas as they have been maintained in the past. At Highland Park, which has been the nucleus of the horticultural program and the work center of the plantsmen of the past, a small crew of dedicated employees is devoting much effort to growing plants for the conservatory displays and for the various flower beds that exist in several areas of the park system. They also are propagating and growing lilacs for replacements as needed in Highland Park. This group of employees is representative of the park plantsmen of the past.

There was a real need, beginning in 1890, for plantsmen such as John Dunbar and, as he gained experience and knowledge, Barney Slavin. With some guidance from Frederick L. Olmsted and his firm of planners, these two men furnished the leadership to accomplish the work involved in converting the acquired land areas into a well-developed system of parks. This was accomplished during a period of approximately fifty years (1890-1940). This type of leadership was continued during the next fifty years; however, the challenge was slightly different. Many of the plantings accomplished by the two pioneers were now matured and some were in need of replacement. Dick Fenicchia, whose career had overlapped with those of John Dunbar and Barney Slavin, not only met this challenge, but also expanded the program of plant breeding and nursery development.

With Dick's retirement now a matter of history, the challenge passes to the younger men who are now on the payroll. Unfortunately, they will not have the benefit of some well-stocked nursery areas from which they can move plants as needed. These have been neglected due to lack of necessary employees to maintain them. Presently there are many acres of undeveloped parkland acquired during the 1960s and 1970s that are in the process of, or awaiting, development. This will add to the challenge facing the park employees assigned to the horticultural aspect of the park system.

Afterword
By Kent Millham, April 2011

I am grateful for the opportunity to add to the story of *The Plantsmen of Rochester Parks*. As mentioned earlier in this book, I began work at Highland Botanical Park in 1975. Since the years from 1975 through the early 1990's have already been related earlier in this book, I will just briefly cover some aspects from my viewpoint working with the plantsman Alvan R. Grant and Richard Fenicchia. Then I will expand on the contributions of the later plantsman just briefly covered by Mr. Grant, and summarize the important additions to the Monroe County arboreta that have occurred from the early 1990's up to 2011.

I began work as a Greenhouse Worker, potting plants and performing other greenhouse tasks at the growing greenhouses at the corner of South Goodman Street and Highland Avenue. My introduction to the arboretum began quickly, when on my third day of employment I began planting rhododendrons in the expanding collection located on Pinetum Drive. The rhododendron planting in this location had begun several years before, and continued for a number of years later. The soil was ideal for rhododendron and ericaceous plant culture, but the soil was further amended with ample quantities of peat moss and sulfur. Many of the rhododendrons planted were unnamed hybrids developed by Richard Fenicchia.

Much time of my early years was spent working at the Smith Road nursery. One side of the property was the growing field and testing ground for many of Dick's hybrid lilacs. The nursery soil was comprised of a very deep layer of Dunkirk silt loam, an extremely fertile soil that was an excellent medium for nursery plants. Later, some of the prime specimens of lilacs, rhododendrons, and evergreens were planted on the north side of the property in a display format, which eventually Dick named the Barney Slavin Arboretum. Unfortunately, the north side had heavier soil, and many of the lilacs planted in that area died or grew poorly. However, the original specimens of Richard's lilacs

'Martha Stewart' and 'Richard A. Fenicchia' (named posthumously) were at one time located here.

Although I worked only a few years for Mr. Grant and Mr. Fenicchia before they retired, their influence had a lifelong effect on my development as a horticulturist. Dick trained me on the techniques of nursery work and plant propagation, along with the art of setting up floral displays in the conservatory. Working so closely with Mr. Fenicchia led to a lifelong interest in lilacs and unusual conifers.

Louis Fenicchia

Louie Fenicchia started working at Highland Park in 1973 and retired in October 2002. Being the son of a horticulturist and the nephew of Richard Fenicchia, he continued the line of plantsmen at Highland. At various times, he was in charge of the Highland Park Greenhouses and /or in charge of the maintenance of Highland Park. Louie had a special interest in the Highland Park arboretum, and the supporting Monroe County nurseries. As a nephew of Richard Fenicchia, he made sure that special care was given to the many named and unnamed hybrids of his uncle.

While serving as a horticulturist at the Highland Park Greenhouses in the 1990's, the annual bedding plant program was expanded to include the entire Monroe County Parks system. Also, annuals were grown for the City of Rochester and Monroe County in Bloom program, although the growing of city annuals by the Monroe County Parks has since been discontinued. Louie, learning important practical horticultural practices from his family, grew high quality plants at the greenhouses using his own soil mixtures, which often incorporated leaf mold that was generated by the Parks Department.

In the arboretum, Mr. L. Fenicchia made sure that the collections were well maintained, with extra care given to the *Syringa* and *Rhododendron* collections. His practical knowledge assured that not only were the arboretum and collections maintained, but that all operations ran smoothly.

217

Robert Hoepfl

As mentioned before, Robert Hoepfl began work with Richard Fenicchia in the early 1960's. He succeeded Mr. Fenicchia when he retired in 1978, and continued as Superintendent of Horticulture until his retirement in 1998. Under Bob's tenure as the Supt. of Horticulture, a number of capital improvement projects were undertaken at Highland Botanical Park.

The Rock Garden was developed from 1978 through 1985, and was located in the Pinetum collection. This new collection was located at the site of the original Herbarium. A winding paved path was created to lead between the evergreen hillside and the collection of dwarf conifers and deciduous shrubs. The rock garden is a hidden gem that is only seen by following the winding path, and is hidden by hillocks on three sides.

As the Rochester Lilac Festival expanded in the late 1970's, a new area to be developed to accommodate the vendors and entertainment. Under Mr. Hoepfl's supervision, Highland Park South was planted with specimen trees by park staff, and the walks and Festival area were planned by EDR. Later expansions at Highland Park South under Bob's supervision included the Viet Nam Memorial and the AIDS Remembrance Garden. These two major gardens incorporate specimen plant material along winding scenic paths.

In the mid 1980's, Mr. Hoepfl helped oversee the first renovation of Lamberton Conservatory. A visitors center was added, along with a new circular traffic pattern that led visitors from the seasonal house to the epiphyte house, tropical rainforest, cacti house, and the house plant and economic plant house. In the center is a courtyard, with the original design by the Federated Garden Club.

In 1989, a level grass path was constructed through the main part of the lilac collection. Along the path a self-guided walking tour of the lilacs was developed, emphasizing the many differences that can be seen in various cultivars and species.

From 1993-1994 the main paved lilac walk was realigned to reflect the original Olmsted design. At the same time, the shrub collections in the rose hollow area were replanted, and the historic views were restored at the pinnacle area where the former Children's Pavilion was located.

As a plantsman, Mr. Hoepfl was taught the art of hybridizing from Richard Fenicchia. Bob has a number of seedlings from the parent 'Flower City' that are worthy of naming. The collective group he calls "FC hybrids". One of his best is 'FC 20', which is a heavy flowering blue hybrid with single florets. 'FC 15' has single dark purple florets, and a compact growth habit. Another very promising seedling has radially doubled florets, but they have delicate, fine petals unlike many of the radially doubled 'Rochester' progeny.

It is also worth noting that Bob is the former president of the International Lilac Society.

Mr. Hoepfl has also been instrumental in registering a number of Richard Fenicchia' s lilac hybrids. Currently, Bob and Kent Millham are involved in registering one of Fenicchia' s most outstanding rhododendron hybrids, 'President Kennedy'.

Thomas Pollock

Tom succeeded Robert Hoepfl as Superintendent of Horticulture in 1999. Mr. Pollock started working for the Monroe County Parks in the late 1970's, and was a graduate of Cornell University, as were plantsmen Alvan R. Grant and Kent Millham.

As superintendent, Mr. Pollock oversaw many important restoration projects, along with some important plant collection enhancements. Tom coordinated the Historic Commemorative Reclamation and Replanting of Durand-Eastman Park using many nurserymen volunteers and plant material donations. These improvements were made along Pine Valley Creek, Rhododendron Valley, the Fruiticeum, the Log Cabin/Dove Tree Area, Sweet Fern/Culver corridor, Sorrel Property and Sunset Point. Many of the plantings were implemented by Park Supervisor Brian Kirchmaier and his very knowledgeable assistant, nurserymen Richard Sage. Mr. Sage made special improvements to the "Archery Range" Maple collection, and was an expert in the grafting of Japanese maples. Dick also made sure that any new plantings at Durand were labeled, a very important task in an arboretum.

Under Mr. Pollock's term as Superintendent, a large crew of dedicated and knowledgeable volunteers was created to tackle the daunting task of removing invasive trees and plants from Durand, as well as many necessary pruning tasks that may not otherwise have been performed. This crew continues to work at the present time.

At Genesee Valley Park, Tom was instrumental in the master plan implementation of the *Historic Olmsted Fabric,* an important landscape design master plan to retain the Frederick Law Olmsted design elements at this park intact.

At Highland Botanical Park, Mr. Pollock continued important restorations with the historic renovation to the stairs in Pinetum, a flowering entranceway to Highland Park lined with large azaleas. Another of Mr. Pollock's volunteer groups, the Friends of the Poet's Border, became an important part of the renovation and maintenance of the Poet's Border, a quiet retreat located across from the Lamberton Conservatory.

Tom enlarged several plant collections at Highland Botanical Park, including major additions to the Magnolia, Rhododendron, and Japanese Maple Collections. A number of the Japanese Maples were grafted by the nurseryman and Durand-Eastman plantsman Richard Sage. New cultivars of Magnolias added included many new pink and yellow hybrids. Along the winding path of rhododendrons to the east of the reservoir, several hundred were added to fill in gaps that occurred in recent years, and to add to the number of cultivars displayed.

In 2004, the Louisiana Iris Beds were dedicated. Mr. Pollock, along with Dr. Edna Claunch, helped secure the donation of approximately 100 cultivars of Louisiana Iris from members of the Society of Louisiana Iris. This donation coincided with a similar donation to Rochester's sister city in Hamamatsu, Japan, and to the University of Rochester. Five beds were planted with the iris, along with companion plants such as hostas and ornamental grasses. One of the beds was a Founders Bed which included newly named cultivars honoring Rochester and Hamamatsu. These included 'Eastman Winds', 'Renee Fleming' 'Susan B. Anthony', 'Frederick Douglass, 'Shizuoka Sunrise', 'Pure Waters' and 'Rochester Lilacs'. This is the largest collection of Louisiana Iris this far north.

Noelle Nagel

Noelle began work in the late 70's at the growing greenhouses at the corner of Highland Avenue and South Goodman Street., and worked at those facilities for about 10 years. Later, she began working at the Lamberton Conservatory after the first renovation around 1988 as a horticultural interpreter, before working with the arboretum crew for about 8 years, pruning many of the collections other than *Syringa*.

Noelle at the current time is the Horticultural Interpreter at the Lamberton Conservatory, returning there in 2007. Because of her educational skills, she is equally adept at teaching youngsters on the requirements for plant growth, or college students on the technical aspects of botany. Noelle also instructs the general public with her signage, often employing humor to illustrate a concept.

Mrs. Nagel is the leader of the docent and volunteer program at the Lamberton Conservatory. The docents are taught about the plants and displays in the various houses at the conservatory, and they relate this information to the public. Volunteers are trained in horticultural tasks in and around the conservatory grounds, and help some in the maintenance.

Kent Millham

Kent is the last of the original plantsmen employed at Highland Botanical Park who has worked in all aspects of horticulture at Highland; the growing greenhouses, Lamberton Conservatory, the Monroe County nurseries, and the arboretum.

Currently Mr. Millham is in charge of planting the floral displays in Highland Botanical Park, designing and planting the pansy bed with 15,000 pansies, planning and designing the seasonal shows at the Lamberton Conservatory, and memorial tree and shrub coordinator. In the arboretum, Kent prunes the lilac collection and keeps the labeling updated, as well as planting lilacs and other trees and shrubs in the arboretum. In October of 2010, he acquired over 130 cultivars of *Syringa* not represented in the collection, to expand the number of lilac cultivars to approximately 630.

With the reinstallation of a mist chamber in a small plastic house at Highland Botanical Park in 2010, Mr. Millham can once again propagate lilacs and evergreens to maintain the collections in the arboretum. In the past, he propagated hundreds of conifers and thousands of lilacs that have been planted in new plantings or as replacements for dead or diseased specimens.

In 2002, a botanical garden data base known as BG-BASE was purchased by Monroe County Parks. Millham is in the process of converting all of the old plant records from index cards to this computer data base. Some of the data being recorded includes plant sources, names, data sources, locations, plant conditions, images, and accession dates. Kent has thus continued the taxonomic work of the arboretum by the updating and expanding of the plant records, assigning of accession numbers to all of the plants in the arboretum, and with the continuation of plant labeling.

Mr. Millham maintains contacts with other arboreta, nurserymen and plant enthusiasts through the International Plant Propagators Society and the International Lilac Society, in which he has been the editor of their quarterly magazine for over 5 years. At the present time, he is in the process of registering several new cultivars of *Syringa* from Highland Botanical Park.

Brief Chronology of Park History from 1993 to 2011

Mr. Grant's original publication historical narrative ended at about 1993. The following brief chronology will bring the reader up-to-date on the important events in the Monroe County Parks since the end of Mr. Grant's narrative.

In 1994, a historic landscape restoration was undertaken at Highland Botanical Park that restored many of the landscape plantings, by replanting of new specimens and pruning existing specimens. Much of this work was done in the Rose Hollow area of the park, which was designated as a mixed bed and collections area of the park by Frederick Law Olmsted, in contrast to most of the arboretum that displays the plants in collections by genera or plant family. The restoration was undertaken by the firm of Trowbridge and Wolfe.

In 1995, the sunken garden area behind Warner Castle was historically renovated. Stonework and railings were restored. Plantings were redone to reflect the landscape materials used at the time of the original plantings, and new pavers were placed. The Warner Castle continues to serve as an important meeting place for area gardeners and horticulturists, and offers many classes and programs to certify area gardeners.

From 1996 to 1999 the Alpine Street area was cleared of scrub trees and brush, and evergreens were planted to screen the adjacent apartments. This planting also served to expand the Pinetum area, with the addition of *Metasequoia, Larix, Thuja,* and *Chamaecyparis.* In 1998, the Labor Day windstorm gave additional importance to this project, as much damage was caused in this area from the damaging winds.

The use of Highland Park South continued to expand with the addition of the Viet Nam Memorial, the AIDS Remembrance Garden, and the Crime Victims Garden. These areas were added circa 1996 and 1997, and augment the plant collections of the park.

In 2002, the historic growing greenhouses at Highland Botanical Park were demolished because of structural problems. New greenhouses were erected at the Fleet Maintenance Center, and later moved to the Monroe County Jail on East Henrietta Road. Annuals for the Monroe County Parks and plants for the seasonal shows of Lamberton Conservatory continue to be grown at these new greenhouses. Monroe County Parks employee Chris Ehmann maintains the plants and supervises chosen inmates in the planting of the floral crops.

As mentioned earlier, BG-BASE was purchased to modernize the plant records of the arboretum. Maintaining accurate records and labeling is one of the most important functions of an arboretum, and the use of this computer database and records assures that Highland Botanical Park will continue to be recognized as an arboretum of scientific importance.

The addition of 5 beds of Louisiana Iris was accomplished in 2004, and they are an important testing ground for Louisiana Iris, and the study of their culture this far north. New cultivars specifically named for the event of the opening were planted, and later another cultivar was named and added to honor one of the coordinators of the project, Edna Claunch.

Circa 2005, a small hoop house was erected near the Highland Botanical Park maintenance center. This house serves as an important house for forcing flowering trees, shrubs and bulbs for the spring shows at the conservatory, as well as other displays such as Gardenscape and the Home Show of Rochester. With the addition of a mist chamber in 2010, propagation of woody plants can once again proceed, augmenting the collections and nurseries of the Monroe County Parks arboreta.

In 2007, a donation to Highland Botanical Park made possible the addition of over 25 dwarf and unusual conifers, expanding the collections of Pinetum. These new cultivars represent an important addition to Highland Botanical Parks recognized collection of diverse mature conifers.

Also, in 2007, Mark Quinn succeeded Thomas Pollock as Superintendent of Horticulture. Mark had served as the Superintendent of Olmsted Parks (Highland and Genesee Valley Parks), and continues the important work of maintaining these two parks, along with Seneca Park, as Olmsted Parks, as well overseeing projects at the important Durand-Eastman arboretum. Mr. Quinn oversees other parks in the Monroe County Park system, and also continues the important interaction with many volunteer groups that help maintain and support specific areas of the arboreta.

From 2009 to 2010, the Lamberton Conservatory underwent a second renovation. This time the central tropical dome was completely renovated from the ground up. All new structural elements and glass were installed, but the original gutter and top vent systems were retained. The staircase that had been installed in the mid 1980's was removed, allowing more light and growing room for the tropical display. This display has already matured, with several specimens reaching near the peak of the dome.

In October 2010, a new expansion of the lilac collection began at a different site in Highland Botanical Park. It is located on a sunny hillside south of the Viet Nam Memorial, and will include about 130 additional lilac cultivars that were not currently in the collection.

Epilogue

Although the horticultural staff of the present day is much diminished in numbers from 25 years ago, the important tasks that need to be done continue to be accomplished by the dedicated staff and volunteers. Important additions and renovations have been made to the plant collections in the arboreta that continue to this day. Kent Millham and Noelle Nagel are now the last of the plantsmen recognized by Alvan Grant that are currently employed by the Monroe County Parks, and it is hoped that the lineage of plantsmen that began with the establishment of the Monroe County Parks arboreta will continue in the future.

APPENDIXES

These appendixes extend the history of the plantsmen of Rochester's park system in two ways. It presents at least a partial inventory of the work of Dunbar, Slavin, and Fenicchia. Secondly, it provides the reader with an opportunity to view these men through their written words.

An index of the subject matter in the appendixes is as follows:

Appendix I
List of Plants Associated with John Dunbar   228

Appendix II
A Talk Given by John Dunbar in the Early 1920s—
    Exact Date Unknown   231

Appendix III
Plants Accredited to Bernard H. Slavin   237

Appendix IV
An Article by Bernard H. Slavin That Appeared in the
    Garden Center *Bulletin*, January 1950   243

Appendix V
Copy of a Handout Prepared by R. Horsey   246

Appendix VI
Copy of a Letter Written to Dr. L. C. Chadwick from
    Richard Fenicchia   248

Appendix VII
Some of the Plants That Can Be Attributed to
    Richard Fenicchia   253

Appendix VIII
Copy of an Article Written for the International Plant
    Propagators Society's Publication, *The Plant
    Propagator*, by Richard Fenicchia   256

APPENDIX I

LIST OF PLANTS ASSOCIATED WITH JOHN DUNBAR

Species and varieties of plants introduced by John Dunbar can be divided into two groupings:

1. Seedlings selected as a result of collecting and sowing large number of seeds, growing on the seedlings until characteristics not formerly found in the existing parent plants could be identified, and then selecting these seedlings as new species or hybrids.
2. Plants discovered during trips taken for the purpose of finding new species or plants with different characteristics.

Plants selected from seedlings that had been grown on by Dunbar consisted of the thirty-one new lilacs that he is credited with introducing and can be divided into four groups according to names, as follows:

1. The Rochester Group—named by Dunbar in honor of members of his family or for members of the Rochester community:
    - 'A. B. Lamberton'—classified as a double-flowering lilac, purple in color, named for a former president of the Rochester Park Commission.
    - 'Adelaide Dunbar'—double flowering, purple with reddish tones, named for a family member.
    - 'Calvin C. Laney'—single flowering, purple with lavender tones, named for the first superintendent of parks.
    - 'Clarence D. Van Zandt'—single flowering, purple (rosy-lilac), named for a former park commissioner.
    - 'George W. Aldridge'—single flowering, pink, named for a former mayor of Rochester.
    - 'Hiram H. Edgerton'—single flowering, light purple, named for a former commissioner and mayor.

- 'Joan Dunbar'—double flowering, white, named for a family member.
- 'William C. Barry'—single flowering, pearly lavender, named for a former park commissioner.
- 'William S. Riley'—single flowering, lavender, named for a former city alderman and commissioner.

2. American Personalities:
   - 'Alexander Hamilton'—double flowering, magenta.
   - 'Elihu Root'—double flowering, azure lavender.
   - 'Henry Clay'—single flowering, white.
   - 'Henry Wadsworth Longfellow'—double flowering, magenta.
   - 'Henry Ward Beecher'—double flowering, pale lilac lavender.
   - 'Patrick Henry'—double flowering, lavender.
   - 'Thomas A. Edison'—single flowering, reddish purple.
   - 'Susan B. Anthony'—single flowering, magenta.

3. Army and Navy:
   - 'Admiral Farragut'—single flowering, reddish purple.
   - 'General Elwell S. Otis'—double flowering, light lilac.
   - 'General Haig'—single flowering, pinkish lilac, judged to be the same as Frau Wilhelm Pfitzer.
   - 'General Kitchener'—double flowering, bluish.
   - 'General John Pershing'—double flowering, bluish lavender.
   - 'General Sheridan'—double flowering, white.
   - 'General Sherman'—single flowering, pinkish lavender.

4. Presidents:
   - 'President Harding'—single flowering, reddish purple.
   - 'President John Adams'—double flowering, white.

229

- 'President Lincoln'—single flowering, bluish, for a long time considered the leading blue lilac.
- 'President Monroe'—double flowering, pinkish lavender.
- 'President Roosevelt' (Theodore)—single flowering, deep purple.
- 'General Grant'—single flowering, light purple.

John Dunbar considered his best lilac to be 'General Sherman,' although 'President Lincoln' probably won him the most credit because it was a real departure in coloring at the time, perhaps the truest blue.

American species or hybrid woody plants associated with Dunbar include the following:
- *Carya Dunbarii*—a cross of *C. laciniosa* and *C. ovata*. One of the hickories named by Dr. Sargent in honor of Dunbar.
- *Cornus Dunbarii*—a cross of *C. macrophylia* and *C. amomum*. One of the dogwoods named by Rehder in honor of Dunbar.
- *Crataegus Dunbarii*—a Dunbar discovery named by Dr. Sargent.
- *Crataegus pedicillata*—discovered by Dunbar while on an exploratory trip throughout Pennsylvania, New York, Connecticut, and Ontario.
- *Halesia monticola*—discovered by Dunbar while on an exploratory trip through North Carolina, Tennessee, and Georgia, a hybrid of *H. caroliniana*.
- *Malus glaucescens*—discovered while on a trip extending from New York to North Carolina and Alabama.
- *Prunus Dunbarii*—a cross of *P. maritima* and *americana*, named in honor of Dunbar by Rehder.

APPENDIX II

A TALK GIVEN BY JOHN DUNBAR IN THE EARLY 1920s
EXACT DATE UNKNOWN

SOME FEATURES OF THE CITY PARKS —
PAST, PRESENT AND FUTURE

It has been fully demonstrated that the establishment of parks in cities with their numerous features for pleasure, recreation, and education are essential factors for the fullest development of the corporate life of a city. Perhaps there is no other city in this country where the people are so closely associated with the features and activities of the public parks as they are in this city.

The growth and development of the park system in this city since its creation by an act of the legislature in 1888 with its many features and attractions is remarkable.

In the great majority of cities where parks are maintained, we believe we can truly say there is a great similarity in their general features. That is, there are lawns, flower beds, meadows, groves of trees, woods, plantations, and opportunities for summer recreations and winter sports, but they have no distinctive or outstanding features. The parks in this city have very prominent and noticeable features which distinguish them from most other municipal parks in this country. Amongst some other things, we will try to show what these important characteristics are.

There are, however, in connection with public parks, certain fundamental and essential features without which parks cannot have any existence. Some of these essential features are meadows, lawns, or turf areas of some kind, woods, groves, plantations, and water in the form of ponds, lakes or streams. These different features in a variety of combinations must exist and must be sacredly maintained at any cost, or parks will soon deteriorate. These necessary features have been and are maintained in excellent condition in the city parks.

Amongst the plans for the development of Genesee Valley, Seneca and Highland Parks thirty years ago, the Park Commissioners had in view the establishment of a shrub collection on the south slopes of Highland Park. It was intended to be an educational feature. Ellwanger and Barry contributed liberally, and shrubs were purchased in different nurseries in this country, Britain, Ireland, France, Belgium and Germany, and from 1891 to 1895, this collection was established, with all the shrubs that could be procured. This included the beginning of the lilac collection which soon afterwards began to attract public attention, and contained 100 varieties at that time. I am sure that the Park Commissioners and the park officials at the time did not dream that the lilac collection would subsequently become so famous, and they did not anticipate that the collections of trees and shrubs would assume in the years ahead the large proportions they have attained in the parks at the present time, and be such a source of educational interest.

In the spring of 1896 the nucleus of the collection of coniferous evergreens was planted on the north side of Highland Park, and with many accessions which have been added to it since that time, it has become a cynosure of much horticulture interest from many parts of the United States.

In May 1899, Dr. C. S. Sargent, Director of the Arnold Arboretum, Harvard University, the world famous dendrologist who knows more about the trees of the world today that any other living man, visited the parks. He was impressed with the collections that had been made. With the approval of the Park Commissioners, he asked the park officials to make investigations of the trees and shrubs in the vicinity of Rochester, Western and Central New York, Ontario, Canada, and elsewhere. Dried specimens were collected and the seed gathered for propagation. Duplicates of these collections were sent to Dr. Sargent with field notes for observation. As a result of this work new species and varieties of hawthorns, crabapples, hickories, dogwoods, June berries, plums, silver bell trees and others were discovered and described by Dr. Sargent and introduced to cultivation. About 1902 Dr. Sargent began sending annual shipments of trees and shrubs to the parks as a compliment for these services. These shipments included many of the new discoveries in the hinterland of China by E. H. Wilson who was sent to China by Dr. Sargent on botanical explorations on several occasions. As a result of these contributions by Dr. Sargent, every part of Highland Park, including the so-called Warner Tract on the west side of South Avenue and the south extension of Goodman Street are occupied with genera and species of trees and shrubs, and also many portions of the large parks, that is, Genesee Valley, Seneca, Durand Eastman, and Cobbs Hill Parks contain areas planted with different family groups, so that in reality a large and comprehensive arboretum is spread throughout the park system, although it does not bear that official title. These are the features in association with Dr. Sargent that have made the Rochester Parks notable in this country and in many parts of Europe. The Park Department has been honored by annual visits from Dr. Sargent, with very few exceptions, in the autumn during the past twenty years.

Many showy flowering plants have been specialized in quantities in the parks to give people enjoyment. The principal group is of course the lilac collection, the flowering of which has been an annual event for many years: Rhododendrons, Azaleas, Crab apples, Magnolias, June berries, Dogwoods, Plums, Cherries, Pearl bushes, Bush honeysuckles, Roses, and Peonies; these, because of their showy flowers, have all been planted largely so that each in turn give delight to the people.

The people of this city were somewhat dismayed when they learned that the State authorities had to cross Genesee Valley Park with the Barge Canal. The canal has been completed. There are a few touches to be added to the restoration next spring. Late this autumn the Park Department planted 1700 oaks along the zone and beyond it, and planted European white willows, flanking the corners of the four handsome substantial bridges that cross the canal so that in a few years time the naked features of these bridges will be softened. We believe in the years to come this plantation of oaks will represent a noble appearance on the banks of the canal, and add a little in concealing its stiff outline. It is now proposed to cover the rip rap stones on the slopes of the banks with the matrimony vine. This is one of the most virile, persistent and rapid-growing of vines, and perhaps there is nothing better to cover up rapidly the bald stone covering along the edge of the canal. Ten or twelve thousand plants will be propagated by the Park Department for this purpose this winter and grown in the nursery for one year or more until they are strong enough to plant out. At the entrance of the park, and at other points where the state engineers had to make important changes, build new slopes, etc., these naked areas have been planted with nearly 1000 Japanese Crab apples.

New features have been added to Durand Eastman Park. Tens of thousands of trees, shrubs and evergreens have been, and are being, planted and mostly propagated in the park nurseries. The topography of this park is of such a nature that its proper treatment necessarily requires a vast amount of planting. It has been ascertained that the soil in this park contains scarcely any lime, and it is therefore adapted to the growth of azaleas and rhododendrons without the great expense of removing the soil for these lime-hating plants, and replacing with humus which had to be done in Highland Park for these plants. Thousands of American azaleas have been planted along the Pine Valley Road and will be a beautiful sight when in bloom as they increase in size in the years to come. About six acres have been planted with the crabapples of the world south of the area occupied by the zoo which, in a few years time, will be a most attractive feature. If conditions are favorable next spring, probably a beginning will be made in planting a collection of Japanese cherries permanently on the west side of Pine Valley Road. In 1914, Dr. Sargent procured a comprehensive set of Japanese cherries from the Japanese empire through Mr. Wilson. These cherries were presented to the Park Department about four years since, and from these original plants, we have been propagating by budding and grafting enough individual cherries to make a plantation. Many of these grafts are now large enough to plant out permanently. A few of the Japanese cherries have been in cultivation and some varieties do very well in Occidental countries. It is a fact, however, that these cherries are much more at home and are more vigorous in Japan than elsewhere. We hope there is a happy future in Durand Eastman Park for them.

Ontario Beach, the latest acquisition in the city parks, has sprung into surprising popularity, and it demonstrates the wisdom of the city administration in making this available to the people, judging by the thousands of people who used it for bathing and picnic purposes last summer. Two hundred and ten American elms were planted all over the grounds last autumn which, in a few years time, will give abundant shade. Ontario Beach Park will be kept in a simple condition. Flower beds or any other ornate embellishment would be out of character in a popular bathing resort like Ontario Beach.

Perhaps not many citizens are aware of the large amount of work connected with the street trees of this city. When we consider that there are considerable over 400 miles of streets, more or less, planted with trees, and many of them trees of large size, the work and problems associated with removing dead trees in dangerous situations, removing overcrowded trees, removing dangerous limbs, general pruning to clear traffic, and spraying in the summer to destroy the larvae of the Tussock Moth, all of this involves a vast amount of labor. The Park Department is considering the question of planting trees on the streets with suitable branching habits. Perhaps the two best all around trees for street tree planting are the American Elm and Norway maple. Sometimes these trees have bad branching habits. That is, they will throw out their branches horizontally or turn their branches downwards. This proves to be a nuisance in a short time, and involves a vast amount of pruning. There is only one way to get around the problem. Select an American Elm or a Norway Maple with a fastigiate or upright growing habit and bud them on young stocks. In this way the trees will be exactly the same as the parent stock. The department has begun budding trees of this type in the park nurseries, and expect to have a large number for planting on the streets in two or three years' time.

A word might be said about the herbarium and its meaning. A herbarium in connection with an arboretum or large collection of trees and shrubs from many parts of the world is necessary for their correct understanding and proper identification. it is just as necessary for this purpose as a laboratory is for chemical experiments. It also serves as an important record. When the flowers, fruits and leaves are dried of a certain tree growing in the parks, if it should disappear by any chance in the future, this shows that it was cultivated in the parks. The native flora is also included. Thirty-two thousand sheets have been mounted. This includes many duplicates of the same species or variety, and shows the extent of its variation.

Nurseries in various parts of the parks have been conducted for many years, and only for growing plant material for the parks. Trees and shrubs have been mainly propagated that are not commonly grown in nurseries. As a matter of fact, some important American trees and shrubs are not propagated in many American nurseries, and where they are grown, only in very limited quantities. The 1700 American oaks, consisting of seven different species mentioned earlier, planted in the Barge Canal zone, Genesee Valley Park, are quoted in nurseries in the same sizes at about $100 per 100. As these oaks were all raised in the park nurseries, the department was fortunate to have them on hand. We are constantly drawing large supplies from the park nurseries to plant in various parts of the parks every autumn and spring. The approximate number of trees and shrubs in the nurseries and frame grounds at the present time, consisting of transplanted stock, seedlings, buds, grafts and rooted cuttings is about 64,000.

APPENDIX III

PLANTS ACCREDITED TO BERNARD H. SLAVIN

Many of these plants were selected from seedlings raised by Barney using seed that he had collected while on plant exploration trips throughout New York, as well as in places farther away (Oklahoma, Arkansas, Missouri, Texas, and Kansas) that he visited as a result of urging by Professor Charles Sprague Sargent of Arnold Arboretum and Harvard University. Two of his selections, which have been mentioned earlier, are his upright form of Norway maple and his upright form of American elm.

As Barney selected plants because of some feature that was different from the true species, he assigned BHS (his initials) numbers to them, and in many cases these numbers can be found even today on plants growing within the parks owned by the City of Rochester but under county jurisdiction. Several of his plants considered of great merit and worthy of introduction on a wide scale are listed below (this list is from a publication printed in 1947):

BHS 1   *Acer platanoides* forma *erectum*—upright Norway maple. Type tree was discovered by Barney in a row of trees planted along the fence-line within Mt. Hope Cemetery at Elmwood Avenue. Several of these maples can be found today growing along Westfield Street and at the approaches to Veterans Memorial Bridge (Ridge Road).

BHS 2   *Ulmus americana* forma *ascendens*—Slavin's Upright Elm. Selected in Seneca Park. According to the County Park Department's plant taxonomist, there may be only one specimen left, in Irondequoit, on the west side of Culver Road north of Titus Avenue.

No number   *Amelanchier grandiflora rubescens*—a seedling of *Amelanchier grandiflora* with flowers purple-pink in bud, tinged with pink when open.

No number   *Carpinus caroliniana*—an upright form of blue-beech or American hornbeam, which he found growing wild in upstate New York.

BHS 51   *Cornus florida*- a seedling form of flowering dogwood with shrub-like growth, branching from the ground; has a compact, dense, round shape.

No number   *Crataegus phaenopyrum fastigiata*—a columnar form of Washington hawthorn growing in Durand Eastman Park.

BHS 3   *Halesia monticola rosea*—pink silverball found among seedlings and named by Dr. C. S. Sargent; type tree in Durand Eastman Park has pale rose flower.

No number   *Acer nigrum* upright form—in park nursery; from seed collected by Slavin near Salamanca; one specimen in Highland Park; bright yellow coloring in the fall; unnamed.

BHS 85   *Magnolia stellats*—*Magnolia stellata* seedling with larger flower than parent; petals slightly broader and coming into bloom a week earlier; named 'Slavin's Snowy' Magnolia by Bernard Harkness.

BHS 4   *Malus coronaria 'Nieuwlandiana'*—double pink crabapple similar to *M. coronaria* 'Charlotte,' but of brighter color; named by Slavin's son Arthur in honor of a favorite professor at Notre Dame.

BHS 6   *Malus ioensis frimbriata*—fringed petals on this double crabapple are outstanding characteristics and give it its name, fringe petal crabapple; differs from related form *Malus ioensis plena* (Bechtal's Crabapple) by this feature and by its shiny spines; the pink flowers are slightly larger than those of Bechtal's and more abundant.

No number   *Malus* 'Katherine'—double-flowered seedling, named by Slavin after his daughter-in-law; conspicuous among crabapples for its regular, somewhat globular shape with dense branching; deep pink buds opening to blush pink fading to white; its heavy flowering makes it a striking white ball; blooms are very fragrant.

BHS 10   *Pinus nigra* 'Hornibrookiana'—dwarf compact plant discovered as a "witch's broom" on an Austrian pine in Seneca Park and named for M. Hornbrook, who had been helpful to Slavin in the determination of dwarf materials in the park.

No number   *Prunus Sargentii,* upright form—originated in Durand Eastman nursery; an existing specimen of this upright Sargent cherry, more than twenty-five years old in 1947 and growing in Durand Eastman Park, had a crown only six feet in diameter although it was thirty feet in height; never formally recorded; could be *Prunus Sargentii fastigiata.*

BHS 17   *Pseudotsuga taxifolia pyramidata* forma *Slavinii*— pyramidal form of Douglas fir selected from a group of seedlings at Cobbs Hill Park; of denser foliage than type; although thirty-three years old in 1947 it was only twenty-two feet in height; regarded as a fine ornamental tree.

No number   *Robinia Slavinii*—hybrid between *R. pseudoacacia* and *R. Kelseyi*; large shrub with rosy pink flowers; found among a group of seedlings of *R. Kelseyi* and propagated by Slavin at Seneca Park.

No number   *Taxus cuspidata minima*—extremely dwarf form of Japanese yew, found as a seedling; type plant at fifteen years was only eight inches tall and broad.

BHS 1   *Tilia   americana   fastigiata*—pyramidal   form discovered among seedlings of American linden; type tree is in Genesee Valley Park; Slavin's Upright Basswood.

The above-listed species are but a few of the seedlings selected by Barney Slavin from among those he started from seeds he collected. There are many more that can be listed. Perhaps it should also be noted that in some instances he probably collected scions rather than seeds. These would have been grafted onto seedlings of the particular species with which he was concerned at the time. A listing of Bernard H. Slavin's selections as compiled by James Kelly, Plant Taxonomist of the Monroe County Park Department (presently responsible for the administration of the principal parks in Monroe County, including many city-owned areas such as Highland, Genesee Valley, and Durand Eastman Parks) during 1988 contains over 150 species of plants. Some of note are as follows:

BHS 3   *Pinus   strobus* forma *contorta*—Slavin's Twisted White Pine; one specimen located in the Durand Eastman arboretum.

BHS 4   *Catalpa x hybrida (C. bignonioides x ovata)*—non-fruiting tree; one specimen located in the Durand Eastman arboretum.

BHS 23   *Pinus nigra* forma *monstrosa*—name changed to *mirabilis* since *P. nigra monstrosa* had already been given to a mutant at the Seneclause Nursery in France in the 1800s; a rapidly growing tree with very long needles; open habit; highly decimate branches and eventually developing two or three heads.

BHS 36   *Pinus ponderosa*, variety *scopulorum* forma *pendula*—Slavin's Weeping Rocky Mountain Ponderosa Pine; one tree in the rock garden at Warner Castle, Highland Park, and one in Durand Eastman arboretum; small tree; ovoid shape; not a vigorous tree.

No number   *Acer nigra* forma *ascendens*—Slavin's Upright Black Maple; a pyramidal tree; one in Highland Park.

No number   *Berberis thunbergia*, cultivar Yellowberry—Yellowberry Japanese Barberry; two in Highland Park collection.

From Jim Kelly's list, one can determine that Barney's interest was indeed comprehensive and widespread. The list includes:

- Forty-six different selections of *Prunus*—collected in New York, Oklahoma, Texas, Kansas, and Missouri.
- *Syringa* (lilac)—seven selections; mostly from Highland Park.
- *Amelanchier*—seven selections from within Durand Eastman Park.
- *Malus* (crabapple)—twenty-four selections; some random selections, some actually the result of hybridizing.
- *Juniperus*—seven selections.
- *Pinus*—fourteen selections.
- *Quercus* (oak)—four selections; includes one collected north of Lawton, Texas, and one collected at Big Bend, west of Milwaukee, Wisconsin.
- *Picea* (spruce)—five selections.
- *Crataegus* (hawthorne)—three selections.
- *Thuja* (arborvitae)—one selection.
- *Halesia* (silverbell)—one selection.
- *Pseudotsuga* (fir)—four selections.
- *Tsuga* (hemlock)—one selection.
- *Abies* (fir)—two selections.
- *Magnolia*—seven selections.
- *Philadelphus* (mock orange)—one selection.

- *Carya* (hickory)—two selections, one shagbark hickory and one pignut.
- *Hamamelis x intermedia* cultivar *superba* (witch hazel)— one seedling, Durand Eastman Park.
- *Sophora* (scholar tree)—one selection; one fruit collected south of Sherman, Texas.
- *Juglans* (black walnut)—two selections.
- *Symphoricarpos albus*, variety *laevigatus* (snowberry)—one selection; collected west of Milwaukee, Wisconsin.
- *Betula* (birch)—one selection with violet bark; seed from Durand Eastman Park.
- *Taxus* (yew)—x media cultivar Slavin's Weeping Yew near Zoo Road.
- *Taxus cuspidata* forma *minima*—Durand Eastman Park.
- *Nyssa sylvatica* (tupelo)—one broad leaf form; one form with dark leaves.
- *Cornus slavinii*—Slavin's hybrid dogwood (*C. rugosa x stolonifera*); in Highland Park.
- *Cornus racemosa* cultivar Slavin's Dwarf—a group planting in the rock garden at Warner Castle, Highland Park.

AN ARTICLE BY BERNARD H. SLAVIN, FORMER SUPERINTENDENT OF THE ROCHESTER PARKS, THAT APPEARED IN THE GARDEN CENTER *BULLETIN*, JANUARY 1950

ACER NIGRUM
THE BLACK MAPLE

The Black Maple, or Black Sugar Maple, (*Acer nigrum*) is a tree of wide distribution that should be better known in cultivation in this county. This is one of the noblest trees of the American forests and is worthy of the highest recommendations as an ornamental shade tree for parks and lawns, also making an excellent street tree. The beauty of its sturdy habit and splendid dimensions is unrivaled in the forests of the northeastern United States and Canada. This tree was long confused with the common sugar maple of which it is still considered a variety by some authors.

Although there are some intergrading forms which are hard to understand, the two species are nevertheless specifically distinct. I was never so impressed with the distinction and beauty of the Black Maple as in the autumn of 1903 when I came upon it in the valley of the Allegheny River near Salamanca in Western New York. Walking through a piece of woods on flat land near the river, I spied a vigorous young maple tree, perhaps from twelve to fifteen years old, which had close, firm bark slightly roughened on the surface, and which had the appearance of a Norway Maple. At first I thought it might be one that had escaped from cultivation, but on examination its large leaves were found to be densely pubescent beneath, even the petioles and young branches being quite hairy.

I then began to consider the Black Maple as being the species. The thought suddenly occurred that if this tree was indigenous, there were likely to be some older specimens of it not far off. On going back through the open woods to make a thorough search, I found more young trees of the same species, and one old giant towering to nearly eighty feet with large limbs radiating over an area of about the same number of feet in spread. A little deliberation soon showed this tree to be a specimen of the most distinct type of the Black Maple (*Acer nigrum*) of F. A. Michaux. Judging by it and others of less size at this station, one would never hesitate to regard it as a species as far removed from *Acer saccharum*, the Sugar Maple, as could be, and still remain a member of the same group.

The broad leaves of this large tree, held forth on long, rather stout petioles, were quivering in the gentle breeze and, as I glanced upward through its massive branches and vigorous orange-brown twigs, the whole tree presented a picture of strength and beauty beyond description. I afterwards found that it is a common tree on the neighboring hills, but is less vigorous on the drier soil, though none the less healthy and beautiful. I also found that it had been considerable planted as a street tree in the Town of Salamanca.

The Black Maple grows to a height of about eighty feet (80') or more, and has a trunk diameter of nearly three feet (3'). It has large spreading branches and stout branchlets which have a lustrous yellow-green or orange-brown bark that becomes dark gray after the third or fourth year. The bark of old trunks is rough, scaly, somewhat furrowed, and nearly black. The leaves from four to six inches wide have from three to five lobes, often drooping and usually pubescent, at least on the under surface and long the petioles. The very ornamental flowers which are akin to those of the Sugar Maple are borne in drooping clusters, and the samaras, or seeds, are much the same as in the Sugar Maple, though having more divergent wings. Its natural range, as given in Professor Charles Sprague Sargent's "Manual of the Trees of North America", is as follows:

"from the valley of the St. Lawrence River in the neighborhood of Montreal, southward to the valley of the Cold River, N. H. through Western Vermont; westward through Northern New York, Ontario, the Southern peninsula of Michigan, Indiana, Illinois and Iowa, to Northeastern South Dakota, Western Missouri, Eastern Kansas; and Southward through Western New York and Pennsylvania, to Southwestern Virginia and Kentucky. It is comparatively rare near Montreal and in Vermont, but more abundant farther West, and almost entirely replacing *Acer saccharum* in Iowa, and it is the only sugar maple of South Dakota."

I later found the Black Maple sparingly planted as a street tree in Rochester, New York, perhaps by accident, but wherever found it seems to be thriving better than the common Sugar Maple. I have seen quite large groves of the Black Maple along the Allegheny River, and it would be difficult to imagine anything grander when their copious leaves turn to a rich yellow in autumn.

APPENDIX V

COPY OF A HANDOUT PREPARED
BY R. HORSEY

PROPAGATION OF TREE PEONIES FROM SEED AS
PRACTICED AT
HIGHLAND PARK, ROCHESTER, NY

Tree Peony seed should be sown in the fall when ripe in seed flats, using greenhouse potting soil with a slight addition of sand, enough to make the soil mellow. The flats should be placed in a cool root or nursery cellar and kept moist, not drying out or over wet. They should be left in the nursery cellar during the next summer and they will come up the next February or March about a year and a half after sowing. Our nursery cellar is not absolutely dark. It is built in the ground to the eaves of the roof, but there are windows in each end and a couple of skylights in the roof.

During the first year the flats containing the Peony seed are placed on strips of wood laid on the concrete floor under a shelf (the wide shelf is about 5 feet from the floor) which extends along the side of the cellar so they receive no direct light the first year. In January when it is nearly time for them to come up, they are placed on this shelf, but not directly under the skylight, receiving a considerable amount of light. This nursery cellar is well aired in summer with the windows open all the time and a slat door which is also opened every warm day in winter.

Leave the plants in the seed flats for the next year, placing outside for the summer, and in the winter put them back in the cellar. Transplant into seed flats the following spring, and leave outside for the summer, wintering in the root cellar again this year. The following spring plant in nursery frames and in a couple of years they will be large enough to plant out and begin to flower.

It takes five or six years to produce sizeable plants, but they are worth it

The above method was described by Mr. Fred Ahrens (deceased), one time propagator for the Park Bureau to R. E. Horsey who wished notes to use in answer to questions about the fine display of tree peonies in Highland Park. These notes were made in 1927.

R. E. Horsey
Highland Park,
440 Highland Ave.,
Rochester, N.Y.

COPY OF A LETTER WRITTEN TO DR. L. C. CHADWICK
FROM RICHARD FENICCHIA

September 12, 1978

Dr. L. C. Chadwick
3634 Olentangy Blvd.
Columbus, Ohio 42324

Dear Chadwick:

I was happy to know that you are in the consulting service. As per your questionnaire, I would like to give you information relating to the subject on the performance of trees both in the city of Rochester and the outlying county parks.

During Barney Slavin's tenure as superintendent of the parks system, he was instrumental in the planting of thousands of trees of all types and descriptions in the city of Rochester, the parks system, and the two main arboretums.

Following in his footsteps, Richard A. Fenicchia planted and developed many new hybrids and species which are being tested in the park system and arboretum.

There exists on a street a planting of English Elms that were planted about 55 years ago. It is a short street, and originally there were about 75 Elms and a good 58 are alive and healthy, and roughly in trunk diameter from 18 to 30 inches. The soil is that of the sandy-loam type, fairly well drained. One of Barney Slavin's elm selections which planted extensively on city streets is known as *Ulmus americana* 'Ascendens'. All of the trees succumbed to the Elm disease in Rochester. Richard, always of the opinion that one or two were alive, finally found one tree on Culver road in Rochester, N.Y. Makes me wonder how the thing survived. Of course, we are in the process of propagating this tree, and if anyone wants scions, they will be given.

248

Another tree tested on the city streets of Rochester was *Tilia americana* 'Fastigiata'. During the course of several years many of the trees planted have made it very well, and they are growing in a soil that is well-drained and sandy-loam in nature.

One tree never tried on a city street, but tried in the Highland Park arboretum, is Acer nigra, known as Slavin's Upright. This tree had done remarkably well planted in a sandy-loam situation.

Hundreds of *Acer platanoides* 'Erectum' have been planted on streets in Rochester. Most of them have done remarkable well in a variety of soils.

Another initial planting that was planted about 60 years ago on small city streets bordering the Genesee River is the *Parrotia persica*. These few trees have done remarkably well, and have been free of disease and natural injuries.

Of course, you are familiar with *Acer saccharum*, Temple's Upright Sugar Maple, which has been extensively planted on many streets of Rochester. A glowing example is the planting of Temple's Upright on an entire street, known as Field Street. The soil in that locality in some areas is clay loam. Parts of the street has remnants of a peaty swampy bog that has been filled in. Trees have done fairly well. Although we know the Sugar Maple is adaptable to many types of soil and density of moisture, I would say it thrives best in a sandy-loam.

Several trees, known as *Quercus cerris*, have been planted on streets bordering Seneca Park and one section of a street in the center of the city of Rochester. This Turkey Oak is very adaptable to conditions in the city of Rochester, and has done remarkably well considering the Oak trees are hard to transplant. The Turkey Oak has the ability to withstand transplanting to the detriment of other Oak trees.

One small street consists of *Tilia petolaris*. The count would be 80 trees on this small street. They were planted possibly

50 years ago. They have done remarkably well, with very little effect by lack of moisture and air pollutants.

Acer rubrum, as a street tree, was planted under a variety of soils, and has done quite well. Related forms of *Acer rubrum* exists on streets of Rochester in fairly large quantities. The closer forms that have occurred, as you know of course, are hybrids between Silver and Red maple. Some forms vary in habit, shape, size and form of growth. Apparently seems to thrive in most soils and localities. Some forms do have selections that are seedless. Of course Chad, I never went along with tailored trees, although they have their place on city streets. I still maintain trees are not only to beautify streets, but also planted to shade areas, to moderate the atmosphere, to augment the formation of oxygen and moisture in the air, and also to add value to surrounding localities.

Another street tree planted about 40 to 50 years ago was the Silver Bells, which has done remarkably well.

Several large Maidenhair trees were planted about 50 or more years ago, are still in existence and in good condition. Would like to mention a condition that exists with one of our Ginkgo trees. This tree planted in Seneca Park, has a diameter of about 25 to 30 inches, and I would say 60' in height. This tree has existed in condition of injury to the bark from height of 5' from the ground to where injury begins, and the injury consists of complete girdling and complete elimination of the cambium layer to width of 10 to 20 inches around the tree trunk. Has survived in this condition for at least 12 years. The only conclusion I arrive at is it must receive nutrients through the pith.

As a small tree planted in many areas of our parks, *Acer griseum* has done remarkable well. It grows principally in a silty soil that exists in Durand Eastman Park, to a heavier sandy-loam that exists in Highland Park. Has a future as a small street tree. At the present time Richard is testing three selections or natural hybrids that have occurred in *Acer griseum* X *Acer nikoense*. Three selections now grow in Highland Park, facing Reservoir Avenue. These three selections have now attained a height of 15' to 18'.

They are a more vigorous grower than either parent, and sturdier looking. Habit of growth more like *Acer griseum*. The bark does not resemble either parent, but the resemblance is closer to *Acer griseum*. I have been testing and observing these hybrids for about 12 years and possibly more testing should be done with them. Has tremendous possibilities as a small street tree. It can also be propagated very readily by grafting on the Sugar Maple.

Several other trees by Richard are a group of natural hybrids that have been selected by Richard A. Fenicchia, known as *Acer cappadocicum* X *Acer Miyabei*. From this group of about 18 plants that were planted about 40 years ago in Durand Eastman Park. Richard has selected three or four unusual forms that are under observation. I think the potential is great for these selections to be planted on streets or in arboretums. The soil conditions are of the silty-loam type.

Acer cappadocicum thrives very well in Highland Park, and has made up to be a remarkable tree. It probably will grow as large as the Norway Maple. Apparently it thrives on a variety of soils, and air pollutants as they exist in the Rochester area. These are sulfur dioxide and ozone. The former produced by burning coal, gas and natural gases and petroleum products. The major cause would result from combustion of gasoline, heating oil, diesel oil, and jet fuel. All these fuels contain small amounts of sulfide and mercaptans, which produce sulfur dioxide upon combustion. so far the only effect some of these pollutants have had on plant life would be leaf curl necrosis, which has attacked mostly lilacs in Highland Park. I have naturally very little pollutant damage on most trees of all types, both on city streets of Rochester and outlying parks, principally Highland and Durand Eastman. some of the injury, as you know on trees in cities, has been caused principally on Norway Maples, some Sugar Maples, and Chestnuts, by sulfides produced by automobiles.

Excessive pollutants have been emitted by conglomeration of industrial plants, and lack of water due to the fact that man has created sidewalks and thousands of covered roads of asphalt and cement; therefore, eliminating air and moisture for the healthful survival of plant material.

Richard has under test and observation a tree on a street known as Reservoir Avenue, through Highland Park a natural hybrid that has occurred between *Acer grandidentatum* and *Acer saccharum*. *Acer grandidentatum* can reach a height of about 12 meters. It tends to be a small, broadly, upright tree. The natural hybrid has characteristics of being fairly compact and broad, resembling *Acer grandidentatum* in habit of growth. These trees have been under observation for about 25 years. There are about 30 trees on Reservoir Avenue. They range in diameter from 6 to 10 inches, after about 25 years of growth. I think they have remarkable potential as a street tree, or for an arboretum. some selections can be made from this group for specific characteristics. Nothing has been done to date. Soil conditions are of sandy loam mix. Air pollution has not affected them.

There is a planting of cork trees on Reservoir Avenue. They were planted possibly 60 years ago. They consist of about 50 trees. some of them attained a diameter of 24 inches or more. They have done remarkably well, and have remained in quite a healthful condition, apparently disregarding air pollution, insect and fungal diseases.

In conclusion, I would like to say that there are many other forms of trees in the parks system in Rochester. Hope I have given you enough information; if more needed, I would be glad to furnish it.

So, I'll sign off by saying I wish you the best in your endeavors, in preparation of this discussion at the National Urban Forestry Conference in Washington. And I wish you the best in your consulting business.

Sincerely,
Richard A. Fenicchia

APPENDIX VII

SOME OF THE PLANTS THAT CAN BE ATTRIBUTED TO RICHARD FENICCHIA

Dick Fenicchia made about 280 crosses of rhododendrons after his return to the Park Department in 1950. These were in addition to the many crosses he made while working under Barney Slavin between the years 1925 to 1934. Most of these early crosses were lost between 1939 and 1950. Many of his crosses made since 1950 have never been named, and many are still under his observation in plantings in Highland Park or in the park nurseries. One rhododendron that he did name and that received an award from the Great Lakes Chapter of the American Rhododendron Society was Rhododendron, President Kennedy, a clone that resulted from the cross of *R. Maximum* x R. Cunningham's White.

By crossing *R. fortunii* with *R. smirnovi* he produced a whole family of cultivars that he named after members of his family.

By crossing *R. fortunii* with R. RAF no. 6 (which is a cross of *R. smirnovi* with *R. Cataubiense Caractacus*), he developed three clones that he named in honor of Alvan R. Grant, Mrs. Alvan R. Grant, and Bernard Harkness.

As already stated, there are many more hybrid rhododendrons produced by Fenicchia, many of which can be found in the plantings in Highland Park under RAF numbers.

A few more of Dick's hybrids or discoveries include the following:
- Upright pyramidal form of Norway maple discovered in Mt. Hope Cemetery in 1950—three specimens planted in Highland Park.
- *Magnolia denudata* hybrids discovered in a batch of seedlings in Highland Park's magnolia collection in 1968.
- *Magnolia Lennei* x *M. lilifolia nigra* hybridized in 1958— specimen planted in the Highland Park collection.

- *Magnolia Kobus* x *M. soulangeana* hybridized in 1958—planted in the Highland Park collection.
- *Acer griseum* x *A. nikoense*—a natural hybrid found in seedlings sown in 1951; three specimens planted in Highland Park.
- *Pinus strobus* Durand Dwarf—discovered in Durand Eastman Park as a volunteer seedling in 1950.
- Douglas fir, pendulus form named Big Flats Fir—discovered in Big Flats, New York, One plant is growing in the Castle grounds at Highland Park; four in the Highland Park pinetum.
- *Cunninghamia lanceolata*—cuttings of this were taken and rooted in 1928 in the lower greenhouses at Highland Park. The rooted cuttings were planted in outdoor beds in the park. Three cuttings survived—one plant was dug and planted on the grounds at the Castle in Highland Park, where it has attained a height of about thirty feet.
- One *Abies Concolor* seedling variation discovered in Durand Eastman Park—a good blue form, planted near the lower Pinetum Road in Highland Park and one also planted in the Smith Road Nursery.

Fenicchia continued:

It would be repetitious to list Dick's hybrid lilacs—the new 'Rochester' strain or family of lilacs. It should be mentioned however that he has many more seedlings that he is watching to determine whether they are worthy of naming. Most of these are planted in the Smith Road nursery:

- Two *Berberis Julianae* natural hybrids resulting from seed gathered in Highland Park; planted on the grounds at Highland Park Castle.
- *Viburnum rhytidophyllum* x *V. lantana*. Hybridizing was done in 1928. There are two plants on the grounds at the Castle and two more in Dick's home nursery.
- *Pinus sylvestris nana* seedling—selected by R. Fenicchia. Five plants are in the rock garden at Highland Park.

- *Juniperus Virginiana* seedling variation discovered at Newport, Rhode Island. Two plants near lower Pinetum Road, Highland Park.
- *Populus alba fastigiata* with twisted branches—discovered in Durand Eastman Park in 1950. Two plants in Highland Park along Goodman Street.
- Twenty trees of *Acer grandidentatum* x *saccharum*—planted along Reservoir Avenue in Highland Park—has great potential as a street or lawn tree. Some variation in form.

The list of plants attributed to Dick could fill many pages. His interest covers a broad range of plants from small potted plants such as begonia to bulbous plants such as amaryllis to the shrubs and trees.

APPENDIX VIII

COPY OF AN ARTICLE WRITTEN FOR THE INTERNATIONAL PLANT PROPAGATORS SOCIETY'S PUBLICATION, *THE PLANT PROPAGATOR*

BREEDING AND GROWING HYBRID LILACS FROM SEED
by
Richard A. Fenicchia
County of Monroe, Department of Parks
375 Westfall Road
Rochester, N.Y. 14620

The 'Rochester' lilac was selected from a batch of so-called French lilacs. It is slow-growing, broad and shrubby, on the dwarf side. Thyrses (ovate panicles) erect, usually in pairs, narrowly conical—7" to 8" tall. Florets white of good substance; corolla lobes often five (occasionally to 17 inches, teratological instances); late blooming, 'Rochester' lilac was used as the female parent for further hybridizing. Male plants used were: 'Madame Charles Souchet', blue; 'Dusk', purple; 'Edward J. Gardner', pink; 'Sensation', purple and white; 'Glory', magenta.

These crosses were made using potted plants, forced into flower in the greenhouse in January, 1960. Under controlled conditions, the other lilacs were brought into bloom about the same time. Emasculation of the 'Rochester' lilac was started by nipping the tender top off of the thyrses; the corolla and anthers of each flower was pulled off by using the thumb and forefinger. Obviously emasculation must take place before the pollen matures. Select between 15 and 20 flowers on each thyrse. Pinch off the other flowers. A brush, thickness of lead in a pencil, may be used to gather the pollen as soon as it has burst from the anther capules; pollination of the stigma to start as soon as emasculation has taken place. Repeat pollination for several days. Thyrses may remain fully exposed without a cover till seeds have ripened. When seed pods have turned brown and brittle, gather seed before carpels fully open. Clean the seeds and store in a cool, dry place until the time for sowing, the first week in January for greenhouse growing.

Cedar flats are used for sowing the seeds. A mixture of sterilized loam and coarse sand is used. Firm mixture in flats with drainage holes in them. Sow seeds by broadcasting evenly or in rows, label and firm seeds in the soil; seeds may be covered with unsterilized coarse sand to a depth of 1/8 inch. Firm sand, place flat in a tank of water below rim of flat. When the soil is wet through, place flat on shelf in greenhouse at a temperature of 65-75 degrees F. Temperature variations may delay germination. A pane of glass may be put over each seed flat. Three days after sowing seeds, the soil should be sprayed with a mixture of captan and malathion; spraying seed flats should continue weekly until seedlings have developed three or four leaves. Seed flats should be kept moist at all times until seed germinates. Good drainage is essential for optimum germination and growth of lilacs in all stages of development.

The pane of glass is removed when the seeds have germinated. When small leaves begin to appear and seedlings are at a size where they can be easily handled, they are potted into 4 inch pots in a soil mix of one part composted soil and one part coarse sand (avoid soil which has an acid test). After seedlings have made additional growth to six inches or more and are well rooted, they can be transplanted into nursery beds at a distance of at least 18 inches apart. When the plants acquire size so that their branches begin to touch, they can be planted farther apart in the nursery where they will remain until moved into permanent locations within the parks.